Society in Question:

Custom Edition

THOMSON

★ ™

NELSON

ISBN-13: 978-0-17-646616-9
ISBN-10: 0-17-646616-9

Consists of:

Society in Questionn
Fifth Edition
Robert J. Brym
ISBN 0-17-610281-7, © 2008, 2004, 2001

Contents

Chapter 2

The Value of a Sociology Degree

SCOTT DAVIES AND DAVID WALTERS

FIELDS AND CAREERS

When university students search for a major, who can blame them for seeking career information on various fields? As individuals and families bear heavier debt loads from rising tuition fees, students are understandably curious about their job prospects. The average cost of a B.A. in Canada is still inexpensive relative to both elite American universities, where annual tuition fees can run up to US$30 000 and to deregulated professional programs (e.g., dentistry, medicine, M.B.A., law), the fees of which have recently soared from $8 000 to $20 000. Nonetheless, the expense of a B.A. is considerably higher than it was 20 years ago, and students are increasingly mindful of its economic potential.

This chapter presents a sociological analysis of the links between university and employment. It compares the job fortunes of Canadian sociology graduates to those from other liberal arts and sets its findings in the context of emerging labour market trends. For reasons of space we focus only on economic payoffs and point interested readers to a recent study of sociology's social, political, and intellectual benefits (Spalter-Roth et al., 2005). We urge students to select a field of study that is compatible with their interests and focus on the economic consequences to help guide their choices.

HIGHER EDUCATION TODAY

Today there is a lot of talk about how the emerging "knowledge economy" requires young people with higher-order cognitive skills acquired through postsecondary schooling. While some sociologists are skeptical about these claims (Livingstone, 1998; Wolf, 2002), Canadian governments are encouraging universities to expand their enrollments at all levels. From a historical vantage point, the sheer growth of university attendance is striking. Enrollments have never been higher and they are projected to grow despite substantial tuition fee hikes.

Faith in the economic value of university education is curious for two reasons. First, many students are choosing fields about which they have little knowledge. For instance, the social sciences attract many students. In fact, they have the highest enrollments in Canadian universities (Statistics Canada, 2005). Fields such as sociology, psychology, economics, business, political science, anthropology, and communications are popular in universities, yet they are not taught much (if at all) in secondary schools. These fields attract many students even though few high-school graduates have a firm sense of what they are about. This situation is quite unlike that of the traditional humanities and natural sciences, such as history, English, biology, and chemistry. Second, when we examine the links between university and job markets, they are remarkably loose. That is, few jobs are directly related to any of the major social sciences and humanities. Check your local newspaper and you won't find many positions for historians, geographers, psychologists, or sociologists. We conclude that the social sciences attract students with little prior knowledge of, and background in, the field and with few role models in the labour market.

The weak connection between the university and job markets is a result of the fact that most university disciplines emerged as research areas, not vehicles for vocational training. They were created to suit the interests of professors, governments, and students, not employers. Their content is shaped by the fascinations of researchers and instructors, not the requests of workplace managers. Their conventions may make sense to academics but not to employers. With the exception of a few professional programs, there are no institutional mechanisms by which economic authorities can influence what is taught in universities. While academic officials may occasionally call for more practical or vocational courses, established universities are governed by powerful norms of academic freedom that grant them considerable autonomy from politicians and employers. As a result, there are few procedures by which employers offer feedback to professors, and few professors are inclined to seek such feedback. To use the language of sociologists who study complex organizations, most university disciplines are "decoupled" from labour markets.

Why do so many students enter the social sciences and humanities given this decoupling? One answer is that a university degree pays off in the labour market. Sociological research shows that university graduates enjoy higher wages and fewer bouts of unemployment compared to graduates from high school, trade colleges, and community colleges (Walters, 2004). In fact, *all* studies of which we are aware reveal such advantages. The trick is to understand how these advantages emerge and persist despite the loose connections between most university fields and the vast majority of workplaces.

WHY SOCIOLOGY PAYS

Sociologists offer three broad explanations as to why social science fields such as sociology are valued in the labour market. The first explanation is that such fields nurture diffuse skills that are useful across a range of service-sector jobs even though they are directly relevant to only a few occupations. Thus, evidence suggests that liberal arts graduates have high levels of decision-making, interpersonal, and communication skills (Axelrod, Anisef, and Lin, 2001; Rush and Evers, 1985; Allen, 1998; Lowe and Krahn, 1995; Giles and Drewes, 2002; Krahn and Bowlby, 1999). They can think critically and explore new ideas with ease. They can think abstractly and theoretically, and quickly absorb different kinds of information. They can work well with others, manage conflict, and relate abstract ideas to real-life situations. They have a capacity to work effectively and assume authority in large organizations. Such skills allow on-the-job training to be quicker and easier. Many argue that today's labour market has a growing need for the abilities of social science graduates. In contrast, graduates from more applied disciplines, particularly those in trade and community colleges, often lack such breadth of knowledge. Graduates from social science fields such as sociology are thus said to enjoy a long-term advantage because their generic skills are portable across many different kinds of jobs. These skills may not be obvious or easily observed. Many students may be unaware that the abilities they develop in sociology courses are useful in any job where written, oral, and critical thinking skills are valued. Yet sociology undoubtedly develops these valued skills in students.

A second reason why general fields like sociology pay off is known as "credentialism" (Brown, 2001). In government and corporate bureaucracies, many applicants compete for few jobs. Employers therefore need legitimate and convenient criteria to whittle down the pool of qualified applicants. Educational credentials are often used as a convenient screening device.

Consider the changing value of the high-school diploma over the past half century. As high-school enrollments grew after World War II, most Canadian-born adults were able to obtain a diploma. Many employers began to demand diplomas as a minimum entry requirement. They did so not necessarily because they associated the diploma with any particular skill but because they associated it with dependability (Berg, 1970). Having a diploma signalled a capacity to follow instructions, complete tasks, and be punctual. However, as more young people with high-school diplomas flooded the job market, employers eventually altered their reasoning. As diploma holders became commonplace, employers interpreted the *lack* of a diploma as potentially problematic. They viewed dropping out of high school as an indicator of potential unreliability. Perhaps, they reasoned, dropouts are incapable of fitting in with people, heeding instructions, and completing tasks.

A similar style of thinking has now been applied to higher education. Before the 1970s, a young person with a bachelor's degree was a rarity in the labour market. Employers often assumed that people with B.A.s were especially able. Their assumption was rooted in the longstanding prestige that higher learning had enjoyed and its association with high status and a sense of social superiority. Employers would sometimes hire university graduates in the hope of bringing prestige to their firm. Before the 1980s, those who lacked university degrees were not stigmatized. High-school graduates could still vie for solid middle-class jobs since most job applicants lacked postsecondary credentials.

This situation appears to be changing. As more and more people graduate from university, degree holders become less rare; and with less rarity comes less prestige (Wolf, 2002). University diplomas no longer offer elite status, even when their holders possess exceptional ability. Such "credential inflation" is sparking a new trend: as long as employers continue to link degrees with some measure of ability, they will increasingly associate someone's lack of degree with mediocrity. Since so many people are earning degrees, employers might suspect that something is wrong with people who lack one. While a degree may no longer buy elite status, it appears to be becoming a general marker of trustworthiness and dependability.

Trust is increasingly important in higher education today, as many new suppliers of educational credentials emerge. These suppliers include online universities, for-profit universities, and private training colleges. Many of these new entrants, such as the online University of Phoenix, offer training only in "practical" fields such as business and information technology that are perceived as being in high demand. The entrance requirements of for-profit institutions are typically lower than those of traditional universities since they need to attract as many fee-paying students as possible to survive. Will their apparent job relevance allow them to take over the higher education marketplace? Will their graduates out-compete traditional liberal arts graduates in the job market? Almost certainly not—and for a stark reason: mainstream universities have the key advantage of being more difficult to enter. This difficulty will remain vitally important as long as employers continue to interpret a degree from a relatively selective university as a general marker of trustworthiness. Credentials from online universities, with their lower entry standards, are less likely to be recognized by employers. In a highly uncertain environment, employers are still inclined to trust a degree from a well-known and respected "brand name" university over a new competitor they may have never heard of and therefore suspect of having lower standards.

A third reason for the continuing popularity of fields of study such as sociology is that they offer a passport to valuable professional and graduate degrees. The highest financial payoffs in university accrue to graduates with advanced degrees in medicine, law, dentistry, and business, or graduates of Ph.D. programs. These programs usually require a previous degree, such as a B.A. or B.Sc. While sociology graduates rarely enter medicine or dentistry given their lack of natural science training (though some medical schools such as McMaster's accept humanities and social science graduates), they commonly enter law, M.B.A., Public Administration, and teaching, all of which offer solid career opportunities and wages (Walters, 2004). Thus, many social science and humanities disciplines continue to thrive by providing a "ticket" for an advanced degree (Collins, 2002). Research shows that humanities and social science graduates are more likely to pursue additional degrees than are other graduates (Statistics Canada, 2001: 27). This tendency seems to be increasingly important as more employers expect workers to return to university and upgrade their skills and credentials. In contrast, a community college diploma is largely a terminal credential and rarely offers eligibility for advanced degrees. Moreover, recent research shows that attending a community college after earning a university B.A. does not usually increase earnings or employability (Walters, 2003).

SOCIOLOGY GRADUATES COMPARED TO OTHERS

The career opportunities discussed previously are those that sociology shares with other liberal arts programs. We next address how sociology graduates compare to graduates from nearby fields. We use the best available evidence, Statistics Canada's *National Graduate Survey*, which for several decades has traced how Canadian university graduates from all fields perform in the work force. We report the latest available data on how individuals who graduated from university in 2000 were faring in the labour market in 2002.

Tables 2.1 and 2.2 compare graduates of several liberal arts fields, including sociology. We

TABLE 2.1 LIBERAL ARTS GRADUATES BY FIELD OF STUDY AND GENDER (IN PERCENT)

FIELD OF STUDY	PERCENT OF ALL LIBERAL ARTS GRADUATES	PERCENT OF ALL MALE LIBERAL ARTS GRADUATES	PERCENT OF ALL FEMALE LIBERAL ARTS GRADUATES	PERCENT MALE IN FIELD	PERCENT FEMALE IN FIELD	TOTAL
Sociology	8	7	9	29	71	100
English	8	7	9	28	72	100
Liberal Arts and Sciences	12	12	12	35	65	100
Fine Arts and Music	7	7	7	35	65	100
Film and Performing Arts	10	11	9	40	60	100
Media and Information Studies	7	6	8	29	71	100
Languages	7	4	9	20	80	100
Philosophy	4	6	3	57	43	100
Psychology	11	6	14	18	82	100
Economics	4	8	3	62	38	100
Political Science	6	6	6	36	64	100
History	7	11	5	52	48	100
Other (Hist/Anthro/ Religion/Geog)	8	9	8	38	62	100
Total	99*	100	102*			

*Does not equal 100 due to rounding.

Source: Adapted from Statistics Canada's 2000 National Graduates Survey (NGS), 2000.

TABLE 2.2 AVERAGE INCOME OF GRADUATES BY FIELD AND GENDER

FIELD OF STUDY	ALL GRADUATES	MEN	WOMEN
Sociology	31 574	33 367	31 137
English	29 437	28 062*	29 917
Liberal Arts and Sciences	31 423	31 668	31 263
Fine Arts and Music	27 477*	25 655*	28 413
Film and Performing Arts	25 046*	27 191*	23 544*
Media and Information Studies	33 740	33 658	33 777
Languages	27 730*	27 411	27 810*
Philosophy	28 811	28 593	29 025
Psychology	30 920	37 450	29 397
Economics	33 528	33 510	33 546
Political Science	32 171	31 007	32 980
History	30 589	31 561	29 803
Other (Hist/Anthro/Religion/Geography)	31 592	37 697	28 239*
All	**30 218**	**31 334**	**29 679**

*Indicates a 95 percent or greater chance that the sample figure is different from the actual figure for sociologists in the population.

Source: Adapted from Statistics Canada's 2000 National Graduates Survey (NGS), 2000.

combined history, anthropology, religion, and geography into an "Other" category because there were too few respondents in the sample from each of these fields to allow for reliable statistical comparisons. "Liberal Arts and Sciences" includes students in general studies, fields that are not classified, and those who did not declare a field. The first column in Table 2.1 shows that the largest group of employed graduates come from combined liberal arts and science programs (12 percent), while economics and philosophy have the smallest proportion of graduates (4 percent). The second and third columns display this information separately for males and females. Males are least likely to hold a degree in languages (4 percent), and most likely to have a combined liberal arts and science degree (12 percent). Females are most likely to hold a degree in psychology (14 percent) and are least likely to graduate in economics and philosophy (both 3 percent). The last two columns in Table 2.1 show that women outnumber men in every field of study except

philosophy, history, and economics. The fields with the largest gender imbalance are psychology (82 percent female) and languages (80 percent female). Males are the majority in economics (62 percent). Sociology graduates make up 8 percent of the liberal arts, representing 7 percent of males and 8 percent of females.

Before going any further we must emphasize that all social surveys examine a part (the "sample") to make generalizations about a whole (the "population"). There is a certain danger in this practice, for a chance always exists that a sample will differ from the population from which it is drawn. To the degree the sample differs from the population, generalizations based on the sample will be inaccurate.

Thankfully, statisticians have developed ways of figuring out the chance of drawing faulty conclusions from different types of samples. In general, sociologists accept a 5 percent chance of being wrong (a 95 percent chance of being right) in the conclusions they draw from sample surveys. We follow that standard here.

In Table 2.2, for example, we report annual earnings in 2002 of graduates who obtained a bachelor's degree in 2000 and were no longer in school in 2002. We created Table 2.2 because we want to know which graduates earn more or less than sociology graduates. Given that each number in Table 2.2 has a certain margin of error, however, we are limited in the conclusions we can safely draw. Specifically, we can be 95 percent confident that the figures marked with an asterisk are actually below sociology graduates' annual income of $31 574. This means that graduates of programs in fine arts and music, film and performing arts, and languages almost certainly earn less than sociology graduates (see column 1; as columns 2 and 3 show, the below-average fields differ somewhat for men considered alone and women considered alone). We cannot, however, state with 95 percent certainty that annual income for graduates of other fields is either above or below that of sociologists in the population as a whole. Thus, economics graduates lead the pack with annual earnings of $33 528, but all we can safely say about them is that their annual earnings are not significantly more than the $31 754 earned by sociology graduates. In other words, in the Canadian population, sociology and economics graduates seem to enjoy roughly the same annual income two years after graduation.

Columns 2 and 3 reveal that, on the whole, men earn more than women. Two years after graduation, male liberal arts graduates earn $31 334, whereas females earn $29 679, about 95 percent of the male average. Most fields have rather small gender pay gaps. Only two fields exhibit big gender gaps in favour of men: males with psychology and "other" degrees earn, respectively, about $8 000 and $9 000 more than their female counterparts. But in seven of the thirteen fields listed in Table 2.2, women report higher annual earnings than men. This finding is consistent with other studies that have found shrinking gender pay gaps among university graduates in recent decades (Walters, 2005).

Overall, the data suggest that the income potential of sociology graduates is roughly the same as that of graduates in most other fields,

and perhaps above average. Graduates of a few fields in the humanities earn significantly less than sociology graduates do. Graduates from no field earn significantly more than sociology graduates do.

CAREERS FOR SOCIOLOGY GRADUATES

We have argued that sociology, like most other subjects in the social sciences and humanities, is both useful and decoupled from the labour market. Decoupling is evident from the fact that only a minority of sociology graduates in Canada and the United States report that their job is directly related to their schooling (Krahn and Bowlby, 1999; Spalter-Roth et al., 2005). Utility is evident in the fact that sociology graduates readily find good work in a variety of fields. We conclude that while employers place few job ads for sociologists, sociology is a flexible field that allows graduates to work in many occupations and organizations.

A study of McMaster University sociology graduates (Davies and Denton, 1997) from various degree levels found them in a great variety of jobs, including social work, teaching, journalism, business administration, health administration, criminal justice, policing, sales, public relations, private polling, government research, and so on. The National Graduate Survey provides data on the percentage of recent sociology B.A.s employed in various occupational categories (see Table 2.3). They illustrate that sociology graduates have opportunities across a broad range of sectors. The largest proportion (35 percent) is in occupations relating to business, finance, and administration. Jobs in the social sciences, education, and government services are the second-largest destination, employing 29 percent of recent graduates. Sales and service jobs are third, accounting for 18 percent of employed graduates; followed by management positions (nearly 7 percent); jobs in the primary industry (almost 5 percent); health (about 2 percent); and art, culture, and sport (about 2 percent).

TABLE 2.3 SOCIOLOGY GRADUATES BY OCCUPATIONAL CATEGORY (IN PERCENT)

OCCUPATION	PERCENT
Management Occupations	6.8
Business, Finance and Administrative Occupations	35.0
Natural and Applied Sciences and Related Occupations	1.2
Health Occupations	2.2
Occupations in Social Sciences, Education, Government Service	29.0
Occupations in Art, Culture, Recreation, and Sport	2.2
Sales and Service Occupations	18.0
Trades, Transport, Primary Industry, and Other	4.7

Source: Adapted from Statistics Canada's 2000 National Graduates Survey (NGS), 2000.

Amid this variety, there are some specific occupations for which sociology prepares its graduates. Most sociology programs have course requirements in research methods and statistics. Such applied research training can be extremely valuable. Many government agencies and companies, such as Statistics Canada, the Centre for Addiction and Mental Health, Proctor and Gamble, Angus Reid, and just about any corporation, federal or provincial ministry, or trade union involved in large-scale research, seek applicants with a strong aptitude for conducting surveys and analyzing data, and they regularly offer excellent employment opportunities to sociology graduates. In fact, every year Statistics Canada offers a national job competition for sociology graduates (information can be found at http://www.statcan.ca/english/employment/emplop.htm). Thus, there is a strong demand for graduates who are capable of administering and analyzing survey data.

In an analysis not reported in detail here, we also found that sociology graduates who specialized in an applied sub-area such as criminology, health, and population studies (demography) had substantially higher earnings than did other sociology graduates. Although the small sample sizes for these subgroups do not permit accurate statistical comparisons with other fields, they suggest both the marketability of applied research areas within sociology and the range of opportunities sociology offers.

Beyond applied and quantitative subfields, many social agencies, hospitals, and market research companies employ graduates with a broad range of research skills that are taught in most sociology undergraduate programs. Many companies want employees with a strong background in qualitative techniques relating to interviewing, organizing, and administering focus groups, and who are capable of communicating research findings to audiences unfamiliar with technical terms. This is why the skills provided in research methods and statistics classes nicely compliment the communication and critical thinking and writing abilities acquired in theory courses.

ADVICE FOR STRATEGIZING IN NETWORKS AND INTERNAL LABOUR MARKETS

What then is the value of a sociology degree? Sociology resembles other social sciences and humanities: it pays off, but largely indirectly. While offering few unique paths to specific labour markets, sociology fosters generic skills, is a recognized credential in bureaucratic settings, and serves as a passport to graduate and professional school. Because it is loosely connected to job markets, sociology is linked to a variety of occupations.

Such wide-reaching links to job markets force graduates to use job search strategies creatively. For example, you have probably heard the old saying that to get a good job, who you know is as important as what you know. Sociological research suggests that there is much truth in that adage. Creating a wide range of social ties can lead to many job opportunities (Granovetter, 1995). For example, if you secure a middle managcmcnt position after you graduate, your newly established contacts may lead to a permanent full-time position. Contacts are particularly useful for securing an interview. Often the people who are offered a job are not the most qualified. Instead, they may be the people with the most interview experience—they knew just what to say, when to say it, and who to say it to. Forming contacts allows you to gain such experience. After an unsuccessful interview—and for most of us there will be many—always follow up with the interviewer to find out how you can improve your performance.

Networking is important when applying to postgraduate programs, especially master's and doctoral programs. Not only do you need to know which programs suit your interests, but also which faculty members conduct research in your area. Having an undergraduate advisor to work with can often be as important as your grade point average for being accepted into a graduate program. The reputation of the professors writing your letters of reference can be extremely important in being admitted into graduate school and even securing a good job in your research area. Faculty members vary widely in their resourcefulness, their ability to fund graduate students as research assistants, and the quality of their connections in the labour market. Select your mentors wisely!

Diverse networks also allow you to obtain advice from multiple sources and thereby improve the breadth of your information. Whether applying to postgraduate studies or entering the labour market, use a variety of sources to research your options. Aside from personal contacts, seek guidance from career counsellors at your university, secretaries in your department, and of course, professors. Draw on as many resources as you can. For example, web sites (such as http://www.sociology.ca) offer information on research and employment opportunities for sociology graduates, as well as links to departments that offer master's degrees. Many departmental web pages provide Internet links to assist students in making academic or career decisions.

Note also that some entry-level jobs lead to better jobs than others. "Internal labour markets" exist when large organizations hire from within (Krahn and Lowe, 2002). Many government and corporate bureaucracies arrange their positions hierarchically, creating promotional paths that lead upward from entry-level jobs to management. This means that a relatively low-paying job can be worthwhile if its leads to something more, and also that seemingly lucrative summer jobs at shopping malls, bars, or factories may yield few long-term benefits. Students may find it difficult to resist such jobs if they pay well, but they are not selling features on a résumé and they offer little advancement potential. Unless you are absolutely confident of being admitted into a graduate or a professional program, you are much better off applying for summer positions at large organizations, even for clerical, volunteer, or unpaid positions, as long as they allow access to an internal labour market. Some initial grunt work may eventually lead to a position with more creative autonomy and authority. A university-educated, hardworking, ambitious employee who already has experience within a company is an ideal candidate for promotion to one of its well-paying full-time positions. If you eventually find fewer openings than you initially anticipated, use this experience to acquire a job elsewhere, and you may benefit from the additional interviewing know-how.

We conclude that although a sociology degree opens up a wide variety of employment opportunities, realizing that potential requires sociology graduates to use job search strategies creatively. Research suggests that social science graduates, including sociology graduates, initially fare less well than graduates with professional degrees, but they catch up somewhat over time (Finnie, 2001). This fact illustrates the importance of building networks and entering internal labour markets. Of course, luck helps in the job market, but you will significantly improve your chance of success by studying sociology and adopting sociological strategies for taking advantage of job market opportunities.

REFERENCES

Allen, Robert C. (1998). *The Employability of University Graduates in Humanities, Social Sciences and Education: Recent Statistical Evidence.* Available on the World Wide Web at http://www.econ.ubc.ca/dp9815.pdf.

Axelrod, Paul, Paul Anisef, and Zeng Lin. (2001). "Against All Odds? The Enduring Value of Liberal Education in Universities, Professions, and the Labour Market." *The Canadian Journal of Higher Education,* 31 (2): 47–78.

Berg, Ivar. (1970). *Education and Jobs: The Great Training Robbery.* New York: Praeger.

Brown, David K. (2001). "The Social Sources of Education Credentialism." *Sociology of Education,* (Extra Issue): 19–34.

Collins, Randall. (2002). "Credential Inflation and the Future of Universities." In Steven Brint, ed., *The Future of the City of Intellect: The Changing American University* (pp. 23–46). Stanford: Stanford University Press.

Davies, Scott, and Margaret Denton. (1997). "The Employment of Masters and Ph.D. Graduates from Eleven Sociology Departments." *Society/Societe,* 21 (1): 9–14.

Finnie, Ross. (2001). "Fields of Plenty, Fields of Lean: The Early Labour Market Outcomes of Canadian University Graduates by Discipline." *Canadian Journal of Higher Education,* 31 (1): 141–76.

Giles, P., and T. Drewes. (2002). "Liberal Arts Degrees and the Labour Market." *Perspectives on Labour and Income,* 13 (3): 27–33.

Granovetter, Mark. (1995). *Getting a Job: A Study of Contacts and Careers,* 2nd ed. Chicago: University of Chicago Press.

Krahn, Harvey, and Jeffrey W. Bowlby. (1999). "Education-Job Skills Match: An Analysis of the 1990 and 1995 National Graduate Surveys." Applied Research Branch for Strategic Policy. Ottawa: Human Resources Development Canada.

Krahn, Harvey, and Graham S. Lowe. (2002). *Work, Industry, and Canadian Society,* 4th ed. Toronto: ITP Nelson.

Livingstone, David W. (1998). *The Education-Jobs Gap: Underemployment or Economic Democracy.* Toronto: Garamond Press.

Lowe, Graham S., and Harvey Krahn. (1995). "Job-Related Education and Training among Young Workers." *Canadian Public Policy,* 21 (3): 362–78.

Rush, J. C., and F. T. Evers. (1985). "Making the Match: Canada's University Graduates and Corporate Employers." *Business Quarterly,* 50 (Winter): 41–47.

Spalter-Roth, Roberta, William Erskine, Sylvia Polsiak, and Jamie Panzarella. (2005). *A National Survey of Seniors Majoring in Sociology.* American Sociological Association. Available at http://www.asanet.org/galleries/default-file/B&B_first_report_final.pdf (12 December 2005).

Statistics Canada. (2001). "The School-to-Work Transitions of Post-Secondary Graduates in Canada: Research Findings Based on the National Graduates Surveys." *Applied Research Bulletin,* (Special Edition).

Statistics Canada. (2005). "University Enrollment." *The Daily,* Tuesday, 11 October. On the World Wide Web at http://www.statcan.ca/Daily/English/051011/d051011b.htm (12 December 2005).

Walters, David. (2003). "Recycling: The Economic Implications of Obtaining Additional Post-secondary Credentials at Lower or Equivalent Levels." *Canadian Review of Sociology and Anthropology,* 40 (4): 463–80.

———. (2004). "A Comparison of the Labour Market Outcomes of Postsecondary Graduates of Various Levels and Fields over a Four-Cohort Period." *Canadian Journal of Sociology,* 29 (1): 1–27.

———. (2005). "Gender, Postsecondary Education and Field of Study." *Higher Education Policy.* In press.

Wolf, Alison. (2002). *Does Education Matter? Myths About Education and Economic Growth.* New York: Penguin.

Chapter 6

Naming and Blaming:

GENDER SOCIALIZATION AND WOMEN'S DEFINITIONS OF SEXUAL HARASSMENT[1]

SANDY WELSH AND JAYNE BAKER

WHEN IS IT SEXUAL HARASSMENT?

Surveys show that between a quarter and a half of Canadian women in the paid labour force experience unwanted sexual attention at work (Welsh and Nierobisz, 1997; Gruber, 1997). Yet not all women define unwanted sexual attention—including sexual touching, jokes, and comments—as sexual harassment (Dellinger and Williams, 2002, Giuffre and Williams, 1994, Welsh et al., 2006). Why is this so? In this chapter we focus on gender socialization as a possible explanation.

To be sure, other factors also play a role. For example, some workplace cultures are less tolerant of sexual harassment than others, and less tolerance may encourage more women to define unwanted sexual attention as harassment (Dellinger and Williams, 2002). In contrast, women from some ethnic and racial groups and women who lack citizenship may be less inclined to define unwanted sexual attention as harassment because of their background and status (Welsh et al., 2006). Women who immigrate to Canada may be initially unaware of what constitutes "sexual harassment" in Canada. They may also be unwilling to label unwanted sexual attention as harassment if it means putting their potential Canadian citizenship status at risk. In our judgment, however, gender socialization plays a primary role in the way women define their experiences and is therefore chiefly responsible for the way women label unwanted sexual attention in the workplace.

Using data from a study of women in Ontario, we demonstrate how gender socialization leads some women to blame themselves for unwanted sexual attention and to dismiss their experiences as unimportant. We begin by defining sexual harassment. We next outline how gender socialization influences women's ability (or inability) to label their experiences as sexual harassment. We then analyze our data, which show how women in Ontario often blame themselves for sexual harassment while others have trouble defining sexual harassment as such. Finally, we demonstrate that gender socialization is not destiny. With the proper social support, some women are able to re-evaluate their experience of sexual harassment as unacceptable behaviour and take action to have it corrected.

SEXUAL HARASSMENT

Sexual harassment involves two forms of behaviour: quid pro quo harassment and hostile environment harassment. Quid pro quo harassment involves sexual threats or bribery linked to getting a job, keeping a job, or receiving a promotion or training opportunity. Hostile environment sexual harassment includes sexual jokes, comments, and touching that may create a sexualized environment or one that degrades women. By law, it is up to the person committing the behaviour to know the difference between welcome and unwelcome sexual behaviours (CHRC, 2004). At its core, sexual harassment lets women know they are not welcome in certain workplaces and that they are not respected members of the work group (Reskin and Padavic, 1994).

GENDER SOCIALIZATION

Gender socialization focuses on how we learn to become male or female according to the cultural standards of the social collectivities to which we belong. While recognizing the existence of biological differences between boys and girls, gender socialization researchers study how children learn the attitudes, behaviours, and expectations associated with masculine and feminine roles by interacting with teachers, parents, and role models, including the role models portrayed in the mass media. Such interactions reinforce behaviours that fit culturally acceptable forms of femininity and masculinity—and punish behaviours that don't. For example, young girls are often given dolls to play with and encouraged to display affection toward them. Such behaviour conforms to cultural expectations about femininity and nurturance. Yet people typically discourage young boys from playing with dolls, reinforcing expectations about a widely accepted form of masculinity that sees men as less nurturing and affectionate than women.

The aspect of gender roles that is most relevant to sexual harassment concerns the way men learn to become relatively dominant, powerful, and competitive while women learn to become relatively nurturing, concerned with the quality of social relations, and passive. As a result of this differential learning, most men learn to treat women as sexual objects or "conquests," while most women learn to believe that being treated as such is normal. For example, women generally learn to be non-confrontational when they are sexually harassed by men; they are inclined not to report such behaviour to the proper authorities. Meanwhile, men come to believe that women want and expect them to flirt, even in the workplace.

Focusing on how people learn gender roles carries with it the danger of emphasizing the existence of only one form of masculinity and one form of femininity—what are often called traditional "gender stereotypes" (Connell, 2002). Said differently, some analysts make it seem as if gender socialization happens to unwitting individuals who lack the capacity to influence, let alone resist, what they are taught. Such analysts downplay the extent to which people enjoy agency and choice. Below, we argue that their determinism is misplaced; people influence and resist traditional gender roles all the time.

GENDER SOCIALIZATION AND SEXUAL HARASSMENT

Early research emphasized how traditional gender role socialization teaches women to tolerate unwanted sexual attention from men and avoid confronting them about it (Gwartney-Gibbs and Lach, 1992; Lach and Gwartney-Gibbs, 1993). From this point of view, by teaching women to avoid conflict and doubt their perceptions, gender socialization makes it more likely that women will not label their experiences as sexual harassment and will not report it (Fitzgerald, Swann, and Magley, 1997; Hotelling and Zuber, 1997).

Researchers then noted that organizational culture contributes to employees' ability and willingness to label certain behaviours as sexual harassment (Folgero and Fjeldstad, 1995). In some masculine work cultures, women may not define their experiences as sexual harassment in order to ensure that they will be seen as competent team players (Collinson and Collinson, 1996). For example, new female coal miners may consider sexualized hazing rituals part of their initiation into work groups (Yount, 1991). In other workplaces, sexual behaviours commonly understood as sexual harassment may be requirements of the job (Williams, 1997: 4). For instance, restaurants may encourage customers to "talk dirty" to waitresses by promoting drinks with sexually loaded names such as "Screaming Orgasm" (Williams, 1997: 22; Giuffre and Williams, 1994: 387) or by requiring waitresses to wear short tight skirts and revealing tops (Loe, 1996). In these sexually charged or permissive work cultures, degrading sexual behaviours become an expected component of work that may not be considered sexual harassment by employees, be they men or women (Williams, 1997). Yet, even in these organizational contexts, gender socialization plays a role since it is part of what leads to the acceptability of sexually harassing behaviours in the first place.

In the remainder of this chapter, we discuss the role that gender socialization plays in how women make sense of the sexual behaviours they experience at work. We show that women's gender socialization affects how women interpret their experience and make decisions about how to respond to it.

METHODS

Our analysis is based on a project designed to evaluate how women define harassment and harassment reporting mechanisms in Ontario. For our study we selected women with a wide variety of social characteristics so we could learn how race, citizenship, class, language, age, disability, and sexuality help to shape their experiences. In the summer and fall of 2000, we conducted six focus groups, following this up with six additional focus groups and seventeen in-depth interviews in the spring of 2002. Data for our analysis comes from these interviews and focus groups, which included a total of 67 women (for details, see Welsh et al., 2006).

RESULTS

NOT NAMING: NORMALIZING UNWANTED SEXUAL ATTENTION

Several women in our study initially viewed their experiences of sexual harassment as "normal" flirting in the workplace or as sexual attention that they simply had to endure. Consider the experience of one francophone woman who worked in a government office. She experienced touching, suggestive talk, and comments from coworkers suggesting she was a sexual "con-

quest." She mentioned that she wasn't even aware at first that she was being harassed. Instead she viewed the behaviour as simply flirtatious:

> I welcomed, contributed to, and responded to the flirting. . . . It wasn't possible to say anything, to do anything because I was so naive, unaware that it was possible to do something, that it was harassment. It didn't happen! I was appealing to the guys. Afterward I told myself that the guys were mean, rather than believing that it was harassment. I minimized the situation, though I warned a new employee to be aware of the two men, so I had some kind of awareness. After the physical confrontation, I experienced a great deal of stress and understood that the situation was serious.

The "physical confrontation" that led her to realize that the men's actions were in fact not "normal" involved their trapping her in a room. She concluded:

> I minimized, I talked about it to my girlfriends, but as if it was flirtation, and that allowed me to vent. [This was] my way of rationalizing and of minimizing, because if I'd seen the situation clearly, I wouldn't have been able to go in to work.

This woman's experience demonstrates how traditional gender socialization can complicate the ability to identify and label behaviour as sexual harassment. What turned out to be sexual harassment was seen as "normal" flirting between men and women, at least initially.

Some women also had initial difficulty naming the sexual harassment due to their race and/or ethnicity or citizenship status. One example of this comes from the group of Filipina domestic workers in our sample. They came to Canada through the Live-In-Caregiver program, which gives them a limited work visa requiring that they hold a domestic worker job for 24 months of a 36-month period in order to apply for Canadian citizenship. One Filipina who cared and cleaned for an elderly man discussed the conflict between her background and Canadian definitions of sexual harassment:

> I remember my first year, he is always telling me why don't you come with me in bed and make me warm? . . . So I just, I don't know the way to take it in Canada, because in the Philippines if somebody say that to you and they don't touch you, nothing happens, it's just a word, but here in Canada, it's something.

These women also talked about how they were unwilling to file a complaint because it might put their employment and future Canadian citizenship in jeopardy. They were afraid that they would be fired from their job and that they would be unable to find a replacement job that would give them the necessary 24 months of work experience. As one Filipina domestic worker stated: "Even if you don't like your situation, you just wait for the time [when you have more permanent citizenship status] to leave."

BLAMING ONESELF

As a result of traditional gender socialization, women often take on a passive role when confronting uncomfortable and unpleasant situations. In the case of sexual harassment, this tendency initially leads most women to blame themselves for unwanted sexual behaviour. This is just what we found in our study. In the words of one white respondent: "I used to blame myself for the harassment and ask myself constantly what I was doing to make them want to treat me this way."

Women did not enjoy sexual advances from male colleagues, yet they believed they were the ones to blame for the men's behaviour (Fitzgerald et al., 1997). Other researchers have shown how blaming oneself for harassment reinforces the way in which women are socialized to respond to issues in a non-confrontational manner. If women blame themselves for the unwanted sexual attention, they will not speak up and attempt to end the harassment.

Like women who experience rape and other forms of sexual violence, the women in our study often blamed their youthfulness or their clothes for inciting men to harass them. Here is what two white women in our study had to say on the subject, the first, anglophone, the second, francophone:

> I did blame myself sometimes for the harassment, asking what it was that made them do this, and also I would think that it was because I was young and the clothes that I wore caused this. I also tried to dress differently so that I wouldn't be attractive at work.

> I asked myself whether the clothes I was wearing were too sexy, even though every day I wore a smock over my clothes since I worked in a hospital setting.

The Native women in our study also struggled to define their experiences as harassment, especially when the perpetrator was in a position of authority, such as a respected elder in the Native community:

> I felt uncomfortable. I don't like doubting myself, I was questioning: maybe that's just the way he is as an elder but it didn't feel right. Sometimes it's just knowing that something doesn't feel right.

This woman experienced sexual comments, touching, and invasion of personal space. Her case illustrates that the authority of the harasser is an important determinant of the victim's ability to identify her experience as harassment: the greater the authority of the harasser, the more difficult such identification becomes (Carr et al., 2004).

NAMING AND NOT BLAMING: BEYOND GENDER SOCIALIZATION

Some women in our study moved beyond blaming themselves. They re-defined their experiences as sexual harassment by talking with someone knowledgeable about the issue.

Women began to understand that what they were experiencing should not be tolerated as normal behaviour between men and women. As one white woman said:

> I worked at a bar and I always kept my looks up, you know, that's where your tips come from. I always thought it was because maybe I was wearing the wrong kind of clothes. I was never trashy looking or anything—but I thought maybe that was what it was. Or I thought maybe I was flirting a little bit with him like when I was being nice to him when he first came in, but then I kept thinking to myself, there's no way. I know I wasn't. And especially I got to see [the support worker] from the sexual assault centre—she really helped me. I realized it was about that.

This case demonstrates how some women resist their early gender socialization. The woman in question decided to re-evaluate behaviour that at first seemed normal to her and, through the assistance of a support worker, was able to reject her initial beliefs and stop blaming herself.

A Black woman who worked in a temporary position demonstrates the same process. She had the following conversation with the interviewer:

Respondent: How did I cope with it? I started going to talk to [the support worker] a lot. But I, you know how you question yourself. I started thinking it was something that I wore or I had too much makeup on or what was it? You know, I don't know why he started off that way. And I said to her, "You know I had my hair down." Sometimes I wore my hair in a bandanna. I wore a scarf. I wore a T-shirt to cover my body like, you know what I mean, and I didn't wear short, short shorts. And I was like "Why was he doing that to me?"

Interviewer: So, did you get an answer to that question?

Respondent: Well she [the support worker] told me that it was nothing that I was wearing or anything. That it didn't have anything to do with that, that it was the person himself.

Interviewer: Do you believe that? Do you believe that it had nothing to do with you?

Respondent: Not at the moment because you know, you question yourself. I guess I questioned myself for a while.

Interviewer: Now how do you look at it?

Respondent: Now how do I look at it? That he was just an ignorant pervert. Stuff like that—he's got some issues he needs to deal with. He's got some problems.

Our interviews show, then, that gender socialization is not the only variable affecting women's ability to define their experience. The nature of workplace culture, the authority of the harasser, the lack of Canadian citizenship, and the intervention of trained support personnel are among the factors that affect the capacity of women to define sexual harassment as such. The fact that some of the women we interviewed first blamed themselves for the harassment they experienced but were later able to re-evaluate their experience and report it to the relevant authorities shows that, while gender socialization constrains self-perceptions, it is by no means a lifetime straight-jacket (Morgan, 1999). For example, by placing support personnel in the workplace—officials who can discuss incidents of harassment with workers, educate them about what constitutes appropriate and inappropriate behaviour, inform them about their rights and mechanisms for seeking a resolution of grievances—organizations can do much to help women who experience sexual harassment. They can help them to recognize it for what it is and do something about it.

NOTES

1. Research for this project was funded by Status of Women Canada. We thank Jacquie Carr, Barbara MacQuarrie, and Audrey Huntley for collaboration on this project. Michael Schreiner and Robert Brym provided helpful comments on this paper. Finally, we are grateful to the women in our study for sharing their experiences with us.

REFERENCES

Canadian Human Rights Commission. (2004). "Discrimination and Harassment." On the World Wide Web at http://www.chrc-ccdp.ca/discrimination/what_is_it-en.asp (31 January 2006).

Carr, Jacquie, Audrey Huntley, Barbara MacQuarrie, and Sandy Welsh. (2004). Workplace Harassment and Violence. Centre for Violence Against Women and Children. University of Western Ontario. On the World Wide Web at http://www.crvawc.ca/research_crvawcpubs.htm (31 January 2006).

Collinson, M., and D. Collinson. (1996). "It's only Dick: The Sexual Harassment of Women Managers in Insurance Sales." Work, Employment and Society, 10: 29–56.

Connell, R.W. (2002). Gender. Oxford: Polity Press.

Dellinger, Kirsten, and Christine Williams. (2002). "The Locker Room and the Dorm Room: The Cultural Context of Sexual Harassment in Two Magazine Publishing Organizations." Social Problems, 49: 242–57.

Fitzgerald, L.F., S. Swann, and V.J. Magley. (1997). "But was it Really Harassment? Legal, Behavioral and Psychological Definitions of the Workplace Victimization of Women." In W. O'Donohue, ed., Sexual Harassment: Theory, Research, and Treatment (pp. 5–28). Boston: Allyn and Bacon.

Folgero, I.S., and I.H. Fjeldstad. (1995). "On Duty—Off Guard: Cultural Norms and Sexual Harassment in Service Organizations." Organization Studies, 16: 299–313.

Giuffre, Patti, and Christine Williams. (1994). "Boundary Lines: Labeling Sexual Harassment in Restaurants." Gender and Society, 8: 378–401.

Gruber, J.E. (1997). "An Epidemiology of Sexual Harassment: Evidence from North America and Europe." In W. O'Donohue, ed., Sexual Harassment: Theory, Research, and Treatment (pp. 84–98). Boston: Allyn and Bacon.

Gwartney-Gibbs, Patricia A., and Denise H. Lach. (1992). "Sociological Explanations for Failure to Seek Sexual Harassment Remedies." Mediation Quarterly, 9 (4): 363–73.

Hotelling, Kathy, and Barbara A. Zuber. (1997). "Feminist Issues in Sexual Harassment." In W. O'Donohue, ed., Sexual Harassment: Theory, Research, and Treatment (pp. 99–112). Boston: Allyn and Bacon.

Lach, Denise H., and Patricia A. Gwartney-Gibbs. (1993). "Sociological Perspectives on Sexual Harassment and Workplace Dispute Resolution." Journal of Vocational Behavior, 42 (1): 102–15.

Loe, M. (1996). "Working for Men at the Intersection of Power, Gender, and Sexuality." Sociological Inquiry, 66 (4): 399–421.

Morgan, Phoebe. (1999). "Risking Relationships: Understanding the Litigation Choices of Sexually Harassed Women." Law and Society Review, 33 (1): 67–92.

Reskin, Barbara, and Irene Padavic. (1994). Women and Men at Work. Thousand Oaks: Pine Forge Press.

Welsh, Sandy, Jacquie Carr, Barbara MacQuarrie, and Audrey Huntley. (2006). "I'm Not Thinking of It As Sexual Harassment: Understanding Harassment across Race and Citizenship." Gender and Society, 20: 87–107.

Welsh, Sandy, and Nierobisz, Annette. (1997). "How Prevalent Is Sexual Harassment? A Research Note on Measuring Sexual Harassment in Canada." *Canadian Journal of Sociology,* 22: 505–22.

Williams, Christine L. (1997). "Sexual harassment in organizations: A critique of current research and policy." *Sexuality and Culture* 1: 19-43.

Yount, K.R. (1991). "Ladies, Flirts, and Tomboys: Strategies for Managing Sexual Harassment in an Underground Coal Mine." *Journal of Contemporary Ethnography,* 19 (4): 396–422.

Chapter 7

Movies and Society

SHYON BAUMANN

THE SOCIOLOGY OF FILM

Quick—name a movie star. Is there anyone who cannot name one, or twenty? Is there anyone who does not know where Hollywood is, or who has not seen an image of the Hollywood sign, spelling out the place name in giant white letters on a hillside? The movies occupy a central place in our popular culture, just as they do in many other cultures around the world. Millions of Canadians see movies in theatres every year, and millions more see movies aired on television or recorded on DVD.

As an integral part of our popular culture, movies merit close sociological examination. The primary question of interest for sociologists of film is, "What is the relationship between movies and society?" There are two secondary questions built into the primary question. First, how do social factors influence the kinds of movies that are made? In other words, how do the social and organizational conditions in which movies are made affect their content? The second question reverses the causal arrow. How do movies influence society, particularly the attitudes and behaviours of audience members? As we will see, there is good evidence for arguing that, just as society influences movies, movies influence society.

TWO PERSPECTIVES ON HOW SOCIETY INFLUENCES FILM

ORGANIZATIONAL ANALYSIS

Do films represent the creative thoughts and actions of filmmakers? Of course they do. For example, the six *Star Wars* films bear the mark of the primary creative force behind them, writer and producer George Lucas. The distinctive characters and plot lines are his inventions. But a sociological perspective can show how movies reflect more than individual creativity. A review of the film industry's organizational history demonstrates that the way in which filmmaking was organized played a role in shaping the kinds of films that were made (Peterson, 1994). The organizational foundations of filmmaking were, in turn, influenced by wider social factors.

Depending on which sources you consult, the invention of a camera that could take moving pictures was either a French or an American invention, though inventors in both countries probably contributed equally to the final product. Regardless of who receives the credit, moving pictures were invented in the final decade of the nineteenth century without any awareness that they would form the basis of a major cultural industry and art form. In fact, moving pictures were first used to document everyday events for scientific and informational purposes. Not long after they were invented, however, cultural entrepreneurs realized their entertainment potential.

To capitalize on audience interest, many owners of shops and lunch counters converted their stores and restaurants into makeshift cinemas. Initially, movies were just a few minutes long, but the new technology so dazzled audiences they would pay just to see footage of a train approaching or a horse galloping. By the second decade of the twentieth century, however, movies had already begun to develop in length and content and to adopt the narrative style with which we are familiar today. As movies evolved, so did the industrial organization of film production and distribution. Movie theatres seating hundreds and even thousands of people were built. A small group of companies emerged as forerunners in film production. Their production facilities were located in Los Angeles to take advantage of the consistently favourable weather for filming.

Before long, this small group of companies was responsible for the vast majority of films being made in the United States, which also meant that they were responsible for the vast majority of films being *seen* in the United States, as well as in many other countries, including Canada. Before television became widespread in the late 1940s and early 1950s, movies were the primary form of mass entertainment. A large proportion of the population attended a movie theatre weekly, and it was not uncommon for people to go to the movies several times a week (Brown, 1995). Movies were big business, and they continue to be big business today even though people see fewer movies than they used to.

Despite the economic success of the film industry, movies were heavily criticized at the time for being formulaic; that is, critics found movies to be bland, predictable, and altogether too similar (White, 1936). Part of their criticism of the movies was directed at the way movies were made.

Because they were the default entertainment option for many people, films were virtually guaranteed a minimum audience size. The incentive for the film companies, then, was to produce a large number of films to meet the high demand. This supply and demand dynamic encouraged a production process for films that resembled that of most other mass-produced goods. For the sake of efficiency, film companies made films in assembly-line fashion. Moreover, the centralization of production by a handful of companies meant that there were relatively few opportunities to create diversity in the kinds of films that were being made. Adding to uniformity was the system of "block booking" that studios forced on

theatre owners (Hanssen, 2000). Theatre owners leased movies from studios, but rather than being allowed to choose which movies they leased, they were required to lease whole "blocks" of films, ranging from three or four to about twenty at a time. Of these blocks of films, only one or two would be "A" movies, and the rest would be cheaply made "B" movies. To book "A" movies, theatre owners had to book the more numerous "B" movies as well. For the most part, this method "encouraged the production and consumption of as vast an avalanche of triviality as has ever been inflicted on a public." The workers involved in producing "B" movies "seemed to consider the assignment a chore below their personal dignity, to be performed perfunctorily, carelessly and ineptly" (Mayer, 1948).

As a whole, the films produced in Hollywood during the era of the "studio system" bear the stamp of the method through which they were created. A "Fordist" assembly-line production model fashioned films that were largely standardized. Unlike cars, however, there were some standout films that exhibited the artistic impulses of particular directors, producers, and screenwriters. Orson Welles, the director of films such as *Citizen Kane* and *The Magnificent Ambersons*, fought hard for his artistic independence from studio executives and was able to make lasting works of art as a result. Walt Disney founded his own studio to pursue the art of animation and was able to create *Snow White and the Seven Dwarfs* and *Fantasia* among many other treasured films. Although these great films are still appreciated today, they are exceptions to the general character of films produced by the studio system.

The studio system came to an end in the 1950s. For a variety of reasons, including the introduction of television, suburbanization, and a rising birth rate, film audiences fell dramatically. In the absence of guaranteed audiences, the assembly-line production method of the studio system was no longer effective. Over the next few decades, new modes of production emerged to suit the changing economic circumstances of the film industry.

The current model for film production is the "blockbuster" model. Production companies make a smaller number of films, and within that smaller pool they select a few to receive most of the funding for production and promotion. In effect, they put most of their eggs in a few baskets. This production logic has, again, an economic foundation. Great uncertainty surrounds every film; producers do not know if an audience will turn up at the theatres. By investing large sums in the production and promotion of certain films, studios increase the likelihood that audiences will flock to them. A recent example is *Batman Begins*, which was made for about $135 million and grossed over $370 million worldwide. Despite these efforts, big budget films often fail. A recent failure was *Catwoman*, starring Halle Berry. It cost approximately $85 million to produce but failed to gross anywhere near that amount. For this reason, the studios hedge their bets and produce smaller budget films on the off chance that they will strike a chord with audiences. While many of these films also lose money, others are surprisingly successful. The original *Texas Chainsaw Massacre*, for example, was made for around $140 000 and grossed over $30 million in 1974. In 2003, the remake of that movie was produced for about $9 million and grossed over $80 million in the United States and tens of millions of dollars more in overseas markets (http://www.imdb.com). The blockbuster production model is profitable for studios because the popular films generate more than enough profit to cover the losses incurred by unpopular films.

As with the studio system, the blockbuster system involves a correspondence between the production model and the nature of the films that are made. The blockbuster system encourages the making of narrative and visual spectacles designed to generate fascination, mass interest, and big profits. Films such as *Titanic*, *Spiderman*, and *The Lord of the Rings* trilogy rely on stunning visual effects and archetypal story lines of good versus evil to appeal to as wide an audience as possible, not just domestically but around the globe. Such films require enormous capital investment, so film studios want to franchise them. After all, spinoff toys, video games, and sequels can add much to the bottom line. Films that can be franchised are more likely to be produced and to be given large budgets.

Films that do not receive as much funding for production and promotion tend to experiment more with narrative elements and lesser known actors. Sometimes these lower budget productions pay off hugely and become hits, as in the case of *My Big Fat Greek Wedding*.

In sum, an organizational perspective offers an important corrective to the conventional view that cultural productions such as movies represent only the work of individual creators. Individual creators surely have an influence on the final product, but if we wish to understand the character of movies it is crucial to take into account the organizational conditions under which they are made.

CULTURAL REFLECTION

A second perspective for understanding how social factors influence the content of films points to the elements of culture reflected in them. In this view, films mirror society for two main reasons. First, filmmaking occurs within a social context and is constrained by that context. Second, films are designed to be popular with audiences and so are made to reflect the interests and concerns of audience members.

As with other artistic media, movies are preoccupied with universal themes such as love and intimacy, family life, growing up, and examining what constitutes true happiness. Because these issues are an integral part of our culture, they enjoy a central place in movies.

Films also mirror society at the level of everyday life. Thus, movies today differ in many ways from the movies of, say, the 1920s. That is partly because the technology of filmmaking has evolved. Today, sound, editing, lighting, camera work, and special effects create movies that look entirely different from the films of the past. Today's movies also look different from movies made in the past because (with the exception of movies set in the future or in the past) they must realistically depict the lives of characters in contemporary social settings, and these settings, including the objects people encounter in everyday life, change over time.

Just as the facts of our everyday existence evolve over time, so do important social problems, concerns, and interests. Consider the villains that populate movies. During the cold war (1947–91), many people in North America felt threatened by Communism, particularly Communist infiltration of Western democracies and nuclear annihilation at the hands of Communists. Films from that period often featured Communists, especially Soviets, as archetypal bad guys. Since the fall of Communism in the Soviet Union and Eastern Europe, these threats no longer loom large in the public consciousness. Communist villains are neither plausible nor interesting to today's audiences. As a result, they generally no longer appear in films. The public is now preoccupied with the threat of terrorism, and that is reflected in an increase in the depiction of terrorist villains in recent films such as *The Sum of All Fears*, *Spy Game*, *The Siege*, and *Collateral Damage*, among many others.

The cold war is just one of many evolving social concerns and interests that are reflected in the movies. Following the rise of feminism in the 1960s, people became more interested in exploring the roles of women in society, and films reflected that interest. The same can be said of such issues as environmental protection, corporate crime, government corruption, genetic engineering, and HIV/AIDS.

Film scholars argue that social concerns also influence films at a deeper, metaphorical level. Accordingly, even films not explicitly dealing with the cold war can be interpreted as expressions of the anxiety associated with it. Science fiction films in which aliens seek to expand their dominion by colonizing Earth were especially popular in the 1950s when cold war anxieties were at their peak. The aliens embodied many of the qualities that were attributed to Communists;

they were godless, emotionless invaders intent on destroying Western democracy, traditions, and prosperity (Hendershot, 1999). Similarly, horror films often depict creatures that afflict humans through implantation or infection. They often end up inside people or they take the form of people. One interpretation of this recurring theme is that it reflects our anxiety over health and illness, particularly illness caused by viruses, bacteria, and cancers that invade and destroy their human hosts (Guerrero, 1990). *Alien* and its three sequels, for example, involve a vicious monster that reproduces itself by inhabiting a human host who is killed when the creature is eventually "born." At a certain level, a film in which people are saved from the dangers of bodily invasion and destruction reassures the audience that it can be saved from the dangers of real-world illness.

HOW FILMS SHAPE SOCIETY

Having considered two ways in which society influences the movies, let us now examine how movies influence society. For almost as long as movies have been made, people have feared that they may corrupt us. Initially, concern arose from the fact that moving images proved to be a captivating and fascinating innovation. Observers predicted disastrous consequences, including the thoughtless imitation of dangerous activities, the learning of criminal techniques, and the rapid deterioration of moral standards.

By the late 1920s, such concern initiated the Payne Fund Studies, which attempted to assess whether going to the movies influenced children negatively. The studies have been thoroughly criticized for their flawed methods and suspect findings. Nevertheless, they indicate the high level of early concern over the possibility—and, in some people's minds, the certainty—that movies were corrupting youth.

Eighty years later, that fear has not abated. New articles about the dangers of movies appear in the popular press without any pretence of social scientific rigour. We often read that movies are responsible for promiscuity, materialism, violence, depression, loss of religion, sexism, agism, racism, and much else. These are serious allegations, but before we conclude that movies actually have these effects, we need strong evidence.

Movies may influence people on both the societal and the individual level. *Societal-level* influences include those that change the nature of our culture, particularly our norms and values. Consider materialism—the view that wealth buys happiness. Some people note that movies typically depict wealthy lifestyles as a source of happiness. The lavish and hedonistic lives of movie stars reinforce the message. How many North Americans envied Jennifer Lopez when Ben Affleck proposed to her with a pink diamond engagement ring worth more than $1 million? People are more inclined to accept the notion that wealth buys happiness when they are surrounded by such images and exposed to such events.

The problem with arguments about societal-level influences is that they are difficult to support or refute with data. There are two reasons for this. First, our culture is affected by many social forces of which the movies are only one. We have no way of separating the effect of movies from all other effects. In the case of materialism, for example, we cannot know if changing values result from changing levels of wealth, changing levels of wealth inequality, messages contained in mass media other than movies, or many other factors. Movies may play a large role, a small role, or no role at all. Given what we know about the complexity of cultural change in general, however, it seems highly unlikely that the movies play a large role in shaping society's values. It is more likely that they reflect existing values.

The second reason for doubting arguments about the societal-level influence of films is that such arguments assume films are understood by members of society in the same way and affect them similarly. We know, however, that some people never or infrequently see films and that different people take away different messages from the same film. For example, do people become more tolerant of promiscuity when they see it portrayed in movies, or more repulsed? Without knowing what messages audience members are receiving from films, it is impossible to form an argument about how films influence society.

Arguments about certain kinds of *individual-level* effects stand on firmer empirical ground. These arguments hold that movies shape the attitudes and behaviours of individuals in specific ways. For example, one vein of research on the effects of movies investigates whether exposure to movies in which the characters smoke increases the likelihood that young people will take up smoking. The most recent study on this topic asked a large number of adolescents about the movies they had seen in recent years, as well as whether they had ever tried smoking (Sargent et al., 2005). It found that increased exposure to movies in which characters smoked was correlated with the likelihood that an adolescent would try smoking, even after taking into account many other factors usually associated with starting smoking. Thus, while movies are by no means the only relevant factor, they seem to have an influence on smoking initiation among some adolescents. Research done in this fashion, however, only gains general acceptance by scholars as reliable after many replications. Time will tell if these initial results hold up.

A much larger body of research conducted over the last 40 years has been done on the topic of violence, again focusing on the potential effects on children. This research attempts to understand whether and in what ways individuals are affected by on-screen violence. Studies take the form of laboratory experiments (in which some children are shown violent content and compared to a control group of children who are shown non-violent content); field experiments (in which the same kinds of comparisons are made in natural social settings); cross-sectional studies (in which surveys allow researchers to examine correlations between exposure to on-screen violence and real-world violence in different segments of the population); and longitudinal studies (in which researchers track samples of people for months or years and look for correlations between exposure to on-screen violence and violent behaviour).

Several recent reviews of the research literature find strong evidence that in the short term, children and adolescents who watch violent films become physically and verbally aggressive. The evidence for long-term effects is significant but requires further research before firm conclusions can be drawn (Anderson and Bushman, 2002; Browne and Hamilton-Giachritis, 2005; Office of the Surgeon General, 2001).

Research shows that violent movies increase the likelihood that *some* audience members will behave more aggressively. Significantly, however, not all individuals are affected in the same way or to the same extent by violent movies. Moreover, violent behaviour has many causes, of which media violence is only one and by no means the most important. It is also important to note that critics have expressed much concern about the graphic nature of violence, as in horror movies where people are butchered. However, on-screen violence tends to have more of an effect on audience members if it is presented without a reasonable moral context. Violence is sometimes presented as a legitimate way to resolve conflict, as an action that goes unpunished, and without a depiction of the devastating emotional consequences that it has on people's lives. It is more the lack of contextualization of violence than its graphic quality that makes on-screen violence problematic (Potter, 1999).

Frequently lost in the conversation about how movies influence society is consideration of their positive effects. Yet movies benefit us by entertaining us and by addressing important issues that deserve public awareness and understanding. *On the Beach* (1959) sparked debate about the nuclear arms race, *Guess Who's Coming to Dinner* (1967) provoked dialogue about interracial relationships, *Philadelphia* (1993) generated widespread discussion about discrimination

against people with AIDS, *The Insider* (1999) raised awareness of the influence of the tobacco industry on the mass media, and *Syriana* (2005) raised questions about the oil industry's manipulation of politicians in the United States and the Middle East. As these examples suggest, the influence of movies on society is often informative and progressive.

REFERENCES

Anderson, Craig A., and Brad J. Bushman. (2002). "The Effects of Media Violence on Society." *Science,* (29 March): 2377–78.

Brown, Gene. (1995). *Movie Time: A Chronology of Hollywood and the Movie Industry from Its Beginnings to the Present.* New York: Macmillan.

Browne, Kevin D., and Katherine Hamilton-Giachritis. (2005). "The Influence of Violent Media on Children and Adolescents: A Public-Health Approach." *The Lancet,* (19 February): 702–10.

Guerrero, Edward. (1990). "AIDS as Monster in Science Fiction and Horror Cinema." *Journal of Popular Film and Television,* 18 (3): 86–93.

Hanssen, Andrew F. (2000). "The Block Booking of Films Reexamined." *Journal of Law and Economics,* 43 (2): 395–426.

Hendershot, Cyndy. (1999). *Paranoia, the Bomb, and 1950s Science-Fiction Films.* Bowling Green, OH: Bowling Green State University Press.

Mayer, Arthur L. (1948). "An Exhibitor Begs for 'B's.'" *Hollywood Quarterly,* 3 (2): 172–77.

Office of the Surgeon General. (2001). *Youth Violence: A Report of the Surgeon General.* Washington, DC: Dept. of Health and Human Services, U.S. Public Health Service.

Peterson, Richard. (1994). "Cultural Studies Through the Production Perspective: Progress and Prospects." In Diana Crane, ed., *The Sociology of Culture: Emerging Theoretical Perspectives* (pp. 163–89). Cambridge, MA: Blackwell Publishers.

Potter, James W. (1999). *On Media Violence.* Thousand Oaks, CA: Sage Publications.

Sargent, James D., Michael L. Beach, Anna M. Adachi-Mejia, Jennifer J. Gibson, Linda T. Titus-Ernstoff, Charles P. Carusi, Susan D. Swain, Todd F. Heatherton, and Madeleine A. Dalton. (2005). "Exposure to Movie Smoking: Its Relation to Smoking Initiation among US Adolescents." *Pediatrics,* 116 (5): 1183–91.

White, William Allen. (1936). "Chewing-Gum Relaxation." In William J. Perlman, ed., *The Movies on Trial* (pp. 3–12). New York: The Macmillan Company.

Chapter 12

How Gender, Class, and Age Affect Self-Esteem

JULIE ANN McMULLIN AND JOHN CAIRNEY

THE PROBLEM STATED

During the early stages of writing this chapter, one of the authors (McMullin) attended a fundraiser for Brescia University College, a small women's school in London, Ontario. The aim of the event was to raise money for scholarships for disadvantaged women. Dini Petty, a famous Canadian journalist, was the guest speaker.

By all accounts, Dini Petty has had a successful career. She began her work as a traffic reporter who flew in a helicopter and reported trouble spots on Toronto's busy streets. Unlike anyone else at the time, however, Ms. Petty decided that she would prefer to both fly the helicopter and report on traffic. Soon she became one of only a few hundred women in the world to have a helicopter license. Ms. Petty subsequently held jobs as a reporter, an anchor for a 6 o'clock TV news show, the host of a Canadian talk show, and most recently, the author of a very good children's story called *The Queen, The Bear, and the Bumblebee*.

When Ms. Petty took the stage at the gala, she presented herself as a confident, self-assured, articulate, and humorous woman. Yet the focus of her talk was on her lifelong struggle to gain self-esteem. "If there were medals awarded for lack of self-esteem," said Petty, "I would have received gold." In her talk, Petty identified two key factors that contributed to her low self-esteem: (1) girls learn at an early age that they need to be nice in order to be liked; and (2) girls face a lot of pressure to be beautiful. Of course, in identifying these factors, Petty concurred with decades of feminist literature. But Petty also talked about her epiphany, the moment at which she looked in the mirror and saw a beautiful person, "both inside and out." She talked about the things she has done over the last few years to gain self-confidence and ultimately self-esteem. Not insignificantly, Petty told the audience that she would soon turn 58, a point which drew applause from some of the listeners, no doubt because she doesn't "look her age."

As Petty noted, self-esteem for young women is linked to cultural notions of beauty and femininity. Young women who perceive themselves as ugly, fat, too short, too tall, and so on, experience lower self-esteem than do those who have more positive assessments of their body (Abell and Richards, 1996). Cultural ideals of female beauty, at least in North America, are also tied to youthful appearance. Women are not considered beautiful if they are wrinkled, grey-haired, or overweight (Abu-Laban and McDaniel, 2001). Hence, one would expect that, among women, self-esteem would diminish with increasing age. Yet this hypothesis stands in contrast to Petty's experience of gaining self-esteem when she was in her fifties.

The fact that Petty's self-esteem did not decline with advancing age, but rather increased markedly, may be tied, at least in part, to her privileged structural location as a white, well-off professional. Most feminist research on self-esteem focuses on young women. Yet in light of what we know about the negative implications of age-discriminating attitudes on perceptions of body and self (Calasanti and Slevin, 2001; Hurde Clarke, 2001), the neglect of research on the relationship between aging and self-esteem is unfortunate.

PREVIOUS RESEARCH

GENDER

Self-esteem is a person's perception of his or her self-worth. The strong and consistent finding regarding gender and self-esteem is that, compared to men, women have lower self-esteem in adulthood (Josephs, Markus, and Tafarodi, 1992). Although boys and girls enjoy about the same level of self-esteem between the ages of 11 and 13, they gradually diverge during the teenage years and adulthood. Boys gain and girls lose a sense of positive self-worth (Rosenfield, 1999).

Several explanations for this relationship exist in the mental health literature. One of the most compelling is Rosenfield's view that men and women have different experiences that begin in early childhood and that are reflections of the *relative power* they enjoy. Relative power, in turn, influences self-appraisal: "Given the power, the responsibility in the public domain, receipt of support, and value placed on masculine pursuits, males generally tend toward high self-esteem" (Rosenfield, 1999: 220).

Two other compelling explanations for gender differences in self-esteem exist. First, people compare their social identities, opinions, and abilities to those of others. To the extent that they feel inferior to those with whom they interact, their self-esteem is negatively affected. This process involves the assessment of self-worth by means of *social comparison*. Second, people assess themselves through their interaction with others. People learn to see themselves as others believe them to be. If significant others do not think highly of a person, that person will come to think poorly of himself or herself. This process is known as the *reflected appraisal* of one's self-worth (Rosenberg and Pearlin, 1978).

Girls and women, more than boys and men, are socially judged on the basis of what they look like. If they diverge from socially constructed cultural ideals of beauty, others may think poorly of them and their self-esteem may suffer (through reflected appraisals). Furthermore, girls and women take part in processes of social comparison whereby they compare their beauty to that of others. If a woman feels less beautiful than the women with whom she interacts, her self-esteem is negatively affected (Abell and Richards, 1996; Furman, 1997). Men also engage in comparative beauty exercises, evaluating the appearance of their body relative to others (Oberg and Tornstam, 1999). But the fact that women place more importance than men on their physical appearance suggests that physical appearance may be more relevant to identity and self-esteem among women than among men.

SOCIAL CLASS

In the literature on the relationship between self-esteem and social class, the latter is typically measured by a person's occupational status, income, and education. In general, adults with low occupational status, income, and education have low social esteem. For instance, as Rosenberg's power theory suggests, individuals who are employed in good jobs that are characterized by high autonomy, prestige, and creativity enjoy higher self-esteem than do unemployed individuals or people who work in "bad" jobs (Gecas and Seff, 1990; Pugliesi, 1995; Rosenberg and Pearlin, 1978; Mirowsky and Ross, 1996).

Explanations of the relationship between self-esteem and social class also consider reflected appraisals and social comparisons (Rosenberg and Pearlin, 1978; Rosenberg, 1981). The reflected appraisals argument suggests that members of the working class have low self-esteem because they are judged negatively by those with whom they interact on the basis of their low-status jobs, incomes, and education. At work, for example, managers tend to see themselves as superior to non-managerial workers and treat them accordingly, while members of the working class are more likely to view themselves as inferior to members of the middle or upper classes. Thus, reflected appraisals and social comparisons negatively influence self-esteem among the working class.

In support of these arguments, Rosenberg and Pearlin (1978) argued that working-class children may not experience the negative perceptions and attitudes about their class as acutely as their parents do. They hypothesized that, as a result, the effects of social class on self-esteem should be greater in adulthood than in childhood. Their research supported their hypothesis. Although their work is now dated, the small body of research that has since been conducted on the relationship between self-esteem and social class confirms their findings (Turner and Roszell, 1994). Perhaps more importantly, the theoretical underpinnings of the argument are sound. The social class homogeneity of many school settings shelters children from social comparisons and reflected appraisals that negatively affect self-esteem.

AGING

Unfortunately, the samples that Rosenberg and Pearlin and others used to test their hypotheses were composed of people under the age of 65. It is therefore unclear how class-based reflected appraisal and social comparison arguments play out in later life. The exclusion of people 65 years old and older is in fact a characteristic of all of the work described above. Only a few studies have explored the relationship between age and self-esteem among the elderly and they have produced mixed results. Some studies show that self-esteem remains stable or increases as people age, others suggest that it decreases, and still others demonstrate that self-esteem first increases with age and then decreases after a certain age (Giarrusso, Mabry, and Bengtson, 2001).

Social scientists have proposed two explanations for the relationship between self-esteem and aging. The *maturation perspective* suggests that as people age they become more accepting of themselves. Proponents of this perspective argue that the process of social comparison is not as pronounced in later life because at that stage individuals develop "ego integrity" and a positive evaluation of their accomplishments

(Dietz, 1996). Consequently, the maturation perspective predicts stable or increasing self-esteem in later life. *Role perspectives* have also been used to explain the relationship between aging and self-esteem. According to role perspectives, the loss of social roles that is associated with old age (e.g., exit from paid work; the so-called empty nest, which involves children growing up and leaving their parents living alone at home) results in lower self-esteem.

A key problem with the maturation and role perspectives is that they do not consider how structured power relations change through the life course and how they influence development processes. Furthermore, cross-time data are required to assess accurately whether either of these perspectives adequately explains the relationship between age and self-esteem. Yet only studies that examine different categories of people at a single point in time have explored the relationship to date. Finally, we are unaware of any research that explores how gender, class, and age combine to produce different effects on self-esteem, although we do know that, in general, these variables create systems of advantage for some people and disadvantage for others in labour markets, health outcomes, and other arenas of social life (Arber and Ginn, 1995; Browne, 1998; Calasanti, 1996; Calasanti and Slevin, 2001; Hill Collins, 2000; Estes, 1999; McMullin, 2000, 2004; Palo Stoller and Campbell Gibson, 1997). Clearly, much research remains to be done on the relationships among gender, social class, aging, and self-esteem.

THE INTERSECTION OF GENDER, CLASS, AND AGE

Our literature review has identified two main types of explanations for differences in self-esteem. First, self-esteem is influenced by the relative control that individuals have over their lives—and gender, class, and age structure this control in complex ways. It is through these complexities that differences in self-esteem emerge.

We might expect, for instance, that positions of authority within families buffer the negative influence of class position on self-esteem for working-class men. We might also expect that the control that professional women have in paid work may buffer the negative effect on self-esteem that comes with their lack of control in determining who is responsible for the under-valued work of caring for children or older adults in families. For older adults, changes in self-esteem may be attributed to changes in power that come with role loss (e.g., retirement) rather than the loss of power itself. But here, class and gender structure these effects. Working-class men may feel a sense of empowerment with positive benefits to self-esteem that come with no longer having to work for anyone. Middle- and upper-class men may feel differently because they no longer have anyone under their control when they retire. The effect of class-based power for women may be similar to that of men in later life but family care and the distribution of power between men and women in the household persist. Thus, the relationship between class, age, and self-esteem cannot be separated from gender.

The second set of explanations for differences in self-esteem that we have identified focuses on the processes of social comparison and reflected appraisal. These processes are themselves influenced by the intersecting structures of gender, class, and age. For instance, research shows that self-esteem operates differently for young women and young men. Relative to young men, young women are more likely to make social comparisons and internalize reflected appraisals of themselves on the basis of socially constructed ideals of feminine beauty. For girls and women, identity is tied to their relationships with boys and men. Hence, to the extent that boys and men believe that a girl or woman is beautiful and therefore worthy of affection, the self-esteem of these girls and women will be heightened. Class is an issue here because processes of social comparison and reflected appraisal may vary if a woman's sense of identity is also linked to her paid work. Because middle-class jobs and professional employment tend to be more meaningful than working-class jobs, the connection between identity and paid work is more likely among middle- and upper-class women than it is among working-class women. Alternatively, economically well-off women, either in their own right or through their relationship with men, may have more resources to invest in maintaining their beauty, in "feeling good about themselves," and in living up to the middle-class ideal of "taking care of yourself." Of course, middle-class men also participate in the cult of self-care, emphasizing physical fitness and nutrition as means of remaining youthful in appearance. Yet the fact remains that bodily appearance is more important for women than for men (Oberg and Tornstam, 1999). As such, perceptions of attractiveness likely figure more into evaluations of self-worth for women.

How does age influence this relationship? In general, beauty is socially constructed with youth in mind (Abu-Laban and McDaniel, 2001; Calasanti and Slevin, 2001). Consumer beauty products are marketed to "combat" the effects of aging—as if we were engaged in a war (Calasanti and Slevin, 2001). For women, and to a lesser extent men, to be attractive and successful is to be young and beautiful. Social comparisons and reflected appraisals of beauty and self-worth are often made with youth as a referent. Indeed, self-appraisals are also made with a younger self as the ideal in comparison with which the older self is judged ("I'm not as young as I used to be;" "I feel younger than I look"). Of course, the connotations of these comparisons are most often negative (Hurde Clarke, 2001). Hence, through processes of self-comparison and reflected appraisal one might expect that older people would have lower self-esteem than younger people.

One of the few studies that explores the relationship between gender, age group, and body image showed that women care more about their appearance than do men, regardless of age (Oberg and Tornstam, 1999). Notably, however, 60 percent of men in the study agreed that their looks were important to them, and compared to younger men, those 75 and older were more likely to agree that their appearance was important. The study also showed that compared to men, women worry more about how their looks will change as they grow older. Except among 75- to 85-year-olds, women were less satisfied with their bodies than were men. Although body satisfaction did not vary by age group among men, older women had higher body satisfaction than did younger women. In short, appearance matters for both men and women of all ages but the relationship between gender, age, and body image is complex. Some of the complexity may be due to the relative influence of competing gender, class, and age identities in people's lives (e.g., professional versus woman, retired person versus professional, and so on).

RESEARCH QUESTIONS

The idea for this chapter was inspired by informal conversations that McMullin has had with women in varying social contexts. When discussions centred on growing old, McMullin noticed an interesting trend. Women in lower socioeconomic groups tended to reflect more negatively on the experience of growing old than did women in higher socioeconomic groups. Their assessments of aging were tied almost exclusively to their bodies. To the extent that their bodies were deteriorating relative to established norms of beauty and youth, such assessments were negative. The self-esteem of these women was threatened by the fact that they saw themselves as "looking old." On the other hand, women in higher socioeconomic groups tended to cherish the experience of growing old. They described the experience as liberating because men no longer paid attention to the way they looked. These women talked about how they loved growing old because of the self-confidence and power they had gained over the years. Like Dini Petty, these women had achieved high self-esteem and self-confidence later in life; in many ways they felt empowered with increasing age (Gibson, 1996; Browne, 1998).

McMullin's discussions with these women and our reading of the literature on self-esteem lead us to explore the following research questions:

- Is there a relationship between age, socioeconomic status, and self-esteem among Canadians? If so, what is it?
- Does gender influence the relationship between age, socioeconomic status, and self-esteem among Canadians? If so, how?

METHOD

Our sample is drawn from the National Population Health Survey (NPHS) conducted by Statistics Canada. The NPHS is a 1994 telephone survey of a representative national sample of Canadians in all ten provinces. Statistics Canada interviewers surveyed 19 600 households in which one person was selected to provide detailed personal information. People living on Native reserves, on military bases, in institutions, and in some remote areas in Ontario and Quebec were excluded.

Self-esteem is the dependent variable in the analysis and is measured by six items. The items assess how strongly one agrees or disagrees with six statements measuring self-worth:

1. You feel that you have a number of good qualities.
2. You feel that you're a person of worth at least equal to other people.
3. You are able to do things as well as most other people.
4. You take a positive attitude toward yourself.
5. One the whole, you are satisfied with yourself.
6. All in all, you're inclined to feel you're a failure.

The independent variables in our analyses include measures of age (at five-year intervals) and gender. Because gender, age, and class influence marital status and because marital status has been found to influence self-worth, we also included it in our analysis. The marital status categories used in the analysis are married (including common-law), previously married (including widowed, divorced, and separated), and single. We used years of education and household income to measure social class.

RESULTS

In support of past research, our results indicate that self-esteem falls with age. Women report lower self-esteem than do men. People who were previously married or single report lower self-esteem than married people. As education and income increase, self-esteem also increases.

To address our two research questions we needed to examine whether and how gender, age, and social class intersect in their influence on self-esteem. We graphed some of our results in Figure 12.1 (for women) and Figure 12.2 (for men). The pattern of association is similar in both graphs. Regardless of sex, the effects of income differences on self-esteem are virtually non-existent in early adolescence through to middle age. By the age of about 62, however, there is a divergence in self-esteem by income groups. Individuals in the highest income groups report higher self-esteem than those in the lowest income group. This gap widens until the age of 90, at which point income differences are most pronounced. Average self-esteem scores are somewhat higher across age groups for men than for women. Moreover, the gap in self-

esteem by income groups at the age of 90 is somewhat wider among men. Finally, the rate of decline in self-esteem and the rate of divergence in income with age appear steeper for women. Education remains significantly and positively related to self-esteem and single people have lower self-esteem than do married people.

DISCUSSION AND CONCLUSION

This chapter takes a modest step toward piecing together the complex relationships among class, gender, age, and self-esteem using Canadian data. We have shown that self-esteem is lower in older age groups, both male and female. This finding is contrary to some past research, which suggests that age has little influence on self-esteem or that self-esteem increases with age. Furthermore, in all age groups, women have lower self-esteem than do men. Corresponding with past research, we found that income tends not to influence self-esteem for young men or women but does for people in middle age. By including persons 65 years old and over in our study we see that the most pronounced income differences are for people in later life.

It is important to note that what influences self-esteem is power, social comparisons, and reflected appraisals—not an individual's gender, income, and age. Gender, class, and age relations determine the relative power of individuals in

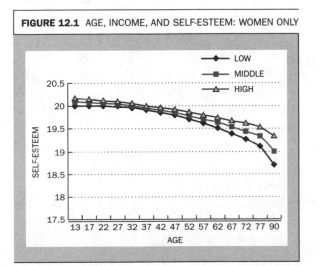

FIGURE 12.1 AGE, INCOME, AND SELF-ESTEEM: WOMEN ONLY

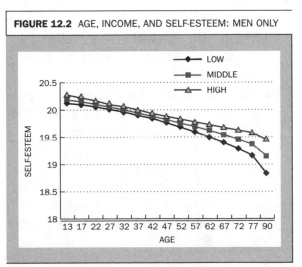

FIGURE 12.2 AGE, INCOME, AND SELF-ESTEEM: MEN ONLY

society as well as the interpersonal processes of social comparison and reflected appraisal. People with less power are poorly positioned to make favourable social comparisons and receive favourable reflected appraisals. Hence, women, members of the working class, and older adults suffer from lower self-esteem because of their structurally disadvantaged position.

This chapter provides only a glimpse into the relationship between social structure and self-esteem, so we can only speculate about how and why gender, class, and age influence self-esteem. More research is needed on this topic. Still, our research contributes to the literature on self-esteem insofar as it moves away from developmental, physiological, and role-loss approaches to aging. Our contention is that an age-based power structure is a detriment to self-esteem in later life. The fact that power decreases in later life, that old age is not highly valued, and that beauty is socially constructed with youth in mind places older people at risk of experiencing low self-esteem relative to younger people.

REFERENCES

Abell, Steven. C., and Maryse H. Richards. (1996). "The Relationship Between Body Shape Satisfaction and Self-esteem: An Investigation of Gender and Class Differences." *Journal of Youth and Adolescence,* 25: 691–703.

Abu-Laban, Sharon McIrvin, and Susan McDaniel. (2001). "Beauty, Status, and Aging." In Nancy Mandell, ed., *Feminist Issues: Race, Class, and Sexuality,* 3rd ed. (pp. 108–33). Toronto: Prentice Hall.

Arber, Sara, and Jay Ginn, eds. (1995). *Connecting Gender and Ageing: A Sociological Approach.* Buckingham: Open University Press.

Browne, Colette V. (1998). *Women, Feminism, and Aging.* New York: Springer.

Calasanti, Toni M. (1996). "Incorporating Diversity: Meaning, Levels of Research, and Implications for Theory." *The Gerontologist,* 36: 147–56.

Calasanti, Toni M., and Kate F. Slevin. (2001). *Gender, Social Inequalities, and Aging.* New York: Altamira Press.

Dietz, Bernadette E. (1996). "The Relationship of Aging to Self-Esteem: The Relative Effects of Maturation and Role Accumulation." *International Journal of Aging and Human Development,* 43: 249–66.

Estes, Carol L. (1999). "The New Political Economy of Aging: Introduction and Critique." In Merideth Minkler and Carol Estes, eds., *Critical Gerontology* (pp. 17–35). Amityville, NY: Baywood Publishing Co. Inc.

Furman, Frida Kerner. (1997). *Facing the Mirror: Older Women and Beauty Shop Culture.* New York: Routledge.

Gecas, Viktor, and Monica A. Seff. (1990). "Social Class and Self-Esteem: Psychological Centrality, Compensation and the Relative Effects of Work and Home." *Social Psychological Quarterly,* 53: 165–73.

Giarrusso, Roseann, J. Beth Mabry, and Vern L. Bengtson. (2001). "The Aging Self in Social Contexts." In Robert. H. Binstock and Linda. K. George, eds., *Handbook of Aging and the Social Sciences,* 5th ed. (pp. 295–312). San Diego: Academic Press.

Gibson, Diane. (1996). "Broken Down by Age and Gender: 'The Problem of Old Women' Redefined." *Gender and Society,* 10: 433–48.

Hill Collins, Patricia. (2000). "Moving beyond Gender: Intersectionality and Scientific Knowledge." In Myra Max Ferree, Judith Lorber, and Beth B. Hess, eds., *Revisioning Gender* (pp. 261–84). New York: Altamira Press.

Hurde Clarke, Laura. (2001). "Older Women's Bodies and the Self: The Construction of Identity in Later Life." *The Canadian Review of Sociology and Anthropology,* 38: 441–64.

Josephs, Robert A., Hazel Rose Markus, and Romin W. Tafarodi. (1992). "Gender and Self-Esteem." *Journal of Personality and Social Psychology,* 63: 391–402.

McMullin, Julie Ann. (2000). "Diversity and the State of Sociological Aging Theory." *The Gerontologist,* 40: 517–30.

————. (2004). *Understanding Inequality: Intersections of Class, Age, Gender, Ethnicity, and Race in Canada.* Toronto: Oxford University Press.

Mirowsky, John, and Catherine E. Ross. (1996). "Economic and Interpersonal Rewards: Subjective Utilities of Men's and Women's Compensation." *Social Forces,* 75: 223–45.

Oberg, Peter, and Lars Tornstam. (1999). "Body Images among Men and Women of Different Ages." *Ageing and Society,* 19: 629–44.

Palo Stoller, Eleanor, and Rose Campbell Gibson. (1997). *Worlds of Difference: Inequality in the Aging Experience.* Thousand Oaks, CA: Pine Forge Press.

Pugliesi, Karen. (1995). "Work and Well-being. Gender Differences in the Psychological Consequences of Employment." *Journal of Health and Social Behavior,* 36: 57–71.

Rosenberg, Morris. (1981). "The Self-Concept: Social Product and Social Force." In Morris Rosenberg and Ralph H. Turner, eds., *Social Psychology: Sociological Perspectives* (pp. 593–624). New York: Basic.

Rosenberg, Morris, and Leonard I. Pearlin. (1978). "Social Class and Self-Esteem Among Children and Adults." *American Journal of Sociology,* 84: 53–77.

Rosenfield, Sara. (1999). "Splitting the Difference: Gender, the Self, and Mental Health." In Carol S. Aneshensel and Jo C. Phelan, eds., *Handbook of the Sociology of Mental Health* (pp. 209–24). New York: Kluwer Academic/Plenum Publishers.

Turner, R. Jay, and Patricia Roszell. (1994). "Psychosocial Resources and the Stress Process." In William R. Avison and Ian H. Gotlib, eds., *Stress and Mental Health: Contemporary Issues and Prospects for the Future* (pp. 179–212). New York: Plenum Press.

Chapter 13

Multiculturalism or Vertical Mosaic?

OCCUPATIONAL STRATIFICATION
AMONG CANADIAN ETHNIC GROUPS

HUGH LAUTARD AND NEIL GUPPY

INTRODUCTION

Canada is primarily a land of immigrants. Most of us trace our ancestral roots to Europe, and more recently to Asia. This has meant, from the outset of our nation, a mixing of people with diverse ethnic roots. How well we have actually mixed is the focus of this chapter.

Our official government policy of multiculturalism implies a wholesome mixing of ethnic groups, an equality among peoples of distinct cultural heritages. Multiculturalism is premised upon a multiplicity of equal cultures.[1] Our diverse cultural heritages are supported through many institutions, including ethnic media outlets, ethnic churches and schools, and ethnic restaurants. The equality among these diverse cultures is most actively promoted by governments but also by, for example, the schools. Multicultural curricula now permeate the school system, in social studies courses, in recognizing different religious holidays, and in celebrating ethnic heritage days. Different cultural traditions provide separate ethnic identities within a common, egalitarian framework. Multiculturalism highlights cultural blending and ethnic equality.

A contrasting vision of Canada was proposed by sociologist John Porter (1965). Writing in the 1960s, he championed the imagery of a "vertical mosaic." "Mosaic" highlights distinct ethnic identities, but Porter saw little mixing or blending. He argued that Canada's ethnic groups were vertically arranged. According to Porter, Canada was composed of distinct social groups defined principally by social class and ethnicity. Furthermore, these social groups were vertically ranked according to income, power, and prestige. The vertical mosaic, Porter argued, accentuates distinct cultures and ethnic inequality.

How useful are the contrasting images of the vertical mosaic and multiculturalism in understanding modern Canada? Canada's population has grown and diversified since 1965, when Porter published *The Vertical Mosaic*, and since 1971, when Canada adopted multiculturalism as official federal government policy.

Section 15.1 of the *Canadian Charter of Rights and Freedoms* (1985) proclaims: "Every individual is equal before and under the law and has the right to the equal protection and equal benefit of the law without discrimination and, in particular, without discrimination based on race, national or ethnic origin, [and] colour. . . ." However, despite the *Charter*'s grounding in multicultural language, the legacy of the vertical mosaic has required additional legislation to help enhance the *Charter*'s equality provisions. So, for example, the *Employment Equity Act* (1986) seeks to erase the subordinate positions of women, the disabled, Aboriginal peoples, and visible minorities. The Act requires employers to hire according to equity targets to overcome ethnic inequality in the labour force. While proclaiming multiculturalism as official policy, the federal government has had to enact laws simultaneously in an attempt to erode the vertical mosaic. If the key proposition of *The Vertical Mosaic* still holds— that ethnicity shapes inequality—then legislation such as the *Employment Equity Act* remains important. This implies, though, that multiculturalism remains more ideology than fact, more rhetoric than reality. Is there a causal link between your ethnicity and your socioeconomic fortunes or misfortunes? We present new data that, when compared with trends published earlier, afford the longest historical perspective yet available on the association between ethnicity and occupation, based on 70 years of census data, from 1931 to 2001. As did Porter before us, we stress both social differences (multiple ethnic groups in a mosaic) and social stratification (vertical alignment of ethnic groups).

IS THE SIGNIFICANCE OF ETHNICITY FOR INEQUALITY DECLINING?

In *The Vertical Mosaic*, Porter described Canada as a nation fractured by ethnicity. He saw the French and the British as two "charter status" groups, commanding greater power and privilege than "entrance status" groups (i.e., other immigrants). He analyzed the asymmetry of power favouring the British over the French and claimed that this asymmetry characterized noncharter immigrant groups, too. For Porter, "immigration and ethnic affiliation . . . [were] important factors in the formation of social classes" (1965: 73).

Porter focused especially on the economic elite, in which he claimed "economic power belong[ed] almost exclusively to [White Protestants] of British origin" (Porter, 1965: 286). More recent analyses of the wealthiest Canadians show less British dominance. While the Thomson family, with its strong British roots, continues to be the wealthiest Canadian family, the corridors of power are now less WASPish (Ogmundson and McLaughlin, 1990; Ogmundson and Doyle, 2001; and Nakhaie, 1997). At one time almost exclusively British, the Canadian elite, almost no matter how it is defined, now contains more people from other ethnic backgrounds.

Porter (1965) also used census data from 1931, 1951, and 1961 to make his case. By tabulating ethnic origin and occupation, he showed which ethnic groups dominated which job categories. For example, in the 1931 census he found British and Jewish groups were overrepresented in professional and financial occupations. Conversely, they were underrepresented in unskilled and primary jobs (e.g., fishing, logging). He wrote that the "French, German, and Dutch would probably rank next, followed by Scandinavian, Eastern European, Italian, Japanese, 'Other Central European', Chinese, and Native Indian" (p. 81). His 1961 census data showed that, save for the French who had slid down a little, "the rough rank order [had] persisted over time" (p. 90).

Why were different ethnic groups represented at higher and lower occupational levels? Porter proposed two complementary explanations. First, newcomers to Canada often brought with them different educational and occupational experiences. People of British heritage frequently came with professional qualifications that were officially recognized in Canada, whereas people from other ethnic backgrounds often arrived with little education and no recognized professional skills. New entrants to Canada would thus reinforce the existing link between ethnic ancestry and social class (Porter, 1965: 86, 1985: 40–51).[2]

Second, Porter argued that social mobility was correlated with ethnicity. Ethnic groups, he argued, either varied in how much they valued economic achievement and upward mobility or found that discrimination dampened their labour market success (Pineo and Porter, 1985: 360–61). Indeed, Porter felt that multiculturalism would impede ethnic assimilation and perpetuate the link between social class and ethnicity (Heath and Yu, 2005).

Much social science research has assessed the adequacy of Porter's vertical mosaic imagery. No doubt insightful in his era, is it an accurate portrayal of ethnic inequality through the last half century? Since the end of the World War II the source of Canadian immigrants has shifted dramatically away from Europe and toward other continents, especially Asia. As well, Canada has changed its immigration policy. Now greater priority is given to the skills new entrants have as opposed to their place of birth. For example, more emphasis is now placed on education and on fluency in at least one of the two official languages. Occupational experience is more valued than birthplace.

Some researchers have concluded that the vertical mosaic imagery simply needs revising to note its "colour coding." They argue that for people of visible minority background the association between ethnicity and social class has been retained. Now we have a "new ethnic mosaic . . . redrafted along lines of race and colour" (Agocs and Boyd, 1993: 333; Lian and Matthews, 1998; Ooka and Fong, 2001; Pendakur and Pendakur, 2002; Reitz, 2001).

Other research traditions have followed Porter's original lead and compared patterns of association between ethnicity and social class in successive census years. For example, Lautard and Loree (1984: 342) used detailed ethnicity and occupation data from 1931 to 1971 and concluded that "occupational inequality is still substantial enough to justify the use of the concept 'vertical mosaic' to characterize . . . ethnic relations in Canada" (Darroch, 1979; Pendakur, 2002). The census data used by Porter and Lautard and Loree combine both the foreign-born and the native-born, thus allowing researchers to examine social change by focusing on trends over time. However, the census data they used provide no test for the two explanations Porter offered about the association of ethnicity and class.

Monica Boyd's (1985) research on the influence of birthplace on occupational attainment offers a test of the immigration interpretation. For foreign-born women and men, Boyd demonstrated that ethnic ancestry was correlated with occupational attainment. Even when immigrants with the same age, education, social origin, and place of residence were compared,

the correlation existed. For women who were foreign-born, Boyd found a "double negative" that reinforced the vertical mosaic. She concluded that birthplace and sex are important factors underlying the Canadian mosaic (Boyd, 1985: 441).

The exact nature of the link between ethnicity and inequality turns, at least in part, on issues of definition and methodology. Porter used the best data available to him but his approach had weaknesses despite his best efforts. Following are the three main problems that any analyst must confront in trying to sort out whether the idea of multiculturalism or the image of a vertical mosaic best characterizes modern Canada.

ETHNICITY

Definitions matter. How broadly or finely one chooses to define ethnicity is critical in these debates. Historically, male ancestral lineage was the defining feature of ethnicity, at least as used by Statistics Canada for measurement purposes. However, this definition is problematic, not only because it privileges male descent lines. Inter-ethnic marriages occur across generations. National borders change. An increasing number of people consider themselves to be of "Canadian" ancestry since they are descendants of people who arrived in Canada generations ago.

Porter's view of the charter status groups, the French and the British, drew no distinction between the English, the Irish, the Scottish, and the Welsh. Likewise, Statistics Canada for a long time was unable to publish distinct numbers for members of different Asian ethnic groups. That is because the number of Koreans and Cambodians, for example, was too small. Typically, the following ethnic categories have been used in the census, with older census years having even fewer distinct groups: British (English, Irish, Scottish, Welsh), French, German, Italian, Jewish, Dutch, Scandinavian, Eastern European (Polish, Ukrainian), Other European, Asian, and Native Indian.

OCCUPATIONS

Porter originally used five broad occupational categories (professional and financial, clerical, personal service, primary and unskilled, and agriculture). Lautard and Loree (1984) used a more detailed occupational categorization with hundreds of separate job categories for each census.

Occupations are, in important ways, just jobs. To show that members of different ethnic groups concentrate in some jobs and not others says nothing about inequality; it is only a comment about different jobs. Only if those jobs have different rewards attached to them does inequality become an issue. But what are the most salient rewards—income, working conditions, prestige, authority? The vertical mosaic clearly implies some hierarchy, but what defines that hierarchy is not specified.

HISTORICAL COMPARABILITY

The number and kinds of occupations in Canada have changed over time. Should researchers use older census categories that tend to be broader or the full range of jobs characterizing the modern division of labour? Likewise, the detail on ethnicity has changed historically, as has the way Statistics Canada collects this information.[3] Should only broad ethnic categories that are strictly comparable over time be used?

MEASURING OCCUPATIONAL STRATIFICATION BY ETHNICITY

With the above limitations in mind you might conclude that using census data to track labour market changes for members of ethnic groups is highly problematic. Our response to this is fourfold. First, these problems must be recognized and the results interpreted cautiously in light of them. Second, even partial insight is better than ignorance. Third, if the findings of this research complement the findings of other researchers using different research methods, then the entire body of research is self-reinforcing. Fourth, if better methods exist to answer the question we are pursuing, then we encourage others to do the research.

We use census information for 1971 and 2001 and compare our results to earlier findings, beginning either in 1931 or 1951. Depending on the availability of data, we discuss changes over a period of up to 70 years. The 2001 analysis involves examining the distribution of the members of 17 different ethnic groups, by gender, across 500 different occupations. This provides enormous detail that we need to summarize. To do so, we measure occupational differentiation by calculating an *index of dissimilarity*, and we examine occupational stratification by using an *index of net difference*.

Here first, by way of analogy, is how to understand the index of dissimilarity. In your college or university, consider the overall percentages of women and men enrolled (assume it is 55 percent and 45 percent respectively). Now think of the percentage of women and men in each of your classes. How well is the overall gender balance of 55/45 reflected in your individual courses? Extend this to all the courses offered at your institution.

To summarize this detail, begin by calculating, for each course, any difference in the percentage of women (or men) from the overall 55/45 average. This tells you how dissimilar each course is from the overall gender balance. Totalling across all courses provides a convenient summary—the higher the index number, the greater the dissimilarity. Comparing the index of dissimilarity across different faculties or different universities would tell you which has the better gender balance.

In our case, we add the percentage differences between the occupational distribution of each ethnic group and that of the rest of the labour force. A separate calculation is done for women and men. The resulting indexes are the percentages of women and men in each ethnic group who would have to be in a different occupation in order for there to be no occupational differences among ethnic groups.

For example, say the index of dissimilarity for women of British origin is 10. This means that only 10 percent of the British women in the labour force would have to be in a different occupation for there to be no difference between their occupational distribution and that of women of other ethnic origins. If the index of dissimilarity for men of Aboriginal origin is 31 percent, this indicates about three times as much difference, with nearly one in three Aboriginal men having to be in a different occupation for them to have the same occupational distribution as non-Aboriginal men. Averaging dissimilarity indexes for ethnic groups in two different census years indicates changes in occupational differentiation among ethnic groups. We present such results for 1971 and 2001, and compare them with earlier findings for 1931, 1951, and 1961, for a combined time span of 70 years.

Dissimilarity, however, does not necessarily mean disadvantage or inequality. As a method of capturing *stratification*, sociologists have adopted other methods. In this chapter, we use two separate methods to examine stratification among occupations. For 1971 we array occupations on a socioeconomic index that measures the prestige of occupations. These prestige ratings are based on the typical education and income of people in particular occupations. For 2001, where such an index is not available, we use a measure constructed by Statistics Canada to rank the variable occupational skill requirements of distinct jobs. Occupation data collected from the 2001 Census are ranked into one of four skill groups, where the groups are arrayed by estimates of educational requirements (i.e., university, college, apprenticeship training, and high school or less). To this, Statistics Canada added a "manager" category, which is unranked since the education levels of managers are diverse.

As a way of summarizing occupational inequality, we use the index of net difference. This measure (unlike the index of dissimilarity, which is always positive) may be either negative or positive. An index of net difference with a minus sign indicates the group for which it was calculated is generally lower on the occupational "ladder" relative to the rest of the labour force, while a positive index indicates higher relative position. The greater the absolute size of the index, whether positive or negative, the greater the degree of stratification, while a net difference of zero would indicate overall equality of occupational status. We use this measure to analyze occupational inequality for 1971 and 2001 and compare our results with earlier findings for 1951, 1961, and 1971.

OCCUPATIONAL INEQUALITY BY ETHNICITY, 1931 TO 2001

Table 13.1 contains indexes of occupational dissimilarity for 16 ethnic groups in 1971 and 17 groups in 2001. These scores summarize results based on just under 500 occupations in 1971 and just over 500 occupations in 2001. Generally, ethnic occupational differentiation is lower in 2001 than 1971. In 2001, average ethnic dissimilarity among men (24 percent) is 6 points lower than in 1971 (30 percent), while it is 8 points lower among women (19 percent, compared to 27 percent). Exceptions to this pattern of declining index scores occur for men and women of German, Dutch, and Scandinavian origin, for men of Ukrainian and Polish origin, and for women of Jewish origin, while the index for women of Polish origin is the same for both years.

Table 13.1 also shows that there is a generally consistent pattern of ethnic occupational differentiation. Groups of North and East European origins exhibit below-average occupational dissimilarity, while, with a few exceptions, groups of South European, Jewish, Asian, Aboriginal, and Black origins show above-average dissimilarity. The generally lower levels of ethnic differentiation in 2001 compared to 1971 are consistent with the decreases reported by Lautard and Loree (1984) for 1931 to 1971, suggesting an easing of differentiation. Nevertheless considerable occupational dissimilarity remains among ethnic groups.[4]

TABLE 13.1 OCCUPATIONAL DISSIMILARITY[a] BETWEEN SELECTED ETHNIC GROUPS AND THE REST OF THE LABOUR FORCE, BY SEX: CANADA, 1971 AND 2001

Ethnic Group	MALE		FEMALE	
	1971	2001	1971	2001
British	15	11	16	10
French	14	10	18	10
German	15	18	11	12
Dutch	16	21	15	16
Scandinavian	17	22	12	16
Ukrainian	15	16	16	12
Polish	15	17	14	14
Hungarian	21	18	20	16
Italian	35	20	38	19
Portuguese	46	29	57	24
Greek	48	31	51	23
Yugoslav	33	23	35	19
Jewish	51	45	32	33
Chinese	52	36	34	26
South Asian	46	27	31	22
Aboriginal	41[b]	31	32[b]	24
Black	NI	26	NI	24
Mean	30	24	27	19
Number of Occupations	(498)	(521)	(464)	(521)

Notes

[a]Each figure in the table indicates the percentage of the ethnic group that would have to have a different occupation in order for there to be no difference between the occupational distribution of that group and the rest of the labour force.

[b]Does not include Inuit.

NI: Not included.

Source: Special tabulations of census data.

TABLE 13.2 NET DIFFERENCE[a] IN OCCUPATIONAL STATUS (1971) AND OCCUPATIONAL SKILL GROUP (2001) BETWEEN SELECTED ETHNIC GROUPS AND THE REST OF THE LABOUR FORCE, BY SEX: CANADA

Ethnic Group	MALE		FEMALE	
	1971	2001	1971	2001
British	0.13	0.06	0.14	0.05
French	−0.06	0.04	−0.02	0.06
German	−0.08	0.04	−0.09	0.01
Dutch	−0.09	0.05	−0.10	0.04
Scandinavian	−0.08	0.07	−0.01	0.05
Ukrainian	−0.09	0.06	−0.13	0.03
Polish	−0.08	0.03	−0.12	−0.02
Hungarian	−0.06	0.07	−0.13	0.02
Italian	0.22	0.01	−0.35	0.00
Portuguese	−0.38	−0.15	−0.62	−0.16
Greek	−0.27	0.02	−0.48	−0.04
Yugoslav	−0.12	0.03	−0.29	−0.03
Jewish	0.36	0.34	0.24	0.24
Chinese	−0.04	0.19	−0.20	0.00
South Asian	0.26	−0.05	0.19	−0.12
Aboriginal	−0.35[b]	−0.15	−0.23[b]	−0.08
Black	NI	−0.10	NI	−0.09
Mean	0.17	0.09	0.21	0.06
Number of Occupational Ranks/Skill Groups	(498)	(521)	(464)	(521)

Notes

[a]A negative figure indicates relatively lower overall occupational status/skill group, a positive figure, relatively higher status/skill group. Zero indicates overall equality of occupational status/skill group. The greater the absolute size of the index, the greater the inequality.

[b]Does not include Inuit.

NI: Not included.

Source: Special tabulations of census data.

Recall that occupational dissimilarity does not necessarily involve occupational stratification. Table 13.2 contains indexes of net difference in occupational status for 1971 and in occupational skill group for 2001 for the ethnic groups discussed previously. In 1971, with the exception of the indexes for men and women of British, Jewish, and South Asian origins, all indexes are negative, indicating the relatively low occupational status of the other groups. Note also that in 1971 both men and women of South European and Aboriginal origin have lower overall occupational status than the other groups.

In 2001, the indexes of net difference are mainly positive. In 1971, they are mainly negative. This is true for both women and men. We conclude that ethnic stratification was less pronounced in 2001 than in 1971.

Note also that the indexes for 2001 exhibit a pattern like that noted above for occupational dissimilarity among ethnic groups. Most men and women of North European origin, as well as those of Jewish origin, tend to be in higher occupational skill groups than people of South European, Aboriginal, and Black origin. Men of Chinese origin are in relatively high occupational skill groups, and women of Chinese and Italian origins are in the middle.[5]

FROM VERTICAL MOSAIC TO MULTICULTURALISM?

Has multiculturalism eclipsed the vertical mosaic? Is ethnic inequality, at least as measured by occupational stratification, only a historical fact in Canada? Our results show that between 1931 and 2001 a decline in the significance of ethnicity, for both occupational differentiation and stratification, has occurred. Yet ethnic origin continues to affect occupational inequality.

The trend in occupational dissimilarity indicates a reduction in the ethnic division of labour of about 30 percent for men and 45 percent for women in 70 years (Figure 13.1). Slowly, but surely, social differentiation based on ethnicity is eroding. With respect to occupational stratification there has been a reduction of approximately

50 percent for men and 45 percent for women, although over a shorter time span (from 1951 to 2001). From 1971 to 2001 the trend has continued. These historical comparisons have the advantage of a 70-year interval of comparison, but such a lengthy interval also makes the specific contrasts cruder than would be ideal.

Do these results imply a "collapse" of the vertical mosaic? No. Between 1971 and 2001 both occupational differentiation and occupational stratification have eroded, but for both women and men, differences persist. Furthermore, these findings are not inconsistent with recent research by Pendakur and Pendakur (2002) showing an increase in the earning gap in the 1990s for both Aboriginals and members of visible minority groups born in Canada as compared to other Canadian-born labour force participants. Also, work by Reitz (2001) shows that recent immigrants to Canada have been faring more poorly than in earlier decades in labour market integration. On the basis of this research there is no firm ground on which to conclude that multiculturalism has eliminated the vertical mosaic.

The research design that we have employed prevents us from investigating which of Porter's two dynamics best explains the continuing level of ethnic inequality: differential immigration or blocked mobility. Our reading of the research literature suggests that differential immigration continues to be the more important factor, especially in terms of visible minorities (Creese and Kambere, 2001; Sorensen, 1995; Davies and Guppy, 2006). That is, ethnicity has less of an effect on inequality for native-born Canadians than it does for immigrants. However, immigration patterns cannot be the sole explanation because our results are also consistent with research showing that some visible minorities, for example, men of Black and South Asian heritage, face earning penalties in the labour market, penalties that are consistent with the blocked mobility thesis (Geschwender and Guppy, 1995; Li, 1990; Lian and Matthews, 1998; Pendakur and Pendakur, 2002). Whatever the extent and

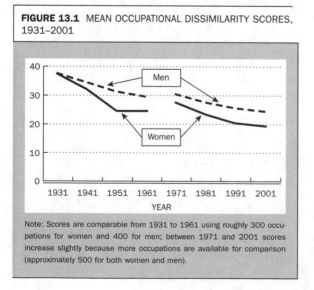

FIGURE 13.1 MEAN OCCUPATIONAL DISSIMILARITY SCORES, 1931–2001

Note: Scores are comparable from 1931 to 1961 using roughly 300 occupations for women and 400 for men; between 1971 and 2001 scores increase slightly because more occupations are available for comparison (approximately 500 for both women and men).

sources of the vertical mosaic, it coexists with other aspects of ethnic and racial inequality beyond the scope of our analysis, including prejudice, hate, and violence, as well as systematic and systemic discrimination in recruitment, interviewing, hiring, promotion, training, and termination practices.

NOTES

The authors gratefully acknowledge the assistance of Jaime Caldwell and Robin Hawkshaw in preparing this paper.

1. The Canadian Heritage Web site provides the government's answer to the question: What is Multiculturalism? "Canadian multiculturalism is fundamental to our belief that all citizens are equal." On the World Wide Web at http://www.pch.gc.ca/progs/multi/what-multi_e.cfm (24 January 2006).

2. For much of Canada's history, foreign-born workers have had a higher level of education than have native-born Canadians (Légacé, 1968; Boyd, 1985). What this average hides, however, is the tendency for immigrants to be either relatively well or relatively poorly educated. Note also that earlier in Canadian history the credentials of immigrants from the United Kingdom in particular were recognized without question. Now the credentials of immigrants are frequently not accepted as legitimate professional qualifications for the Canadian labour market (Boyd and Thomas, 2001).

3. In the 1971 and earlier censuses, the census question to determine ethnic origin was: "To which ethnic or cultural group did you or your ancestor (on the male side) belong on coming to this continent?" In 1981 the question was: "To which ethnic or cultural group did you or your ancestors belong on first coming to this continent?" Notice how difficult it is for Aboriginal people especially to answer such a question accurately. Beginning in 1981, multiple ethnic origins were accepted, and the

2001 question read: "To which ethnic or cultural group(s) did this person's ancestors belong?" Our ethnic categories for 2001 are based on single responses and exclude those reporting multiple ethnic or cultural origins, except for multiple origins involving only constituent groups of certain categories. For example, "British" includes persons who report their origin(s) to be British or any one or more of English, Irish, Scottish, Welsh, and so on, but no non-British origin(s). Scandinavian includes persons who report their origin(s) as Scandinavian or any one or more of Danish, Icelandic, Norwegian, Swedish, and so forth, but no non-Scandinavian origin(s). Although the 2001 Census Guide still made it clear that ethnic origin did not refer to citizenship, "Canadian" was among the examples listed with the question itself. Our data, however, corroborate Li's (2003: 128) observation that "the growth of people reporting Canadian origin . . . did not have a measurable impact on the reporting of ethnic minorities."

4. Just as Lautard and Loree's (1984) average dissimilarity for men in 1961 (29) was about double that reported by Darroch (1979), our 1971 averages for men (30) and women (27) are roughly double Darroch's 1971 average for men and women combined. This shows why trend comparisons are so important; the dissimilarity measure is sensitive to the number of occupations used (Lautard and Lorree, 1984: 336). The level of dissimilarity reported by other authors is important as a statement about ethnic differences (i.e., how big or small they might be), but it is comparison over time, using a consistent methodology, that answers questions about how ethnic divisions are changing in Canada.

5. Data for the intervening census years, 1981 and 1991, indicate the overall decline and pattern in ethnic inequality is comparable to those reported by Lautard and Loree (1984) for the census years studied by Porter (1951 and 1961) as well as 1971 (Lautard and Guppy, 2004).

REFERENCES

Agocs, Carol, and Monica Boyd. (1993). "The Canadian Ethnic Mosaic Recast: Theory, Research and Policy Frameworks for the 1990s." In J. Curtis et al., eds., *Social Inequality in Canada: Patterns, Problems, Policies* (pp. 330–52). Toronto: Prentice-Hall.

Boyd, Monica. (1985). "Immigration and Occupational Attainment." In M. Boyd et al., eds., *Ascription and Attainment: Studies in Mobility and Status Attainment in Canada* (pp. 393–446). Ottawa: Carleton University Press.

Boyd, Monica, and Derrick Thomas. (2001). "Match or Mismatch? The Employment of Immigrant Engineers in Canada's Labor Force." *Population Research and Policy Review,* 20 (1–2): 107–33.

Creese, Gillian, and E. N. Kambere. (2001). "What Colour Is Your English?" *Canadian Review of Sociology and Anthropology,* 40 (5): 565–74.

Darroch, Gordon. (1979). "Another Look at Ethnicity, Stratification and Social Mobility in Canada." *Canadian Journal of Sociology,* 4 (1): 1–25.

Davies, Scott, and Neil Guppy. (2006). *The Schooled Society: An Introduction to the Sociology of Education.* Toronto: Oxford University Press.

Geschwender, Jim, and Neil Guppy. (1995). "Ethnicity, Educational Attainment, and Earned Income among Canadian-Born Men and Women." *Canadian Ethnic Studies,* 27 (1): 67–83.

Heath, Anthony, and S. Yu. (2005). "Explaining Ethnic Minority Disadvantage." In A.F. Heath, J. Ermish, and D. Gallie, eds., *Understanding Social Change* (pp. 187–224). Oxford: Oxford University Press.

Lautard, Hugh, and Neil Guppy. (2004). "Multiculturalism or Vertical Mosaic: Occupational Stratification among Canadian Ethnic Groups." In Robert J. Brym, ed., *Society in Question: Sociological Readings for the 21st Century,* 4th ed. (pp. 165–75). Toronto: Nelson.

Lautard, Hugh, and Donald Loree. (1984). "Ethnic Stratification in Canada, 1931–1971." *Canadian Journal of Sociology,* 9 (3): 333–44.

Légacé, Michael D. (1968). "Educational Attainment in Canada." Dominion Bureau of Statistics, Special Labour Force Survey No. 7. Ottawa: Queen's Printer.

Li, Peter. (1990). Ethnic Inequality in a Class Society. Toronto: Thompson.

———. (2003). *Destination Canada: Immigration Debates and Issues.* Don Mills: Oxford University Press.

Lian, Jason, and David Ralph Matthews. (1998). "Does the Vertical Mosaic Still Exist? Ethnicity and Income in Canada, 1991." *Canadian Review of Sociology and Anthropology,* 35 (4): 461–81.

Nakhaie, M. Reza. (1997). "Vertical Mosaic among the Elites: The New Imagery Revisited." *Canadian Review of Sociology and Anthropology,* 34 (1): 1–24.

Ogmundson, Richard, and M. Doyle. (2001). "The Rise and Decline of Canadian Labour/1960 to 2000: Elites, Power, Ethnicity and Gender." *Canadian Journal of Sociology,* 27 (3): 413–25.

Ogmundson, Richard, and J. McLaughlin. (1990). "Trends in the Ethnic Origins of Canadian Elites: The Decline of the BRITS." *Canadian Review of Sociology and Anthropology,* 29 (2): 227–42.

Ooka, Emi, and Eric Fong. (2001). "Globalization and Earnings among Native-Born and Immigrant Populations of Racial and Ethnic Groups in Canada." *Canadian Studies in Population,* 29 (1): 101–22.

Pendakur, Ravi. (2002). *Immigrants and the Labour Force: Policy, Regulation, and Impact.* Montreal: McGill-Queen's University Press.

Pendakur, Krishna, and Ravi Pendakur. (2002). "Colour My World: Have Earning Gaps for Canadian Born Ethnic Minorities Changed Over Time?" *Canadian Public Policy,* 28 (4): 489–512.

Pineo, Peter, and John Porter. (1985). "Ethnic Origin and Occupational Attainment." In M. Boyd et al., eds., *Ascription and Achieve-*

ment: Studies and Status Attainment in Canada (pp. 357–92). Ottawa: Carleton University Press.

Porter, John. (1965). *The Vertical Mosaic: An Analysis of Social Class and Power in Canada.* Toronto: University of Toronto Press.

———. (1985). "Canada: The Social Context of Occupational Allocation." In M. Boyd et al., eds., *Ascription and Achievement: Studies in Mobility and Status Attainment in Canada* (pp. 29–65). Ottawa: Carleton University Press.

Reitz, Jeffrey G. (2001). "Immigrant Skill Utilization in the Canadian Labour Market: Implications of Human Capital Research." *Journal of International Migration and Integration,* 2 (3): 347–78.

Sorensen, Marianne. (1995). "The Match Between Education and Occupation for Immigrant Women in Canada." *Canadian Ethnic Studies,* 27 (1): 48–66.

Chapter 14

Tapping Immigrants' Skills

JEFFREY G. REITZ

TRENDS AND ISSUES IN THE ECONOMIC STANDING OF IMMIGRANTS

Canada selects immigrants partly on the basis of their labour force skills but underutilizes those skills once newcomers settle here. A valuable opportunity is thus squandered: analysts estimate that the Canadian economy loses about $2 billion annually because immigrants' qualifications are insufficiently recognized in the workplace (Reitz, 2001a; Watt and Bloom, 2001).

The overall employment situation of immigrants is becoming worse. For more than a decade, immigrants have faced declining earnings and employment success despite rising skill and education levels (Reitz, 1997a, 1997b, 2001b; Dougherty, 1999). In 1980, the earnings of newly arrived male immigrants were about 80 percent of the earnings of Canadian-born men. By 1996, that figure fell to 60 percent. In 1980, the employment rate for newly arrived immigrant men was 86.3 percent, close to the 91 percent for Canadian-born men. By 1996, the comparable figures stood at 68.3 percent for newly arrived immigrant men and 85.4 percent for Canadian-born men. The trends for newly arrived immigrant women are similar (Reitz, 2001b: 590–95). Note too the high poverty rates among several immigrant groups, particularly in big cities such as Toronto (Kazemipur and Halli, 2000). In 1996, the poverty rate in Toronto for families of non-European origin was 34.3 percent, more than double the rate for families of European origin (Ornstein, 2000). The poverty rate for some categories of non-European families was more than 50 percent.

Educational credentials among recent immigrants are higher on average than those of the Canadian-born work force and are rising. Recent immigrants' levels of fluency in an official language have not changed. Yet the trends in immigrants' employment and earnings are downward. This pattern suggests that the problem we are facing is not so much one of immigrants' skill levels as the extent to which those skills are accepted and utilized in the Canadian workplace.

The difficulties confronting immigrants are a problem for Canada not only in economic terms, but also because of their social and political repercussions. The fact that the great majority of immigrants to Canada today belong to racial minorities probably magnifies the impact. Overall earnings disadvantages and the extent of skill underutilization are greater for immigrants who belong to racial minorities than they are for immigrants of European ethnic origin. Thus, comparing Black immigrant men and European immigrant men *with the same level of education and other qualifications*, I found that Black men earned $6 476 less in 1996. Nearly a quarter of that difference was due to differences in access to skilled occupations (Reitz, 2001a: 367–69). In any society, the correlation between ethnic or racial status and economic success over extended periods of time is bound to become divisive and to affect intergroup relations.

Source: Adapted from Jeffrey G. Reitz, "Tapping Immigrants' Skills: New Directions for Canadian Immigration Policy in the Knowledge Economy," *IRPP Choices* (11, 1: February 2005). Reproduced with permission from IRPP (www.irpp.org).

Clearly, the emphasis in Canadian government policy on points-based immigrant selection and, in particular, on ever-higher educational standards for immigrants, is not resulting in higher employment and earnings for immigrants. One possible response would be to fine-tune the immigrant selection process. But given that sustained efforts to do so have proven ineffective, it seems inadvisable to rely entirely on that approach. There are three other alternatives to the current policy, two of which could have negative consequences.

The first option is to accept downward employment trends among current immigrants and hope for a better future for their children. The expectation of better prospects for the second generation is based in part on the importance highly educated immigrants attach to education, an attitude they tend to pass on to their children. Also, employers are more likely to accept the second generation because their education will have been acquired in Canada. Data on the offspring of immigrants generally confirm this optimism (Boyd, 1992).

The downside of this option is that even if poverty among immigrant parents does not impede their educational aspirations for their children, immigrants living in poverty could create pressures—or at least the perception of pressures—on the social welfare system. That could lead to public demands for a reduction in social programs and other support, which would affect the native-born as well as immigrants.

The second option is to cut immigration levels so as to reduce its negative social impact. For most of the period since World War II, Canada has pursued an expansionist immigration policy, and the current government is continuing that approach with a target immigration level of 1 percent of the population per year (about 300 000 immigrants annually). For much of the past decade, the actual immigration level has ranged between 200 000 and 250 000 people. On a per capita basis, these numbers are high—about three times the immigration rate of the United States, for example. Critics of Canadian immigration suggest cutting these numbers to between 150 000 and 200 000 immigrants per year (Collacutt, 2002; Stoffman, 2002: 191).

The difficulty with doing so is that it would force Canada to forego much of the potential future economic benefits of immigration. Due to its small size and low fertility rate, Canada has relied heavily on immigration as a development strategy. Demographic projections show that, for the most part, labour force growth in Canada for the foreseeable future will stem from immigration.

Recent experience in Australia illustrates the downside of cutting immigration. Australian opposition to immigration resulted in the number of immigrants being reduced from approximately 140 000 per year in the late 1980s to between 70 000 and 90 000 in the mid-1990s. However, there was political resistance against reducing family-class immigration, so it was easier to reduce the skilled-worker-immigrant category. Consequently, out of economic necessity, Australia soon resumed accepting a larger number of immigrants. Its recent target has been in the range of 100 000 to 110 000 per year (Castles and Vasta, 2004: 146). Cutting immigration levels also had the negative consequence of reinforcing negative perceptions of immigrants, thereby exacerbating domestic race-relations problems.

By comparison, Canadians have a positive view of immigration (Simon and Lynch, 1999: 461). Surveys show that over the past 25 years most Canadians have wanted to maintain or increase immigration levels (Reitz, 2004). Arguably, popular support for immigration in Canada has helped ease the settlement process, and the absence of intense public debate over immigration levels has helped to maintain a supportive environment.

I conclude that accepting downward employment trends among immigrants and cutting immigration levels would not be advisable. The third alternative—augmenting the institutional capacity to utilize immigrants' skills more effectively—makes most sense, as I will now argue.

EFFECTS OF LABOUR MARKET CHANGE IN THE KNOWLEDGE ECONOMY

Canada's current immigration strategy rests largely on human capital theory. This theory was developed to increase our understanding of labour markets in a knowledge economy, but its weaknesses when applied to immigrants have become evident. Human capital theory suggests that workers' earnings reflect the productive value of their skills, particularly skills based on formal education and work experience. Yet immigrants' recent labour market outcomes contradict that expectation, as we have seen.

One reason for the weakness of human capital theory as applied to immigrants is that it assumes employers have effective means of assessing the productive value of prospective workers' skills. The underutilization of immigrant skills suggests that, for immigrants, they lack such means (Li, 2000; Reitz, 2001a).

Historically, immigration policy in Canada has reflected the country's stage of economic development. When agriculture was the economic priority, Canada recruited immigrants for farm work. When priorities shifted to those of an industrializing economy, Canada recruited immigrants for construction and manufacturing. Now that Canada is moving toward a postindustrial or knowledge economy, immigrants are being recruited to respond to that imperative. In the agricultural and industrial eras, it was sufficient to recruit immigrants on the basis of their capacity for physical labour and acquiring the limited skills necessary for manual work. Assessment of foreign credentials was irrelevant. In the knowledge economy, immigrants' credentials are important, and assessment of these credentials is critical to the success of the immigration program.

Any analysis of the integration of immigrants in the knowledge economy should take into account how organizational changes in the labour market and in the workplace are affecting immigrants. For example, employers place more emphasis on credentials insofar as they reflect specific skills that increase productivity (Hunter, 1988; Hunter and Leiper, 1993); organizational decision making is becoming more attentive to employee opinion; the most highly skilled employees are gaining more autonomy in their work; there is greater use of personal networks in recruitment; and there are closer links among universities, governments, and employer organizations. These changes will likely affect workers in the most highly skilled occupations, particularly in the most skill-intensive industries.

Statistics Canada defines "knowledge occupations" as those in which a high proportion of workers have a university education. They include the science and engineering professions, health and education, as well as a variety of other professional fields. "Knowledge industries" have a high proportion of knowledge workers and high levels of investment in research and development. Among them are the high-tech pharmaceutical, chemical, instrument, electronics, and machinery and equipment industries. Management is often considered a knowledge occupation too, particularly when the activities managed involve highly skilled or professional work. Between 1971 and 2001, the proportion of Canadian workers in knowledge occupations almost doubled, increasing from 14 percent to 25 percent. Education levels in these occupations also increased. At the same time, educational requirements and levels have risen in many occupations outside the knowledge category (Baldwin and Beckstead, 2003: 5; Beckstead and Vinodrai, 2003; Beckstead and Gellatly, 2004).

Because of changes in recruitment and hiring practices, qualified immigrants appear to be facing increasing difficulty gaining access to work in knowledge occupations (Reitz, 2003). As a result, they end up working in less-skilled occupations than do comparably qualified native-born Canadians. In 1996, 59 percent of native-born men with bachelors' degrees were working in knowledge occupations, compared with only 35 percent of recent immigrants with bachelors' degrees. The corresponding figures for women were 57 and 28 percent. Of men with postgraduate degrees, 79 percent of those who were born in Canada were working in knowledge occupations, compared with only 59 percent of recent immigrants. The corresponding figures for women were 78 and 49 percent. Between 1981 and 1996, as the importance of knowledge occupations increased, differences between the income levels and representation in knowledge occupations of native-born Canadians and immigrants have grown as well. Despite increases in the skill levels of new immigrants, their representation in knowledge occupations was lower in 1996 than it was in 1981. Within the knowledge occupations, immigrants have greater difficulty gaining access to managerial than to professional positions (Reitz, 2003: 485, 487; Beck, Reitz, and Weiner, 2002).

These barriers to access in professional and managerial occupations and the earnings disadvantages within these fields clearly have the effect of decreasing immigrants' earnings. Less known, but at least as important, are the earnings disadvantages of highly educated immigrants in occupations outside the knowledge sector, which are actually larger and more financially consequential than those within the knowledge sector. For example, in the knowledge occupations, the net earnings of immigrant men with bachelors' or postgraduate degrees (professions and management) are 12 to 16 percent lower than are those of native-born Canadians with similar education, but in all other occupations, they are 25 to 34 percent lower. Over time, negative earnings trends in occupations outside the knowledge sector have contributed substantially to the overall downward trend in immigrant earnings (Reitz, 2003: 493, 500).

The stereotype of immigrants with Ph.D.s driving taxis reflects the most extreme consequence of barriers to immigrant employment. Instead of working in knowledge occupations, and often experiencing greater barriers in lower level skilled work, university-educated immigrants often do unskilled work. For recent immigrants with a university degree who were employed between 1991 and 2001, "at least one in four had a job requiring no more than a high school education" (Galarneau and Morissette, 2004: 13). Most immigrants with degrees who came to Canada in the 1990s worked in just 29 occupations, including restaurant and food-service managers, taxi and limousine drivers and chauffeurs, truck drivers, security guards and related occupations, and janitors, caretakers, and building superintendents (Statistics Canada, 2003: 13). Their earnings were substantially below those of native-born Canadians in the same occupations.

Immigrants' relative success in the professions (as opposed to management and non-knowledge jobs) implies that rigorous credential assessment processes are advantageous to them. Moreover, immigrants' difficulties outside the professions indicate that addressing the problem of credential assessment must go beyond the issue of barriers to licensing. Policy reform should also focus on sectors of the work force outside the knowledge sector, where the processes are often much less formal.

I conclude that the new knowledge economy is far from entirely immigrant-friendly. There is a well-known commitment to universality in knowledge-producing institutions such as the sciences, but the validation of knowledge-based skills in labour markets is inevitably performed by local institutions. The question is whether these local institutions can better develop the capacity for validation of skills. Employment success increasingly depends on high levels of educational attainment, but only if that education is properly assessed and utilized. The increased emphasis on education-based skills in many occupations, both inside and outside the professions, as well as the increased supply of domestically educated workers, means that immigrants now face significant competition in the labour market and cannot escape the problem of skills transferability. Creating labour market institutions that can handle a diverse work force will require institutional innovation and change.

INSTITUTIONAL CHANGE: COMPLEXITY, TIMING, AND RACIAL ATTITUDES

The success of Canada's immigration policy depends on the existence of institutions that link workers to jobs and provide for the international transferability of skills. To that end, employers need access to accurate information about the skills reflected in credentials acquired from educational institutions abroad; reliable information about people's performance in acquiring their credentials; and sound performance assessments of comparably qualified individuals who are already employed here.

While in today's labour market there should be incentive enough for employers to participate in gathering such information processes, three stumbling blocks exist. First is the complexity of the required changes. Second is the timing of the changes in relation to the decision-making processes involved and also to the different priorities of employers and immigration policymakers. Third is the effect of racial attitudes in the host society. Let us consider each of these issues in turn.

INSTITUTIONAL COMPLEXITY

In discussions of barriers to immigrant skill utilization, the role of licensing bodies has probably received the most attention. Immigrants who worked abroad as professional engineers, for example, may encounter difficulty obtaining a licence to practice in Canada. Although there has been progress in this area, more work is needed. However, important as it is, access to professional and trade licences is only a small part of the problem. Possession of a licence does not guarantee a job, and those who do get jobs in licensed occupations are not guaranteed professional advancement or promotions. As several studies have shown, the career path leading from professional to managerial responsibility, which is often successfully followed by native-born workers, is blocked for many immigrants (Reitz, 2003; Beck, Reitz, and Weiner, 2002).

Immigrants also experience difficulty in gaining a licence when there are specific gaps in their training or when specific skills are not transferable. Frequently in such cases, they are required to repeat the entire training program in Canada, which, of course, is wasteful. A more efficient way to fill specific skills gaps would be to provide some form of bridge training, such as occupation-specific programs involving collaboration among educational institutions, governments, and regulatory bodies. The University of Toronto's Faculty of Pharmacy has developed such a program. It enables pharmacists trained outside North America to take university-based courses, thereby facilitating their preparation for professional practice in Ontario. There are a few similar programs in the health professions, and others are being developed.

Recognition of foreign educational credentials is also a problem in occupations that are not licensed or regulated. These occupations frequently require substantial educational qualifications, even though the requirements may be less specific or explicit. They include some knowledge-based occupations, such as managerial positions in knowledge-based industries. Since this labour market sector is less formally organized, institutional change may be more difficult to achieve.

One useful type of institution that is widely available in the less-regulated sector of the labour market is the credential assessment service, available in nearly all high immigration areas in Canada. For about $100, they offer immigrants an authoritative assessment of the Canadian equivalence of their foreign educational credentials. Although immigrants have so far made limited use of these services, credential assessment is making inroads and could play an important role in breaking down barriers to immigrant skill utilization. At the same time, these organizations need to gain wider acceptance among employers. For their part, the assessment services may not be providing some of the information employers need, such as information about distinctions in quality among foreign universities. Hence, it is difficult to judge the effectiveness of these services, and it would be useful if they were subjected to systematic evaluation.

The shortcomings of the institutions that certify immigrants' qualifications and promote skill utilization are epitomized by employers' notorious demand for Canadian experience. This demand has been a source of particular frustration for immigrants because of its Catch-22 character (you need Canadian experience to get Canadian experience) and also because of the suspicion that it hides prejudice against immigrants and minorities. Yet employers have a legitimate interest in knowing whether a job candidate can function effectively in the local context. In judging native-born job applicants, employers get information by means of recommendations from previous employers or well-known local educational institutions. Understandably, hiring immigrants in the absence of such information may be seen as a significant risk.

In this context, programs promoting the mentoring of new immigrant employees by more senior colleagues may well be useful. These are a kind of on-the-job training that is similar to apprenticeships or internships—a means by which the mentor can pass on knowledge about local practices in a given occupation. While employer-sponsored apprenticeship programs are not yet as common in the Canadian labour market as they are in some other countries, such as Germany, they could potentially be very useful in addressing immigrants' needs. But they must be carefully designed: programs and processes will have to be set up to match mentors with immigrants effectively. It may also be necessary to provide subsidies.

In most large and complex organizations, human resource managers are responsible for ensuring effective utilization of the skills of job applicants and employees. Increasingly, this task involves "diversity management," that is, addressing employment issues related to gender, disability, sexual orientation, ethnicity, and immigration status. Although human resource managers are likely to support and promote the institutional changes sketched above, there are limits to what they can achieve on their own. For instance, human resource managers may have the expertise to initiate immigrant mentorship, but they will need resources to do so. As well, setting up these programs may require collaboration with groups other than the employer organization.

Information is a key issue in many of these changes, and developing the means for effective communication between immigrants and employers is part of the necessary institutional response. On the immigrant side of the equation, Citizenship and Immigration Canada is creating a web site that is intended to serve as a one-stop source of information for prospective and recent immigrants. It includes information on a range of topics related to work, credential assessment, regulated professions and trades, and other labour market issues. It also features links to information about local labour markets and employers. Still in the experimental stage, neither the effectiveness of the web site in reaching its target audience nor the usefulness of the information it contains has yet been assessed. Comparable information sources for employers and other interested groups might also be useful.

Finally, institutional change requires a supportive environment. Attitudes matter. A high degree of positive commitment is necessary to bring about meaningful institutional change, inasmuch as general sympathy with the issue may or may not translate into support for concrete action in workplaces where the actual financial risks are taken. In effect, positive actions and incentives may be required to reinforce supportive work environments. Although public attitudes may provide some of these incentives, recognition of employers who develop effective best practices could be useful. *Canadian Business* magazine, in collaboration with OMNI Television, recently took a step in this direction by publishing a list of the "best employers for visible minorities" ("Minority Report," 2004).

TIMING AND DECISION-MAKING STRUCTURES

Given the complexity of the changes required, questions of timing and decision making arise. Can the institutional changes needed to avert or reverse the decline in immigrant employment outcomes be made before their negative consequences become difficult to reverse? Are the necessary decision-making processes in place? Of course, given enough time, employers might become more familiar with foreign-acquired qualifications. But working against this is the very complexity of the institutional changes needed to accommodate foreign-trained workers and the rapid increase in the supply of highly skilled native-born workers, which reduces the incentives for employers to innovate in the area. Thus, from the employer's perspective, the issue of immigrant skill utilization may be much less pressing than it is for those concerned with the broader goals of the immigration program, or for the rest of society, if there are negative economic and social consequences of declining immigrant employment outcomes.

The decline in immigrants' employment outcomes has been fairly rapid, and its negative impact could translate into a number of social problems. First, we can expect demands on the social safety net to increase. Although immigrants are known to be self-reliant and reluctant to take advantage of the social assistance for which they are eligible, high rates of poverty and social disadvantage will inevitably translate into high rates of social-service use. Second, we can expect public perceptions of immigrants as a liability or social problem to become more widespread. That perception would be heightened if social problems associated with poverty were to emerge. Third, immigrants themselves may react politically to their employment conditions. Although the time frame for these outcomes is unknown, the risks are clear. It would be prudent to ensure that the steps taken are adequate to address the problem fully.

If change is more urgent for governments than it is for employers, and if the process must be kick-started, adequate decision-making structures must be in place. Intergovernmental collaboration is crucial. In Canada, no one agency has clear responsibility for immigrant skill utilization. Responsibility resides with different levels of government and different agencies at different levels of government. At the federal level, for example, Citizenship and Immigration Canada is responsible for immigration. Yet current immigration policy is designed to minimize government involvement in matters related to the integration of immigrants in the labour force. Other federal agencies are responsible for industrial development, which includes employment issues. For example, in 2002, Human Resources and Development Canada, in cooperation with Industry Canada, committed $40 million over five years to the integration of immigrants in the labour market (Canada, 2002). More recently, further initiatives have been announced. Public statements make it clear that action on this front depends on cooperation with provincial governments because regulation of employment is formally a provincial responsibility. Unfortunately, such cooperation is far from automatic, and to date it has been minimal.

Recently, federal and provincial governments have concluded a number of agreements on immigration (in addition to the long-standing agreement involving Quebec). Much attention has been focused on two issues that are tangential to skill utilization: immigrant selection and the allocation of settlement funds. There have also been moves toward greater federal–provincial collaboration in developing a more effective immigrant employment policy. These are promising, but rapid progress is needed.

Municipalities also share the responsibility. They provide many of the services. But they are resource-poor and are fragmented among the metropolitan areas in which immigrants settle. In Toronto, for example, the need for coordination of immigration-related issues has only recently emerged as an item on the local agenda as part of a broader resurgence of attention to urban needs. While progress is being made, the question remains whether the pace of change is sufficient given the task at hand.

RACIAL ATTITUDES

Underlying all these issues are questions arising from the interrelation between immigration issues and increasing ethno-cultural and racial diversity. Because the groups affected by skills underutilization are primarily composed of racial minorities, the potential exists for inter-group tensions and prejudice to emerge. Indeed, there is already much evidence of racial prejudice and employment disparities in Canada (Boyd, 1992; Christofides and Swidinsky, 1994; Reitz and Breton, 1994; Li, 1998; Baker and Benjamin, 1994, 1997). Ethnic and racial stereotypes may affect perceptions of immigrant qualifications. Cultural differences and misunderstandings can impede efforts at cooperation. And the minority status of individual groups may have an effect on the attention they receive in the political process.

Although recognition of immigrants' foreign qualifications has not been widely viewed as a problem of racial discrimination, racial discrimination is a cause of skill underutilization. Racial discrimination occurs when negative employment decisions are based on candidates' racial origins rather than their skills. Racial discrimination is not necessarily based on racial prejudice but could arise from other individual and organizational circumstances.

The context of race relations suggests that in some circumstances resistance to better utilization of immigrant minorities' skills is not only a problem of institutional barriers in labour markets, but also one of intergroup relations. This is evident in the controversy over whether racial attitudes underlie employers' requirements for Canadian experience. Virtually any employer's judgment that a foreign-acquired qualification reflects a lower standard than its Canadian counterpart could be viewed as discriminatory.

The issues of race and employment emerged as part of the debate in Canada over employment equity. It was highly controversial, and the resulting policy initiatives have been weak, confused, and fragmented. These policy shortcomings are compounded by the fact that employment equity legislation operates differently at the federal and provincial levels. At the federal level, it was introduced in 1985 and originally included "visible minorities," among other target groups. Since then, it has been adminis-

tered, with periodic adjustments, under federal employment jurisdiction. Ontario introduced legislation in the mid-1990s similar to the federal law, but a later government scrapped it on the grounds that it amounted to the introduction of racial quotas. This disarray shows that Canadian governments have had great difficulty in directly confronting issues related to race. It illustrates how race relations complicate the process of addressing the employment circumstances of immigrant minorities.

TOWARD A NEW CANADIAN MODEL FOR IMMIGRATION

The Canadian immigration model developed as a result of the country's substantial commitment to immigration, which was dictated in part by geography and political economy. It consists essentially of two main components: immigrant selection—specifically, the points system—and the policy of multiculturalism. Today, as Canada pursues mass immigration in the context of a knowledge economy and declining employment outcomes for immigrants, the sustainability of the immigration program in the global labour market is in question.

The range of institutional innovations that will be necessary to create a global knowledge credentials network is complex. These innovations include:

- Improved Internet-based and other information sources for immigrants, both before and after they arrive in Canada.

- More support for providers of credential assessments to improve the labour market effectiveness of their services.

- Bridge-training programs to top up immigrant skills or fill gaps across a range of occupations.

- Subsidized workplace internship and mentoring programs for immigrants.

- Upgraded human resource management training programs that include training about ethnic diversity issues.

- Employer recognition of best practices.
- Improved public awareness of the problems faced by skilled immigrants in integrating into the Canadian labour market and the social and political consequences of those problems.

Broad support exists for many of the proposals just listed, but to bring about institutional change and create a new Canadian model for immigration, the various agencies and levels of governments must work together. To develop the initiatives outlined here, government leadership will be required to coordinate the institutional players that share responsibility for various aspects of the utilization of immigrants' skills: the federal government for immigration and broad economic and social policy; provincial governments for employment, education, and municipal affairs; and municipal governments for immigrant settlement and delivery of services.

To a large degree, the success of our immigration policy depends on our ability to meet the challenges outlined above. If we do not do so in a timely fashion, several consequences are likely to follow. In the short term, there may be increased pressure to reduce the size of the immigration program and its place in the nation's overall development strategy. In the longer term, there is the potential for social and political unrest. Whether Canada becomes a leader in this field remains to be seen. Several countries have been working on this issue for some time. Initiatives in Europe and the United States focus on credential assessment and recognition. The ultimate policy objective, however, is effective utilization of immigrants' skills in labour markets, which in turn depends on the broader development of labour market institutions. Fully functioning global labour markets are becoming a priority. Our heavy reliance on immigration for expansion and growth gives us a considerable incentive to focus our energies in this area.

REFERENCES

Baker, M., and D. Benjamin. (1994). "The Performance of Immigrants in the Canadian Labor Market." *Journal of Labor Economics,* 12: 369–405.

———. (1997). "Ethnicity, Foreign Birth and Earnings: A Canada/U.S. Comparison." In M.G. Abbott, C.M. Beach, and R.P. Chaykowski, eds., *Transition and Structural Change in the North American Labor Market* (pp. 281–313). Kingston: John Deutsch Institute and Industrial Relations Centre, Queen's University.

Baldwin, J. R., and D. Beckstead. (2003). *Knowledge Workers in Canada's Economy, 1971–2001.* Catalogue no. 11-624-MIE no. 004. Ottawa: Statistics Canada.

Beck, J. H., J. G. Reitz, and N. Weiner. (2002). "Addressing Systemic Racial Discrimination in Employment: The Health Canada Case and Implications of Legislative Change." *Canadian Public Policy,* 28 (3): 373–94.

Beckstead, D., and G. Gellatly. (2004). *Are Knowledge Workers Found Only in High-Technology Industries?* Catalogue no. 11-622-MIE no. 005. Ottawa: Statistics Canada.

Beckstead, D., and T. Vinodrai. (2003). *Dimensions of Occupational Changes in Canada's Knowledge Economy, 1971–1996.* Catalogue no. 11-622-MIE no. 004. Ottawa: Statistics Canada.

Boyd, M. (1992). "Gender, Visible Minority and Immigrant Earnings Inequality: Reassessing an Employment Equity Premise." In V. Satzewich, ed., *Deconstructing a Nation: Immigration, Multiculturalism and Racism in the 1990s Canada* (pp. 279–321). Toronto: Garamond Press.

Canada. Human Resources Development Canada. (2002). *Knowledge Matters: Skills and Learning for Canadians.* Ottawa: Human Resources Development Canada.

Castles, S., and E. Vasta. (2004). "Australia: New Conflicts around Old Dilemmas." In W. Cornelius, J. Hollifield, and P. Martin, eds., *Controlling Immigration: A Global Perspective,* 2nd ed. (pp. 141–73). Palo Alto, CA: Stanford University Press.

Christofides, L. N., and R. Swidinsky. (1994). "Wage Determination by Gender and Visible Minority Status: Evidence from the 1989 LMAS." *Canadian Public Policy,* 22: 34–51.

Collacutt, M. (2002). *Canadian Immigration Policy: The Need for Major Reform.* Vancouver: Fraser Institute.

Dougherty, C. (1999). "New Entrants to the Labour Market: A Comparison of the Labour Market Performance of Immigrants Landed in the 1980s and 1990s." Paper presented at the 4th International Metropolis Conference, Washington, DC, 7–11 December.

Galarneau, D., and R. Morissette. (2004). "Immigrants: Settling for Less?" *Perspectives on Labour and Income,* 5 (6): 5–16.

Hunter, A. A. (1988). "Formal Education and Initial Employment: Unravelling the Relationships between Schooling and Skills over Time." *American Sociological Review,* 53: 753–65.

Hunter, A. A., and J. M. Leiper. (1993). "On Formal Education, Skills, and Earnings: The Role of Educational Certificates in Earnings Determination." *Canadian Journal of Sociology,* 18: 21–42.

Kazemipur, A., and S. S. Halli. (2000). *The New Poverty in Canada: Ethnic Groups and Ghetto Neighbourhoods.* Toronto: Thompson Educational Publishing.

Li, P. S. (1998). "The Market Value and Social Value of Race." In V. Satzewich, ed., *Racism and Social Inequality in Canada* (pp. 115–30). Toronto: Thompson Educational Publishing.

_____. (2000). "Earnings Disparities between Immigrants and Native-born Canadians." *Canadian Review of Sociology and Anthropology,* 37 (3): 289–311.

"Minority Report: The First Canadian Business-OMNI Round up of Top Workplaces for Visible Minorities." (2004). *Canadian Business* (March).

Ornstein, Michael. (2000). Ethno-racial Inequality in Toronto: Analysis of the 1996 Census. Prepared for the Chief Administrator's Office of the City of Toronto.

Reitz, J. G. (1997a). "Priorities for Immigration in a Changing Canadian Economy: From Skill Selectivity to Skill Utilization." Workshop on "New Selection Criteria for Economic Stream Immigrants," held by the Department of Citizenship and Immigration Canada, Ottawa, 30–31 October. (Pages 189–206 in proceedings published by Citizenship and Immigration Canada.)

_____. (1997b). "Measuring Down: The Economic Performance of New Canadians Is Declining; If We Want to Change That, We Need to Rethink Immigration Policy." *Financial Post,* 8 November. Reprinted (1998) in Charles Davies, ed., *Post 2000: Business Wisdom for the Next Century* (pp. 157–63). Toronto: Key Porter Books.

_____. (2001a). "Immigrant Skill Utilization in the Canadian Labour Market: Implications of Human Capital Research." *Journal of International Migration and Integration,* 2 (3): 347–78.

_____. (2001b). "Immigrant Success in the Knowledge Economy: Institutional Change and the Immigrant Experience in Canada, 1970–1995." *Journal of Social Issues,* 57 (3): 579–613.

_____. (2003). "Occupational Dimensions of Immigrant Credential Assessment: Trends in Professional, Managerial, and Other Occupations, 1970–1996." In Charles Beach, Alan Green, and Jeffrey G. Reitz, eds., *Canadian Immigration Policy for the 21st Century* (pp. 469–596). Kingston: John Deutsch Institute for the Study of Economic Policy.

_____. (2004). "Canada: Immigration and Nation-Building in the Transition to a Knowledge Economy." In W. Cornelius, J. Hollifield, and P. Martin, eds., *Controlling Immigration: A Global Perspective,* 2nd ed. (pp. 97–133). Palo Alto, CA: Stanford University Press.

Reitz, J. G., and R. Breton. (1994). *The Illusion of Difference: Realities of Ethnicity in Canada and the United States.* Toronto: C.D. Howe.

Simon, R. J., and J. P. Lynch. (1999). "Comparative Assessment of Public Opinion Toward Immigrants and Immigration Policy." *International Migration Review,* 33 (2): 455–67.

Statistics Canada. (2003). *Earnings of Canadians: Making a Living in the New Economy.* Catalogue no. 96F0030XIE2001013. Ottawa: Minister of Industry.

Stoffman, D. (2002). *Who Gets In: What's Wrong with Canada's Immigration Program—and How to Fix It.* Toronto: Macfarlane, Walter and Ross.

Watt, D., and M. Bloom. (2001). *Exploring the Learning Recognition Gap in Canada. Phase 1 Report. Recognizing Learning: The Economic Cost of Not Recognizing Learning and Learning Credentials in Canada.* Ottawa: Conference Board of Canada.

Chapter 15

What Is a Family?

NEW CHALLENGES IN DEFINING AN EVERYDAY TERM

ADIE NELSON

On the surface, answering the question "What is a family?" does not seem to pose much of a challenge. Regardless of what type of family we grew up in or what type of relationship we are currently involved in, the image of the "ideal" family comes readily to mind: the benevolent but firm father who sits at the head of the table and the household, the emotionally expressive wife/homemaker/mother and, of course, their two children. The imagery is especially potent because it is sheathed in the "charm of hominess," or a vision of Home Sweet Home in which the family is a haven in an often heartless world (Gottlieb, 1993: 270). The scene is reminiscent of a Norman Rockwell painting—the white picket fence, the gingham-clad daughter and denim-clad son playing happily with the frolicking puppy, mom's chocolate chip cookies cooling on the window sill, dad cutting the festive turkey—and creates an enticing portrait of comfort and security.

The patriarchal heterosexual nuclear family is routinely extolled by conservative political parties (Conway, 1990: xi). It is championed as universal, idyllic, and sacred. However, one of the subtle consequences of heralding this image of the family is that it constructs an evaluative framework by which all relational forms are to be judged (Abbott and Wallace, 1992: 73). Thus, a particular type of family, characterized by a gendered division of labour (that is, the male "breadwinner" and the female "housewife") is depicted "as the normal, natural and inevitable family form." Implicitly, forms of relationships that depart from or challenge this imagery are viewed as "deviant" (Gavigan, 1997)—even

though Canadian families are much more varied than this image of the family suggests. Moreover, inasmuch as "good people" enter into "good" (that is, conventional) relationships, those involved in non-traditional family forms may be regarded as suspect or inferior.

The word "family" stems from *famulus*, Latin for "servant" (Gottlieb, 1993: 7). The word *familia* was used originally in classical times to refer to the live-in staff of a household, and from there it came to mean the household itself or its members. The term *pater familias* was so commonly used to refer to a "householder" that it took on the connotation of "an ordinary citizen." *Mater familias* was also commonly used to refer to the "woman of the house" in the sense of the person who directed its domestic affairs. The gendered division of household responsibilities (man's realm was public, woman's was private) was already evident.

Our ideas of what is and is not a family are products of our society, reflecting dominant ideologies about the social roles of men and women, about their sexuality and sexual behaviour, about fertility and procreation, and about the care and socialization of children. Given that these issues intersect in discussions of the family, any attempt to answer the question "What is a family?" inevitably provokes debate.

For example, the issue of whether a long-term homosexual relationship between adults can constitute a family has considerably agitated people who categorize homosexuality as a "sexual perversion" and view homosexuals as a threat to social order (Cossman, 1996; Lancaster, 2003). Accordingly, some analysts maintain that the family must include "adults of *both* sexes, at least two of whom maintain a socially approved sexual relationship, and one or more children of their own, or adopted, of the sexually cohabiting adults" (Murdock, 1949: 1, emphasis added).

Canada's first widely publicized, unofficial gay "marriage" took place in 1977, when two gay men were married by a Unitarian-Universalist minister in Winnipeg (Jackson and Persky, 1982). Until recently, however, Canada has not been guided by a concept of "different, but equal" when it comes to same-sex relationships (Kinsman, 1996). It was only in 1969, following Prime Minister Pierre Trudeau's famous comment that the "state has no place in the bedrooms of the nation," that homosexual acts committed in private, between two consenting adults of at least 21 years of age, were decriminalized. However, it is telling that, as of 2006, the "age of consent" for engaging in the act of anal intercourse is still set higher (18) than the age at which one can legally engage in heterosexual acts (14). It is also notable that, in 1993, when Gallup Canada first attempted to gauge public attitudes toward same-sex marriage, 76 percent of Canadians expressed opposition. It was only in February 2000 that less than half (48 percent) opposed homosexual marriage. Another polling milestone was reached in June 2001, when a Leger marketing poll found majority support for gay adoption. Yet as recently as 1988 only 25 percent of Canadians agreed that gays should be allowed to adopt children (Bricker and Greenspon, 2001: 267).

Throughout the 1990s, and with growing momentum in the new millennium, many of the rights and obligations that were once exclusively associated with marriage (e.g., the right to spousal support; the right to benefit from a partner's job benefits plan) were extended to couples living in marriage-like relationships. In 1990, the Ontario government extended full coverage of supplementary health, hospital, and dental benefits to the same-sex partners of provincial government employees. In 1995, the federal government amended its policies, extending leave-related benefits (e.g., bereavement leave, leave for family-related responsibilities) to the same-sex partners of federal civil servants. In that same year, an Ontario provincial court judge ruled that, under the *Child and Family Services Act*, homosexual couples have the right to adopt a child. In the 1996 case of *M. v. H.*, the opposite-sex definition of "spouse" in Ontario's *Family Law Act* was struck down when, both at trial and on appeal, the courts ruled that M. was entitled to sue H. for support following the breakdown of their lesbian relationship. In 1998, the province of British Columbia enacted changes to its *Adoption Act* and *Family Relations Act* that gave same-sex couples who had cohabited for a period of two years the same rights and responsibilities as their opposite-sex counterparts, including pension and inheritance rights. Other changes in that year were prompted by an Ontario Court of Appeal ruling that declared the federal government's definition of "spouse" in the *Income Tax Act*, which excluded same-sex survivor benefits from employers' pension plans, was unconstitutional. A year later, the Supreme Court of Canada dismissed an appeal by Ontario's Attorney General of the 1996 *M. v. H.* Decision, upholding the right of same-sex couples to seek and obtain spousal support in the same way as opposite-sex common-law couples and informing the Ontario government that it had six months to ensure that its legislation in this area was constitutional. Although the Ontario government, in response, passed an omnibus bill in 1999 that amended 67 of its laws to include same-sex couples, it did so by creating a separate class of "same-sex partners" rather than providing same-sex couples with all of the rights of opposite-sex common-law couples. When the Quebec National Assembly unanimously passed Bill 32 in June 1999, the Quebec government became the first Canadian province to ensure that same-sex couples would receive all the benefits and responsibilities of opposite-sex couples, excluding the right to marriage. Other notable changes in that year occurred when the Alberta government joined with Ontario and British Columbia in allowing same-sex couples to jointly adopt a child and when the British Columbia government introduced the "Definition of Spouse Amendment," which expanded the definition of a spouse in that province to ensure that "persons of the same gender" would be treated the same as opposite-sex couples in relation to such matters as wills, estates, and inheritance. Although that year also witnessed the federal Parliament voting to preserve the opposite-sex definition of marriage, the tides of change were clearly moving in the opposite direction.

In 2000, for example, the federal government of Canada enacted the *Modernization of Benefits and Obligations Act*, which equalized the treatment of same-sex and opposite-sex common-law couples under 68 federal laws (EGALE, 2000). In separate legislation that year, the *Immigration Act*'s "family class" provisions were expanded to include same-sex couples. Also in that year, Nova Scotia introduced legislation that revised the definition of "spouse" in family law to include common-law and same-sex partners who had cohabited for a period of one year. The following year, Nova Scotia's same-sex couples became the first Canadians to be able to register their unions under registered domestic partnership legislation. In 2001, Quebec extended the definition of spouse to same-sex couples in a "de facto" union in 39 of its laws.

Further evidence of a shift in thinking on the question of what constitutes a family may be found in the Canadian census (EGALE, 2001). While the 1981 Census was the first to report on common-law marriages, the 2001 Census included two questions that recognized same-sex, common-law unions. It also recognized that children were being raised in same-sex households—even in jurisdictions where provincial or territorial laws did not permit same-sex couples to formally adopt or share guardianship of their children. According to Statistics Canada, a "census family" is "a now married couple (with or without never-married sons and/or daughters of either or both spouses), a couple living common-law (again, with or without never-married sons and/or daughters of either or both

partners), or a lone parent of any marital status, with at least one never-married son or daughter living in the same dwelling."

Perhaps the most noteworthy legal change has occurred in relation to the definition of marriage itself. Under the *Constitution Act*, the federal Parliament of Canada controls who may marry (i.e., the capacity of persons to marry), while the provinces regulate the technical aspects of the "solemnization of marriage" (e.g., who can perform the ceremony, how the deed is registered) (EGALE, 2004). In July 2002, three Ontario Superior Court judges made Canadian legal history when they ruled that the opposite-sex limitation in common law (which restricted marriage to the union of one man and one woman) was unconstitutional. This decision was echoed in 2003 by courts in British Columbia, Quebec, the Yukon and, in 2004, in Manitoba, Nova Scotia, Saskatchewan, Quebec, and Newfoundland and Labrador. In the fall of 2004, the federal government of Canada presented a "Reference re Same-Sex Marriage" to the Supreme Court of Canada, requesting that the Court clarify whether the opposite-sex requirement for marriage was consistent with *Charter* guarantees of equality. In response, the Supreme Court stated that the federal government had the power to change the definition of marriage to include same-sex couples and that their doing so would be constitutional. The Supreme Court of Canada likened our systems of laws to a "living tree which by way of progressive interpretation, accommodates and addresses the realities of modern life," noting that the definition of marriage in Canada's constitution "does not exclude same-sex marriage." The Court also observed that clergy could, as an expression of freedom of religion, refuse to conduct marriage ceremonies involving same-sex couples. With the passage of Bill C-38, Parliament changed the definition of marriage to comply with the *Charter* and, on July 20, 2005, the *Civil Marriage Act* received Royal Assent.

Although a November 2005 survey conducted by CBC and Environics found that two-thirds of Canadians feel that the issue of same-sex marriage has now been settled in this country and should not be revisited (EGALE, 2006), it is apparent that others hold a different opinion. For example, it is noteworthy that on the very first day of the 2006 federal election campaign, Conservative Party leader Stephen Harper declared that, if elected Prime Minister, he would reopen the equal marriage issue and ask Parliament to approve an amendment that would limit the definition of marriage to opposite-sex couples. One hundred and thirty-five law professors from across Canada issued an open letter to Harper challenging his remarks and his desire "to enact clearly unconstitutional legislation" and accused him of "playing politics with the Supreme Court and the Charter" (Choudhry et al., 2005).

For some Canadians, objections to same-sex marriage are anchored in the belief that the rights of same-sex couples to marry under the equality provisions of the *Canadian Charter of Rights and Freedoms* are secondary to the "main purpose of marriage, which is to provide a structure within which to raise children"—a view expressed in a 2001 Supreme Court of British Columbia decision (quoted in Arnold, 2001). Earlier, in 1995, the Supreme Court of Canada had expressed a similar view and identified procreation as the "ultimate purpose of marriage" in the case of *Egan v. Canada*. The flaw in this argument is that, while opposite-sex partners are uniquely able to procreate, infertile heterosexual couples or those who simply do not wish to have children are not legally prohibited from marrying. Moreover, "extending marital rights and obligations, or even marital status, to same-sex couples will not derail the state objective of encouraging procreation" (Bailey, 2000: 20).

It is also the case that gays and lesbians can and do become parents in a variety of ways. For example, new reproductive technologies allow for gay and lesbian parenting; the "lesbian baby boom" that began in the mid-1970s is largely the result of artificial insemination by donor sperm (Taylor, 1997: 75). In an attempt to genetically link the baby to both female partners, one partner in a lesbian couple may be inseminated with the sperm of a male relative of the other partner (Salholz, 1993). The new reproductive technologies have not only made possible a growing number of lesbian co-parents but (albeit less commonly) children born to gay biological fathers and surrogate mothers. Science may also hold additional breakthroughs for gay couples. For example, in September 2000, newspaper headlines reported that gay male couples may, in the near future, be able to sire "motherless" children through cell nuclear replacement, a technique originally designed to treat infertility and metabolic disorders. This procedure allows scientists to "replace the nucleus from the egg of a female donor with the nucleus from a sperm cell. The resulting 'male egg,' which would contain only male DNA, would then be fertilized in vitro by sperm from another man and implanted in the womb of a surrogate mother who would carry the child to term" (Honore, 2000).

In general, people who applaud the legalization of same-sex marriage in Canada maintain that granting gays and lesbians the right to marry is important both in practical and symbolic terms. Beyond the economic and practical advantages that marriage confers, it is believed that the right to legally marry will promote increased social acceptance of sexual minorities and function as an important source of social support for gays and lesbians as they pursue long-term relationships. As noted by Justice L'Heureux-Dubé in a dissenting opinion in *Egan v. Canada*: "Given the marginalized position of homosexuals in society, the metamessage that flows almost invariably from excluding same-sex couples from such an important social institution is essentially that society considers such relationships to be less worthy of respect, concern and consideration than relationships involving members of the opposite sex." Allowing same-sex couples the right to marry, she maintained, could go a long way toward redressing this situation and "may be of greater value and importance to those affected than any pecuniary gain flowing from that recognition" (quoted in Bailey, 2000: 46).

In marked contrast, for religious fundamentalists and other conservative groups, the case against gay marriage is unambiguous: marriage is a union of opposite-sexed persons and attempts to recognize gay families must be vigorously repelled. Consider, for example, that in June 1999, a Baptist preacher from Topeka, Kansas, announced that he and a group of his followers would be leading a demonstration on the steps of the Supreme Court of Canada to protest its decision to extend the definition of "spouse" to same-sex couples. According to the preacher, Canada had become the "sperm bank of Satan" (Anderssen, 1999). On other occasions, like-minded people have wielded posters proclaiming such sentiments as, "God made Adam and Eve, not Adam and Steve" (Smolowe, 1996). In addition, not all gay activists in Canada or elsewhere support the legalization of same-sex marriage. Some oppose same-sex marriage on the grounds that it is too derivative of heterosexual unions and mimics a traditionally repressive institution that is based on property rights and institutionalized husband–wife roles (Johnson, 1996). Such gay activists also argue that legalizing same-sex unions could further stigmatize homosexual relations that occur outside of committed, long-term relationships. Will the legalization of same-sex marriages result in further stereotypes of homosexuals and define "good gays" as those who confine themselves to sexual relations with a spouse and who parent children, and "bad gays" as those who do not? (Allen, 1997; Cossman, 1996, 1997). As one observer notes, "when same-sex couples present themselves as 'normal' in pursuit of formal recognition, the polarization of 'family' and 'not family' is effectively cemented." She rhetorically asks, "Are queers 'family?' Could queers be 'family?' Should queers be 'family?'" (Owen, 2001: 96).

Until recently, researchers studying families tended either to ignore gay families or depict them as pathological. Although in recent years there has been a knowledge explosion in this area (e.g., Arnup, 1997; Beals, Impett, and Peplau, 2002; O'Brien and Weir, 1999; Kurdek, 2003), there also exists a counter-tendency to "present fairy tale versions of our lives in which [gays and lesbians] are all happy individuals, partners and family members" (Williams, 1995: 98–99). Although research on gay and lesbian families in Canada has largely tended to draw upon small, nonrepresentative samples of white, middle-class, well-educated respondents, this body of research clearly suggests that the families of gays and lesbians may be most remarkable for their utter ordinariness (Nelson, 1993).

In 2003, the Vatican released "Considerations Regarding Proposals to Give Legal Recognition to Unions Between Homosexual Persons." The document maintained that "the absence of sexual complementarity in these [homosexual] unions creates obstacles in the normal development of children who would be placed in the care of such persons. They would be deprived of the experience of either fatherhood or motherhood. Allowing children to be adopted by such persons living in such unions would actually mean doing violence to these children, in the sense that their condition of dependency would be used to place them in an environment that is not conducive to their full human development" (Section III.7). In response, the Canadian Psychological Association (CPA) issued a press release refuting the Vatican's claim. It stated: "Psychological research into lesbian and gay parenting indicates that there is no basis in the scientific literature for [the Vatican's] perception." According to the CPA, the psychological research on lesbian and gay parenting indicates that there are "essentially no differences in the psychological development, gender identity or sexual orientation between the children of gay or lesbian parents and the children of heterosexual parents." It also emphasized that "[s]tatements that children of gay and lesbian parents have more and significant problems in the areas of psychosocial or gender development and identity than do the children of heterosexual parents have no support from the scientific literature" (Canadian Psychological Association, 2003; see also Malone and Cleary, 2002).

Similarly, despite research proclaiming lesbian couples the most egalitarian of all forms of intimate partnerships (Huston and Schwartz, 2002; Shumsky, 2001), it appears that these relationships are not immune to the violent and abusive behaviour that occurs among heterosexual and gay male couples (Ristock, 2003). Paralleling the patterns found in heterosexual relationships, violence in lesbian relationships also tends to increase in both frequency and severity over time and to be associated with the dynamics of power and dependency and the use of alcohol and other drugs (West, 2002; Fortunata and Kohn, 2003).

There can be no doubt that same-sex families challenge many of our taken-for-granted assumptions. They challenge the common-sense assumption that human beings have a heterosexual destiny and that the way in which most of us conduct our sexual affairs is both natural and morally right. They challenge classification systems surrounding the family and marriage, gender, love, and sexual experiences. Said differently, same-sex families remind us that human behaviour is not as simple as those who believe in a "natural order" suggest. The term "family" has become a very fluid concept indeed.

REFERENCES

Abbott, Pamela, and Claire Wallace. (1992). *The Family and the New Right.* London: Pluto.

Allen, Katherine R. (1997). "Lesbian and Gay Families." In Terry Arendell, ed., *Contemporary Parenting: Challenges and Issues* (pp. 196–218). Thousand Oaks, CA: Sage.

Anderssen, Erin. (1999). "Gay-Bashing Preacher Calls Off Protest." *The Globe and Mail,* 29 June. On the World Wide Web at http://www.egale.ca/archives/press/9906299gm.htm (10 January 2003).

Arnold, Tom. (2001). "B.C. Court Says No to Gay Marriage." *National Post,* 4 October, A1, A15.

Arnup, Katherine. (1997). "In the Family Way: Lesbian Mothers in Canada." In Meg Luxton, ed., *Feminism and Families: Critical Policies and Changing Practices* (pp. 80–97). Halifax: Fernwood Publishing.

Bailey, Martha. (2000). *Marriage and Marriage-Like Relationships.* On the World Wide Web at http://www.lcc.gc.ca/research_project/00_relationships-en.asp (10 January 2006).

Beals, K. P., E. A. Impett, and L. A. Peplau. (2002). "Lesbians in Love: Why Some Relationships Endure and Others End." *Journal of Lesbian Studies,* 6 (1): 53–63.

Bricker, Darrell, and Edward Greenspon. (2001). *Searching for Certainty: Inside the New Canadian Mindset.* Toronto: Doubleday Canada.

Canadian Psychological Association. (2003). "Gays and Lesbians Make Bad Parents: There Is No Basis in the Scientific Literature For This Perception." 6 August. On the World Wide Web at http://www.cpa.ca/documents/GayParenting-CPA.pdf (10 January 2006).

Choudhry, Suhjit, Jean-Francois Gaudreault-DesBiens, Wendy Adams, et al. (2005). "Open Letter to The Hon. Stephen Harper from Law Professors Regarding Same-Sex Marriage." 16 December. On the World Wide Web at http://www.law.utoronto.ca/same-sexletter.html (10 January 2006).

Conway, John F. (1990). *The Canadian Family in Crisis.* Toronto: James Lorimer and Company.

Cossman, Brenda. (1996). "Same-Sex Couples and the Politics of Family Status." In Janine Brodie, ed., *Women and Canadian Public Policy* (pp. 223–78). Toronto: Harcourt Brace and Company.

———. (1997). "Family Inside/Out." In Meg Luxton, ed., *Feminism and Families: Critical Policies and Changing Practices* (pp. 124–41). Halifax: Fernwood Publishing.

EGALE. (2000). "Omnibus Federal Law Recognizes Same-Sex Couples." On the World Wide Web at http://www.egale.ca/index.asp?lang=E&menu=21&item=400 (10 January 2003).

———. (2001). "Press Release: 2001 Census to Recognize Same-Sex Couples." 10 May. On the World Wide Web at http://www.egale.ca/pressrel/010510-e.html (10 January 2003).

———. (2004). "Quebec Becomes Third Province to Allow Same-Sex Couples to Marry." 19 March. On the World Wide Web at http://www.egale.ca/index.asp?lang=E&menu=1&item=952 (10 January 2006).

———. (2006). "Egale Asks Harper to Clarify Murky Position on the Notwithstanding Clause." 8 January. On the World Wide Web at http://www.egale.ca/index.asp?lang=E&menu=1&item=1266 (10 January 2006).

Fortunata, B., and C. S. Kohn. (2003). "Demographic, Psychosocial and Personality Characteristics of Lesbian Batterers." *Violence and Victims,* 18 (5): 557–68.

Gavigan, Shelly A. M. (1997). "Feminism, Familial Ideology and Family Law." In Meg Luxton, ed., *Feminism and Families: Critical Policies and Changing Practices* (pp. 98–123). Halifax: Fernwood Publishing.

Gottlieb, Beatrice. (1993). *The Family in the Western World from the Black Death to the Industrial Age.* New York: Oxford University Press.

Honore, Carl. (2000). "'Male Egg' Couple Enable Two Men to Conceive a Child." *National Post,* 26 September 26, A1, A12.

Huston, M., and P. Schwartz. (2002). "Gendered Dynamics in the Romantic Relationships of Lesbians and Gay Men." In A.E. Hunter and C. Forden, eds., *Readings in the Psychology of Gender: Exploring Our Differences and Commonalities* (pp. 167–278). Needham, MA: Allyn & Bacon.

Jackson, E., and S. Persky. (1982). *Flaunting It: A Decade of Gay Journalism from the Body Politic.* Toronto: Pink Triangle Press.

Johnson, Fenton. (1996). "Wedded to an Illusion: Do Gays and Lesbians Really Want the Right to Marry?" *Harper's,* November, 41–50.

Kinsman, Gary. (1996). *The Regulation of Desire: Homo and Hetero Sexualities,* 2nd ed. Montreal: Black Rose Books.

Kurdek, L. A. (2003). "Differences Between Gay and Lesbian Cohabiting Couples." *Journal of Social & Personal Relationships,* 20 (4): 411–36.

Lancaster, Roger N. (2003). *The Trouble with Nature: Sex in Science and Popular Culture.* Berkeley: University of California Press.

Malone, K., and R. Cleary. (2002). "(De)Sexing the Family: Theorizing the Social Science of Lesbian Families." *Feminist Theory,* 3 (3): 271–93.

Murdock, George. (1949). *Social Structure.* New York: Free Press.

Nelson, Fiona. (1993). *Lesbian Motherhood: An Exploration of Canadian Lesbian Families.* Toronto: University of Toronto Press.

O'Brien, Carol Anne, and Lorna Weir. (1999). "Lesbian and Gay Men Inside and Outside Families." In Nancy Mandell and Ann Duffy, eds., *Canadian Families: Diversity, Conflict and Change* (pp. 111–39). Toronto: Harcourt Brace.

Owen, Michelle K. (2001). "'Family' as a Site of Contestation: Queering the Normal or Normalizing the Queer?" In Terry Goldie, ed., *In a Queer Country: Gay & Lesbian Studies in the Canadian Context* (pp. 86–102). Vancouver: Arsenal Pulp Press.

Ristock, J. L. (2003). "Exploring Dynamics of Abusive Lesbian Relationships: Preliminary Analysis of a Multisite Qualitative Study." *American Journal of Community Psychology,* 31 (3–4): 329–41.

Salholz, Eloise. (1993). "For Better or For Worse." *Newsweek,* 24 May, 69.

Shumsky, E. (2001). "Transforming the Ties That Bind: Lesbians, Lovers and Chosen Family." In E. Gould and S. Kiersky, eds., *Sexualities Lost and Found: Lesbians, Psychoanalysis and Culture* (pp. 57–69). Madison, CT: International Universities Press.

Smolowe, Jill. (1996). "The Unmarrying Kind." *Time,* 29 April, 68–69.

Taylor, Ronald L. (1997). "Who's Parenting? Trends and Patterns." In Terry Arendell, ed., *Contemporary Parenting: Challenges and Issues* (pp. 68–91). Thousand Oaks, CA: Sage.

West, C. M. (2002). "Lesbian Intimate Partner Violence: Prevalence and Dynamics." *Journal of Lesbian Studies,* 6 (1): 121–27.

Williams, Karen. (1995). "The Good Mother." In Katherine Arnup, ed., *Lesbian Parenting: Living With Pride and Prejudice* (pp. 98–110). Charlottetown, PE: Gynergy books.

Chapter 16

Love Online[1]

ROBERT J. BRYM AND RHONDA L. LENTON

THE BIRTH OF A NEW SOCIETY

It is not often that one gets to witness the birth of a new society. Yet the birth of a new society is exactly what is happening on the Internet today.

The society is growing quickly. Numbering 40 million people in 1996, it reached 375 million in 2000. It grew to more than 700 million in 2005. In 2005, only China and India were bigger than the society of the Internet.

But is it really a society? A society is a large, enduring network of social interaction that survives by accomplishing five main tasks: (1) preserving order, (2) producing and distributing goods and services, (3) teaching new members, (4) providing its members with a sense of purpose, and (5) replacing old members (Aberle et al., 1950). Bearing this definition in mind, does the Internet form a society? We believe it does.

Internet society accomplishes many of the same tasks as other societies. For example, although control of members is much less centralized and extensive than in other societies, Internet society has established governing structures, such as those that regulate conventions in the use of HTML code, the allocation of domain names, and user behaviour on specific sites. Similarly, although e-commerce is still only a fraction of economic activity in the world of bricks and mortar, it is growing much more quickly than the economy as a whole. Meanwhile, distance education is becoming increasingly popular (some universities already offer entire degrees online), and the Internet has become an important agent of informal socialization. Thus, the first three tasks of an enduring

society—preserving order, producing and distributing goods and services, and teaching new members—are all performed by Internet society.

So is society's fourth task—providing members with a sense of purpose. More precisely, Internet society provides its members with *many* senses of purpose by enabling social interaction in a wide variety of contexts. Today, Internet users interact socially by exchanging text, images, and sound via e-mail, Internet phone, video conferencing, computer-assisted work groups, mailing lists, and chat groups. Some forms of computer-assisted interaction operate in delayed time. "A" sends a message to "B." "B" receives the message when he or she logs on, responding when convenient. Other forms of computer-assisted interaction operate in real time; people communicate by means of instant messaging.

The proliferation of computer-assisted communication in delayed and real time has resulted in the creation of "virtual communities." Virtual communities are associations of people, scattered across the country or the planet, who communicate via computer and modem about subjects of common interest. Membership in virtual communities is fluid but the communities endure. They are self-governing bodies with their own rules and norms of "netiquette" (McLaughlin, Osborne, and Smith, 1995; Sudweeks, McLaughlin, and Rafaeli, 1999). Members of virtual communities form social relationships. They exchange confidences, give advice, share resources, get emotionally involved, and talk sex. Although their true identities are usually concealed, they sometimes decide to meet and interact in real life. In the 1980s, most observers believed that social interaction by means of computer would be restricted to the exchange of information (for a review and critique of this literature, see Wellman et al., 1996). It turns out these observers were wrong. Internet society can provide its members with a sense of purpose, giving them new freedom to shape their selves as they choose (Turkle, 2001).

THE RISE OF ONLINE DATING

The fifth task of any enduring society involves replacing old members. That is, people ensure the survival of their society by dating, courting, forming long-term offline relationships, and reproducing. With respect to this task, too, Internet society is now beginning to measure up to other societies. Online dating is a growth industry, and cases of online relationships resulting in long-term relationships are increasingly common.

The first online dating services started up around 1996. Wherever the Internet extends, people now use these services. For example, China's Xinhua News Agency ran a story a few years ago about two handicapped people, one in China and the other in California, who met thanks to an online dating service and eventually married ("Internet Dating," 2000). By the middle of 2000, the seven largest online dating sites on the Internet boasted over 12 million registered members and many more "guests" or "visitors." Of these seven large sites, four are based in the U.S. The U.K., Israel, and Canada host the other three large sites. The Canadian site, Webpersonals, and its associated Womanline.com and Manline.com sites, have more than one million members, about a quarter of them Canadian residents. Advertising revenues aside, membership subscriptions generate up to $450 000 per month per million registered members. *Business Start-Ups* magazine ranked online dating as one of the top five business ideas of 2000 and beyond ("Market Overview," 2000; "Mediametrix's," 2000; "DatingClub.com," 2000; Rogers, 2000; "uDate.com," 2000).

How does an online dating site work? Typically, any Internet user may browse the ads free of charge. However, to place an ad and interact with others, one must pay to become a site member. Some sites charge a monthly fee while others operate on a fee-per-use basis. Ads include text and an optional photograph and sound recording of the member. Members may correspond by e-mail or instant messaging.

Members create a public identity—a name by which others may identify them and a user profile by which others may determine their level of interest in specific individuals. The user profile usually includes such information as the member's sex, age, locale, marital status, type of relationship preferred (e.g., romantic involvement, marriage, casual sex, online sex), sexual preferences, and so forth. The online dating service also categorizes this information and allows members to search for other members with specific characteristics. For example, one may search for heterosexual single Christian men between the ages of 35 and 44 living within a 50 km radius of one's home and wanting a romantic involvement. Some smaller sites are devoted exclusively to Christians, Blacks, Jews, gay men, and so forth (Briscoe, 2000; Crary, 2000).

Four main social forces appear to be driving the rapid growth of online dating.

A growing proportion of the population is composed of singles. Statistics Canada divides the Canadian population into four categories by marital status: married (including common-law unions), single, widowed, and divorced. Of these four categories, "married" has been growing slowest and "divorced" has been growing fastest for decades. Between 1995 and 1999, the number of married Canadians grew by 3.3 percent. The number of single, widowed, and divorced Canadians grew by 4.4 percent. With more single, widowed, and divorced people in the population, the dating and marriage markets have grown apace (Statistics Canada, 2000a).

Career and time pressures are increasing. In the 1970s, many observers predicted the advent of a "leisure society" by the end of the century. In reality, many people are working longer hours

(Schor, 1992). Among the world's rich countries, Canada ranks in the middle in terms of hours worked per week and near the bottom in terms of paid vacation days ("Mild Labor," 1999). According to a 1998 Statistics Canada survey of more than 11 000 Canadians over the age of 14, a third of Canadians identify themselves as "workaholics" and more than half worry they do not have enough time to spend with their family and friends. Nearly a fifth of Canadians reported "severe time stress" in 1998, up significantly since 1992 (Statistics Canada, 1999). Increased pressure from work makes it more difficult to find the time to engage in conventional dating methods, such as meeting eligible partners in athletic clubs and bars. People are looking for more efficient ways of meeting. Online dating has emerged as a credible alternative.

Single people are more mobile. According to the 1996 Census, more than a fifth of Canadians were not living in the same census subdivision as five years earlier. Nearly 7 percent said they had moved from another province or another country (Statistics Canada, 2000b). These numbers reflect the fact that single people, who compose nearly 80 percent of online daters, form an increasingly flexible work force, more willing to uproot and relocate in response to job market demands than in the past. (Dual careers may make it more difficult to relocate so it is questionable whether married people are more mobile.) Moreover, a growing number of jobs require frequent travel. As a result of increasing geographical mobility, single Canadians are finding it more difficult to meet other people for dating and sustained intimate relationships. Online dating is increasingly seen as a possible solution to this problem.

Workplace romance is on the decline. Due to growing sensitivity about sexual harassment in the workplace, it is more difficult to initiate workplace romances. Increasingly, people understand that sexual or romantic overtures may be interpreted as sexual harassment and result in disciplinary action or suspension. This encourages the search for alternative milieux in which to meet people for sexual and romantic involvements. Again, online dating benefits (Luck and Milich, 2000).

In short, while demand for dates is on the increase, social circumstances often make it difficult for people to find good dating partners. Thus, a 1999 Toronto Sun/COMPAS poll found that fully 52 percent of Toronto's singles were not dating, while 75 percent said they are finding it difficult or very difficult to find a good dating partner (Mandel, 1999).

A SOCIAL PROFILE OF ONLINE DATERS

To find out more about online daters in Canada, we conducted two surveys late in 2000. First, between 7 and 29 November 2000 we organized a telephone survey of 1200 randomly selected Canadians living outside the northern territories (400 in Quebec and 800 in the rest of the country). Second, we organized an online survey at the web site of Webpersonals, Canada's largest Internet dating service, between 31 November and 5 December 2000. Members and visitors to the Webpersonals sites were presented with a pop-up window when they logged on. It asked if they were willing to participate in the survey and informed them that the survey was restricted to Canadian residents. Exactly 6 581 people completed our questionnaire. From respondents who completed the questionnaire, we selected 185 men and 105 women who said online dating is "a great way to meet people" and said they were willing to be interviewed in depth by telephone. Eleven individuals were subsequently selected at random from this group of 290. They participated in 20-minute taped interviews from which we quote below.

The two surveys show that online daters differ in significant ways from the general Canadian population and from Canadian Internet users who do not use online dating services. People who use the Internet at least once a month comprise about 40 percent of the Canadian population. However, Internet users are younger, better educated, more likely to be employed in the paid labour force, and more likely to earn a higher income than Canadians in general. Using the online survey, it is also possible to compare online daters with Internet users who are not online daters. This comparison shows that the two groups are similar in some respects but different in others. Online daters are more likely to be male, single, divorced, employed, and urban. They are also more likely to enjoy higher income.

One of the enduring myths about avid computer users is that they are social isolates in the real world, locked in their basements alone for hours on end, with windows tightly sealed and shuttered. Similarly, online daters are sometimes characterized as "losers" or "lonely hearts," people who are unable to form normal social ties and enjoy normal social interaction. In this view, they pursue online dating out of desperation.

There may have been some truth to these observations when online dating was in its infancy (Klement, 1997). However, our online dating survey found little evidence to support these generalizations. It turns out that, as of the end of 2000, Canadian online daters are sociable and self-confident. Offline, they tend to be joiners of organizations. They often visit family members. They frequently engage in social and leisure activities with others. These findings are consistent with the results of other recent Canadian research on avid computer users. It turns out that the myth of the socially isolated computer enthusiast is just that—a myth (Hampton and Wellman, 1999, 2000; Wellman and Hampton, 1999).

About 30 percent of Canadians claim to belong to churches, synagogues, mosques, and temples. Membership is concentrated among people 35 years of age and older, and especially among people 55 years of age and older. Only about 15 percent of Canadians under the age of 35 say they attend church, and so forth, weekly (Bibby, 2001: 128, 132). Set beside these figures, it is surprising that almost 24 percent of online daters say they belong to churches and so forth.

That is because more than half of online daters are under the age of 35, compared to just 29 percent of the population. It seems that online daters are more likely to belong to churches and so on than non-online daters of the same age.

Additional evidence of sociability comes from a question on club membership. Respondents were asked to indicate whether they had been "a member of any clubs, such as a bridge club or athletic club, within the past year." Fully 41 percent of respondents said they belonged to such clubs. Of those who said they belonged to such clubs, 61 percent said they belonged to more than one. In striking contrast, a recent Statistics Canada study shows that only 18 percent of Canadians aged 15 and over belonged to one or more "sports and recreation organizations" (Hall et al., 1998: 43).

When respondents were asked how often they visit family or distant relatives in a typical month, only 18 percent replied that they do not visit them even once. This cannot be considered a high figure in a society with high geographical mobility. In Canada today, people often live a considerable distance from family members and cannot visit regularly. More than 82 percent of online daters visit family or relatives at least once a month and 39 percent visit them weekly or more often.

Finally, respondents were asked how often they go out with one or more people for social or leisure activities in a typical month. Only 4 percent said they typically do not go out with others at all. Roughly speaking, a quarter of respondents go out with others zero to two times per month, a quarter go out three to four times a month, a quarter go out five to eight times a month, and a quarter go out nine or more times a month. So, on average, online daters go out for social and leisure activities with others a lot. Some 53 percent typically go out with others for social or leisure activities more than once a week.

It is interesting to compare these results with comparable data from the telephone survey. About 86 percent of respondents in the telephone survey said they have never read personal or dating ads on the web or "checked out" an online dating site. These people are much more likely than online daters to belong to a religious organization (40 percent vs. 24 percent) and visit their families and relatives one or more times per week (60 percent vs. 39 percent). However, Internet users who have never read personal or dating ads on the web or checked out an online dating site are somewhat *less* likely than online daters to belong to a club (37 percent vs. 42 percent). They are also somewhat less likely to go out once a week or more for social or leisure activities (68 percent vs. 65 percent). Thus, online daters are less sociable in terms of religious and family activities but more sociable in terms of friendship and intimate activities.

Sociable people tend to be self-confident. It should therefore come as no surprise that online daters are, in general, a very self-confident group. Specifically, 70 percent of respondents said they would feel comfortable making a speech in public. Of these, 45 percent said they would feel very comfortable. Only 30 percent of respondents said they would feel uncomfortable making a speech in public. Of these, 36 percent said they would feel very uncomfortable.

Respondents were also asked about how others see them: "In terms of your personality, how do you think that people who know you well would rank your self-confidence, say, on a scale from 0 to 6, where 0 is not self-confident and 6 is very self-confident?" Only 5 percent of respondents answered in the "not self-confident" range (0–2). Another 10 percent gave a neutral response (3). Fully 86 percent of respondents answered in the "self-confident" range (4–6).

In terms of self-confidence, Internet users who have not read personal or dating ads on the web and have not checked out an online dating site are slightly more self-confident than online daters. Seventy-five percent of Internet users who have not read personal or dating ads on the web or checked out an online dating site said they would feel comfortable making a speech in public and 89 percent said that others regard them as self-confident.

In sum, the picture that emerges from these data goes a long way toward dispelling the myth of the online dater as a social isolate lacking social skills. On the whole, online daters are joiners. They often socialize with family and friends. They see themselves as self-confident. And they believe others see them that way. Although Internet users who have not read personal or dating ads on the web or checked out an online dating site differ from online daters in some ways, the two groups differ little in terms of overall sociability and self-confidence.

THE PROS AND CONS OF ONLINE DATING

People use online dating for a variety of reasons. Allowing multiple responses, the online daters we sampled often use online dating services to meet someone (78 percent), find someone for a long-term relationship (58 percent), find sexual partners (43 percent), out of curiosity or fun with no intention of making face-to-face contact (41 percent), for casual online chatting and flirting (36 percent), and to find a possible marriage partner (31 percent).

More than a million Canadians over the age of 17 have at least visited an online dating site. (21.9 million Canadians over the age of 17 × 39.1 percent Internet users × 13 percent of respondents in the telephone survey who said they had at least visited an online dating site = 1.1 million people.) What do these people see as the main advantages and disadvantages of online dating? Respondents were asked to evaluate nine possible advantages of online dating on a scale from 0 to 6. We calculated the percentage of respondents who gave each item a score between 4 and 6. For online daters, and allowing multiple responses, the three main advantages of online dating are as follows:

• It creates the opportunity to meet people one would otherwise never meet (89 percent of respondents gave this item a score of 4 to 6).

- It offers privacy and confidentiality (75 percent of respondents gave this item a score of 4 to 6).

- It's a lot more convenient than other ways of trying to meet people (74 percent of respondents gave this item a score of 4 to 6).

We conducted 11 in-depth telephone interviews of online survey respondents. When asked "What prompted you to use online dating?" they virtually unanimously stressed its convenience and the way it allows users to be selective. Typically, one woman in her twenties from Montreal said: "I feel that online I can find someone more compatible because I'm very much into the computer field and if someone has an ad up on the Internet that means that he knows how to use a computer. . . . [Also] you can get to know the person first [before dating] and sometimes see a picture, which helps." In the words of a Toronto man, also in his twenties: "You see right away if you have some compatibility. It's not like a random chance where you walk into a bar. You know right away if they're a smoker or a non-smoker, you know if they participate in some of the same activities you participate in. Some of them have photos. You can see if there's a physical attraction. Quite a long list! You can assess the person more easily." Or as a woman in her thirties from Calgary put it: "You don't have to have these lengthy, drawn-out conversations at a bar with one person. Via the Internet you can start up five or six or seven different conversations with people and kind of weed them out."

Respondents were also presented with a list of five possible disadvantages of online dating. The two biggest disadvantages:

- People online might not tell you the truth about themselves. Eighty-two percent of online daters found this a big disadvantage. Women were significantly more likely than men to find this a big disadvantage. There were no other noteworthy differences between subgroups.

- The people you meet online might be hiding something. Seventy-two percent of online daters found this a big disadvantage. Again, women were significantly more likely than men to find this a big disadvantage and there were no other noteworthy differences between subgroups.

The 11 people interviewed in depth agreed unanimously that the number one disadvantage of online dating is that some people misrepresent themselves. As one respondent put it when asked about the disadvantages of online dating: "I can't really think of any [disadvantages] other than a few people will, shall I say, exaggerate the truth."

CONTACT, MEETING, AND MISREPRESENTATION

Some people read online personal ads merely for fun, out of curiosity, or to engage in erotic verbal fantasies with no intention of meeting their correspondents. Over a third of our online survey respondents said "chatting and flirting" are important reasons why they use online dating services.

Chatters and flirters aside, other people actually meet one or more correspondents face to face. Let us now see how often people establish contact with others through online dating services and how often they meet face to face. We then discuss misrepresentation in online contacts.

Contact. Respondents in the online survey were asked how many people they had contacted by e-mail or other means as a result of an online personal ad or dating service. They were also asked how many people had contacted them. Nearly a quarter of respondents never initiated a contact. Over a third initiated one to five contacts. Nearly a fifth initiated six to ten contacts, and just over a fifth initiated more than ten contacts. Women were more likely than men to be contacted by others. Thus, nearly 16 percent of men but only about 12 percent of women had never been contacted. At the other extreme, 3 percent of men but nearly 12 percent of women had been contacted more than fifty times.

Meeting. We asked respondents how many people they had asked to meet in person as a result of online dating and how many people had asked to meet them. About a quarter of respondents said they requested no meetings with others and about half said they requested meetings with one to five other people. The remainder said they requested meetings with more than five other people. The figures are much the same for meetings requested by others. In both cases, the median number of requested meetings is two. About 2 percent more men than women asked to meet others and 8 percent more women than men were asked to meet by others.

How many people actually meet face to face as a result of using online dating services? A third of respondents reported no face-to-face meetings as a result of online dating. Nearly half reported one to five face-to-face meetings and nearly a fifth reported more than five face-to-face meetings. The median number of face-to-face meetings was two. Men reported fewer than 2 percent more face-to-face meetings than women.

About two-thirds of online daters exchanged pictures and 86 percent talked on the phone before agreeing to go out on a date. Some 55 percent of respondents spoke on the phone three or more times before first getting together with someone they met online. Only 2 percent of respondents met face to face the same day they established contact. About a third met within a week and a quarter within two weeks of first contact, with the remaining 40 percent taking more than two weeks to meet. This suggests that most respondents approach online dating cautiously, taking the time to collect information and grow comfortable before going out on a first date. On the other hand, a minority is quick—in our judgment, too quick—to date.

Misrepresentation. People do not always give accurate information when they place personal ads online. Some people misrepresent them-

selves to stimulate interest. In the online survey, people who had placed personal ads were asked if they had ever given inaccurate information about their appearance, job, education, income, age, marital status, interests and hobbies, and whether they have children. Multiple responses were allowed. Over a quarter of respondents said they had misrepresented themselves. This is a somewhat smaller percentage than we expected to find. We were also somewhat surprised not to discover big differences between men and women in their propensity to misrepresent themselves. The only sex difference worth mentioning is that slightly more men than women (11 percent vs. 8 percent) misrepresented their marital status. Age is the number one issue people misrepresent. Fourteen per cent of respondents said they had misrepresented their age. Tied for the number two spot as topics of misrepresentation are marital status and appearance (10 percent each).

SOME CONSEQUENCES OF ONLINE DATING

We asked respondents about the kinds of relationships they formed with people they met online. Multiple responses were allowed.

Of those who met other online daters face to face, 63 percent had sex with at least one person they met online. Having sex with a person first encountered online is somewhat more likely for men than women (66 percent vs. 58 percent) and for Canadians living in the East than those living in the West. Thus, 69 percent of Atlantic Canadians, 67 percent of (mainly anglophone) Quebeckers, 65 percent of Ontarians, but only 60 percent of respondents from the Prairies and British Columbia say they have had sex with someone they met online. A higher proportion of gay men (79 percent) than heterosexuals (62 percent) and lesbians (61 percent) said they have had sex with people they met online. As far as age is concerned, it is people in their forties who are most likely to have sex with someone they met online (67 percent) and people under the age of 25 who were least likely to do so (58 percent).

Sex aside, 60 percent of those who met other online daters face to face formed at least one long-term friendship. Thirty-seven percent met at least one person they regarded as a "partner." Three percent met someone they eventually married. The probability of marrying someone whom one first encounters online falls with age. The people most likely to marry a person first encountered online are in their twenties. The people least likely to do so are more than 39 years old. The probability of marrying an online date is not associated with one's income or education. However, the people most likely to marry someone they meet online tend to live in small towns near major cities or in the suburbs of major cities. Such people compose 25 percent of all online daters but 56 percent of online daters who married someone they met through an online dating service.

What pre-dating practices are associated with the establishment of long-term relationships among online daters? We asked respondents: "How many, if any, of the people that you have met as a result of online dating have become a long-term friend, a partner, or a spouse?" Our data show that people who formed long-term relationships were more likely to have taken a long time to get to know other people online. They were also more likely to engage in a protracted exchange of information and emotion before the first date. Specifically, people who found long-term friends, partners, and spouses online were more likely than others to have sent photos to people they eventually dated, seen photos of those people, talked to them on the phone ten or more times, and waited more than a month before first meeting them. It may be that daters looking for long-term relationships are generally more selective than daters looking for casual relationships. It may also be that people who spend more time getting to know others before meeting them face to face inadvertently increase the chance of finding a good match and therefore forming a long-term rela-

tionship. In either case, the duration and intensity of pre-dating "courtships" is likely to be greater for people who eventually form long-term relationships.

Despite the apparently high "success rate" of online daters, 42 percent of people who went out on a date with someone they met online reported at least one bad experience on a date. For 38 percent of people who went out on a date, the bad experience involved "disappointment" at least once. Another 33 percent "felt uncomfortable" at least once. More seriously, 10 percent said they felt "frightened" at least once and 26 percent said they were "pestered" at least once after a date. (Multiple responses were allowed.)

It is important to note that the 10 percent of daters who said they were frightened at least once on a date were not frightened enough to change their positive opinion about online dating in general. There was no difference in attitude toward online dating between people who were frightened and those who were never frightened. The same finding—no difference in attitude toward online dating—held for the 26 percent of daters who reported being pestered at least once after a date. It also held for men and women considered separately. We conclude that, in the great majority of cases, the more serious negative experiences reported by our respondents were not all that serious.

They were almost certainly less common than the kinds of negative experiences people have during conventional dates. For example, one nationwide survey of dating in Canadian universities found that, in the year preceding the survey, more than half the men and women who dated were insulted or sworn at by a date and more than half experienced a date throwing, smashing, or kicking something. Nearly 12 percent of men and 20 percent of women were pushed, grabbed, or shoved by a date in the year preceding the survey (DeKeseredy and Schwartz, 1998: 60). Seen in this context, it is quite possible that online dating is safer than conventional dating. That was certainly the strong consensus of the 11 online daters we interviewed in depth. "It just seems safer doing it this way. . . . Online dating gives you more control," said one woman in her forties from Northern Ontario. When asked whether she would recommend online dating to others, a woman in her thirties from Calgary replied: "Oh, definitely, yes. Because it's safe. . . . It's risk free. You can get to know somebody anonymously before you meet them." These responses must be taken with a grain of salt because the 11 individuals interviewed in depth were selected on the grounds that they thought Internet dating is "a great way to meet people." Still, if seen in the context of other data presented above, it seems reasonable to conclude that Internet dating is rarely the risky activity sometimes portrayed by the mass media.

NOTE

1. This article summarizes a report published in 2001. For the full report, see Robert J. Brym and Rhonda L. Lenton, *Love Online: Digital Dating in Canada* (Toronto: MSN.CA, 2001), on the World Wide Web at http://www.nelson.com/ nelson/harcourt/sociology/newsociety3e/ loveonline.pdf. This summary is published with permission of Donna Hindson and MSN.CA.

REFERENCES

Aberle, D. F., A. K. Cohen, A. K. Davis, M. J. Levy, Jr., and F. X. Sutton (1950). "The Functional Prerequisites of a Society." *Ethics,* 60: 100–11.

Bibby, Reginald. (2001). "Religion." In Robert J. Brym, ed., *New Society: Sociology for the 21st Century,* 3rd ed. (pp. 117–43). Toronto: Harcourt Canada.

Briscoe, Connie. (2000). "Mr.right.com." *Essence,* 31, 4: 112–14.

Crary, David. (2000). "Weary Christian Singles Also Find Love on Internet." *Florida Times Union,* 1 September, B4.

"DatingClub.com Reaches One Million Members on Eve of Third Anniversary On Internet." (2000). *Business Wire,* 24 July.

DeKeseredy, Walter S., and Martin D. Schwartz. (1998). *Woman Abuse on Campus: Results from the Canadian National Survey.* Thousand Oaks, CA: Sage.

Hall, Michael, Tamara Knighton, Paul Reed, Patrick Bussière, Don McRae, and Paddy Bowen. (1998). *Caring Canadians: Highlights from the 1997 National Survey of Giving, Volunteering and Participating.* Ottawa: Statistics Canada.

Hampton, Keith N., and Barry Wellman. (1999). "Netville On-Line and Off-Line: Observing and Surveying a Wired Suburb." *American Behavioral Scientist,* 43: 475–92.

———. (2000). "Examining Community in the Digital Neighbourhood: Early Results from Canada's Wired Suburb." In Toru Ishida and Katherine Isbister, eds., *Digital Cities: Technologies, Experiences, and Future Perspectives* (pp. 475–92). Heidelberg, Germany: Springer-Verlag.

"Internet Dating Leads to Marriage of Handicapped Couple." (2000). *Xinhua News Agency,* 14 July.

Klement, Jo Anne. (1997). "Love at First Byte: Internet Romance is Cheaper, Less Stressful Than a Blind Date." *The Salt Lake Tribune,* 8 September, B1.

Luck, Adam, and Emily Milich. (2000). "Lonely Heart Britain Floods Dating Firms." *Sunday Times,* 2GN edition, 13 August, 9.

Mandel, Michele. (1999). "The Dating Game: Your Place or Mine?" *Toronto Sun,* 24 September. On the World Wide Web at http:// www.canoe.ca/CNEWSLifeSexSurvey/six. html (22 December 2000).

"Market Overview." (2000). On the World Wide Web at http://corporate.udate.com/udatecorp. asp?MenuItem=3,0 (23 December 2000).

McLaughlin, Margaret L., Kerry K. Osborne, and Christine B. Smith. (1995). "Standards of Conduct on Usenet." In Steven G. Jones, ed., *CyberSociety* (pp. 90–112). Thousand Oaks, CA: Sage.

"MediaMetrix's July 2000 Statistics Confirm uDate.com as the Fastest Growing Online Matchmaking Site." (2000). *PR Newswire,* 23 August.

"Mild Labor: The World at Work and Play." (1999). *Wired,* 7 (12): 144.

Rogers, Scott. (2000). Team Director, Webpersonals. com. Personal communication, 15 September.

Schor, Juliet B. (1992). *The Overworked American: The Unexpected Decline of Leisure.* New York: Basic Books.

Statistics Canada. (1999). "General Social Survey: Time Use." *The Daily,* 9 November. On the World Wide Web at http://www.statcan. ca/Daily/English/991109/d991109a.htm (23 December 2000).

———. (2000a). "Population by Marital Status and Sex." On the World Wide Web at http://www.statcan.ca/english/Pgdb/ People/Families/famil01.htm (23 December 2000).

———. (2000b). "Population 5 Years and Over by Mobility Status, 1991 and 1996 Censuses." On the World Wide Web at http://www.statcan.ca/english/Pgdb/People/ Population/demo42a.htm (18 December 2000).

Sudweeks, Fay, Margaret McLaughlin, and Sheizaf Rafaeli, eds. (1999). *Network and Netplay: Virtual Groups on the Internet.* Menlo Park, CA: AAAI Press.

Turkle, Sherry. (2001). "Identity in the Age of the Internet." In Robert J. Brym, ed., *Society in Question: Sociological Readings for the 21st Century,* 3rd ed. (pp. 49–55). Toronto: Harcourt Canada.

"u.Date.com Reports Record 309% Growth in Third Quarter Revenues." (2000). On the World Wide Web at http://www.stockgenie. com/udatrel.htm (23 December 2000).

Wellman, Barry, and Keith N. Hampton. (1999). "Living Networked in a Wired World." *Contemporary Sociology,* 28: 648–54.

Wellman, Barry, Janet Salaff, Dimitrina Dimitrova, Laura Garton, Milena Gulia, Caroline Haythornthwaite. (1996). "Computer Networks as Social Networks: Collaborative Work, Telework, and Virtual Community." *Annual Review of Sociology,* 22: 213–38.

Chapter 17

Political Volatility in Canada:

BROKERAGE PARTIES AND A DEALIGNED ELECTORATE

LAWRENCE LeDUC

THE 1993 "EARTHQUAKE"

From the early 1960s until 1993, the Canadian party system comprised two strong parties—Liberal and Progressive Conservative—and a weak New Democratic Party. In the 1993 Canadian federal election, however, two new parties appeared to shatter the old system. The Bloc Québécois and the Reform Party emerged as major players on the Canadian political scene and made it more difficult to weave together a national majority. Reassembling the much-weakened Progressive Conservative Party was found to be a more difficult task than anyone imagined. Three successive leaders sought to construct a new party that could compete against the Liberals—first as the Reform Party, then the Canadian Alliance, and finally the new Conservative Party of Canada. A foreign visitor familiar with the old "two-and-a-half" party system might easily be convinced that Canadian federal politics had changed beyond all recognition.

But how different, in reality, is the new political world from the one that it replaced? In this chapter, I examine several competing interpretations of the federal party system in the light of recent political events, including the 2006 federal election, which saw the defeat of the Liberal Party after 12 consecutive years in power. I argue that, despite the political turbulence of recent years and the dramatic victory of the Harper Conservatives in 2006, older interpretations of Canadian party politics hold up well when tested against these events. While powerful changes have taken place in federal party politics, the source of those changes remains deeply embedded in the very

nature of Canadian political parties. Set alongside other dramatic periods of change in modern Canadian history—the Diefenbaker victories in 1957–58, the ups and downs of the Trudeau years, or the Mulroney landslide of 1984, for example—the political events of 1993 and 2006 are more readily understood.

THREE INTERPRETATIONS OF CANADIAN POLITICAL PARTIES

A NEW PARTY SYSTEM

Some scholars interpret the 1993 election as the start of a major political realignment in which the foundations of an entirely new party system were formed. One group of researchers refers to the new configuration as Canada's "fourth party system."[1] In this view, each party system has had distinctive characteristics that produced attachments to political parties spanning several elections. Other observers argue that the new party system, with its entrenched bases of regional support, "looks like Canada." One would expect a party system that so clearly reflects the political realities of the country to have considerable staying power.

Superficial evidence supports the view that the 1993 election signalled the advent of a new party system. Thus, after four federal elections (1993, 1997, 2000, and 2004) producing broadly similar electoral patterns, it became increasingly difficult to argue that 1993 was a temporary aberration similar to those of 1962 or 1979. Right through the 2006 federal election, the Bloc Québécois has retained its appeal among Quebec voters, and the new Conservative Party of Canada has captured most of the electoral support won by its predecessors, Reform and the Canadian Alliance. The Liberal share of the vote has fluctuated only between a high of 41 percent in the 1993 and 2000 elections and a low of 30 percent in 2006 despite the Liberals' fall from power in the most recent election. The new, highly regionalized alignment makes it increasingly difficult for *any* party to win a majority of votes, or even of seats, across the country. Accordingly, minority governments of the kind elected in 2004 and 2006 may become the new norm, heralding more frequent elections and weaker and more unstable federal governments. But partisan attachment in such a system could well be stronger, because voters would be less likely in any given election to move outside the prevailing regional alignments.

LIBERAL HEGEMONY

The second interpretation of Canadian political parties is the theory of Liberal hegemony. Liberal Party has been in power federally through much of Canada's modern history and has been extraordinarily successful at bridging the regional, ethnic, and linguistic divisions of Canadian society and adapting to new political and economic circumstances. One might argue that, despite the Liberal minority government that emerged from the 2004 election and the loss of the Liberals in the 2006 election, the recent period still resembles other long periods of Liberal hegemony, punctuated by occasional setbacks. Parties that are primarily "power seeking," as the Liberals historically have tended to be, are often particularly good at adapting to changed political circumstances.[2]

Contemporary analysts of the 1958 or 1984 landslide elections, or even of Joe Clark's defeat of Trudeau in 1979, might easily have misread those events as signalling the demise of the Liberals. But in each instance, the Liberals were back in power within a few years. Surveys of the electorate consistently show that more Canadians

identify with the Liberal party than with any of its competitors. Some analysts thus argue that the Liberal support base continues to be wide and deep.[3] In their view, Liberal continuity has been evident despite the 1993 shattering of the old party system. Despite his victory in 2006, Stephen Harper may find his tenure in office cut short by a reinvigorated Liberal Party under an appealing new leader. The race within the Liberal Party to bring about precisely that outcome was under way within weeks of the 2006 election. Those who have seen the Liberal Party rise time and again from electoral defeat expect to see yet another rebirth of what many analysts regard as "Canada's natural governing party."

BROKERAGE POLITICS

The third and final interpretation of Canadian political parties is the theory of brokerage politics. Canadian political parties of the past have traditionally been brokerage parties. Lacking stable support groups in the electorate, and avoiding clear ideological and even issue differentiation from their competitors, the parties and their leaders approach each election anew, hoping to cobble together a winning coalition of support across the electorate.[4] In election campaigns, brokerage parties do not seek to appeal to voters on the basis of long-standing principles or ideological commitment. They are not bound by positions or actions they have taken in the past, and they sometimes appear inconsistent as they search for electorally successful formulations or respond to new versions of old problems. They organize around leaders rather than around principles or ideologies, and expect the leader to work out the many compromises required for electoral success. A variety of conflicting and contradictory policy stances may sometimes coexist inside a brokerage party.

Some analysts have suggested that the Canadian preoccupation with issues of national unity, ethnic and/or linguistic relations, and federal–provincial divisions of responsibility has prevented the emergence of an electoral politics of social class or ideology.[5] In the past, the major parties have generally attempted to accommodate interests on the opposing sides of important social, linguistic, or regional cleavages. Under this interpretation, the success of the Liberals throughout Canadian history has come, not from the natural dominance of the party, but from its success at fashioning new coalitions of support. However, brokerage politics, by its very nature, leads to weak parties, limited commitments from voters, and considerable volatility, or at least the potential for volatility, in elections.[6]

Arguably, recent events suggest that brokerage politics is returning to the federal political arena. The 2003 merger of the Canadian Alliance with the remnants of the old Progressive Conservative Party provided the framework for the construction of a new brokerage party with a potentially broader range of appeal than its immediate predecessors. As the 2006 campaign waged by the new party demonstrated, the key to its victory lay in refashioning old political coalitions and mobilizing short-term discontent. Any long-time observer of Canadian federal politics might well say, "Plus ça change, plus c'est la même chose."

THE 2006 ELECTION: TESTING THE HYPOTHESES

At first, the post-1993 world seemed very different from the traditional world of brokerage politics to which Canadians had long been accustomed. With the Canadian Alliance promoting an agenda of a "united right" and the Bloc Québécois committed to its long-term project of achieving Quebec sovereignty, Canadian federal politics appeared to have become segmented into parties and groups representing narrower and more specific ideological, interest, or issue positions than had been the case in the past. Even the Liberals, with weaker representation from Quebec and the West, appeared increasingly to speak largely for the interests of Ontario or the major urban centres. In this political world, it seemed that the Liberals could win

national elections by default as long as they could portray themselves as the only credible alternative to smaller parties with narrow appeal.

The 2006 election, however, saw a return to the practice of brokerage politics and yielded a result that is likely to revive and reaffirm the predominance of brokerage parties in Canada. Stephen Harper fashioned his victory not by uniting the right but by deliberately positioning his party closer to the centre of the ideological spectrum and appealing directly to interests outside of his secure western base. The Bloc, although running candidates only in Quebec, sought to broaden its appeal to federalists and other voters, emphasizing in its campaign not sovereignty but rather the sponsorship scandal. And both the NDP and the Liberals pitched large parts of their 2006 campaign to each other's voters, de-emphasizing issue and ideological positions and appealing instead for "strategic" votes.

Given that the "new party system" of the post-1993 period had seemingly become solidified, many of these developments came as something of a surprise. At the beginning of the 2004 election campaign, the new Conservative Party of Canada surged ahead of the Liberals in the polls, only to fall back in the final weeks of the campaign.[7] The weakness of the Liberals in that campaign, and the minority outcome, should have provided clues as to what lay ahead. In 2006, the Harper-led Conservatives moved from an initial deficit of about eight percentage points at the time of the government's defeat in Parliament to a lead of as much as twelve percentage points at the start of the final week of the campaign (Figure 17.1). Unexpectedly, the Conservatives suddenly became a force in Quebec, ultimately winning ten seats and a stunning 25 percent of the popular vote in a province where they had all but been written off and where support for the Bloc seemed unshakable. Volatility and uncertainty had made a dramatic return to the Canadian federal political arena.

But the surface evidence available from the events of the 2004 and 2006 federal elections is of course not in itself a definitive test of the var-

FIGURE 17.1 PUBLIC OPINION POLLS IN THE 2006 FEDERAL ELECTION CAMPAIGN

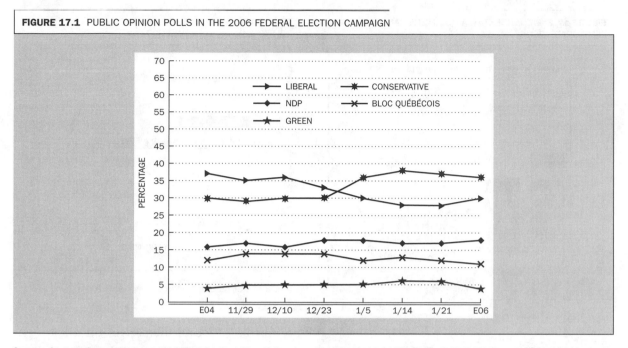

Sources: Strategic Counsel/*Globe and Mail*; Ekos Research/*Toronto Star*; Ipsos Reid/*National Post*; SES Research/*CPAC* (29 November 2005–21 January 2006). E04, E06 denote actual vote percentages in the 2004 and 2006 elections (Ottawa: Elections Canada)

ious theoretical interpretations of the Canadian party system discussed earlier. It is entirely possible that the 2006 election represented something of an aberration, given the role played by the sponsorship scandal and other events of a purely short-term nature. There is however other evidence available that speaks more directly to these issues, and which is not affected by the specific issues and events of 2004 and 2006. Further evidence can be found in data from some of the recent Canadian National Election Studies, which shows that the Canadian electorate since 1993 continues to be largely dealigned, and thus highly susceptible to brokerage appeals.[8] Neither the "liberal hegemony" hypothesis nor the "new party system" line of argument stands up well when examined in the light of available survey data revealing the attitudes and attachments of Canadian voters. Given the right electoral circumstances, significant numbers of Canadian voters can still be moved by short-term appeals emanating from an election campaign or other sources.

A DEALIGNED ELECTORATE

As Figure 17.2 shows, about a third of Canadian voters identify in some way with the Liberal Party. But just over 6 percent of respondents consider themselves "very strong" Liberals. In fact, in 2004 fewer than 15 percent of Canadians saw themselves as "very strong" supporters of *any* party, and another fifth of the electorate held no partisan attachment at all.[9] Added together, there are more weak partisans or non-partisans in the Canadian electorate than there are Liberals, and the percentage of Canadians who do not identify with any of the federal political parties has risen substantially, from about 12 percent of the total in surveys conducted during the 1980s to more than 20 percent in 2004 (Figure 17.3).

In short, if we are searching for a solid base of party support in the Canadian electorate, it is increasingly difficult to find one. While the Liberals enjoy an advantage over all competitors, they find it increasingly difficult to win an election through appeals to partisans alone, includ-

FIGURE 17.2 PARTY IDENTIFICATION IN THE CANADIAN ELECTORATE, 2004

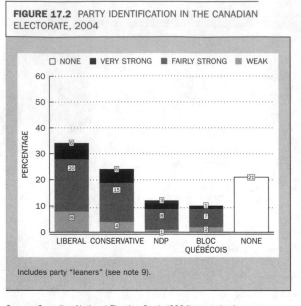

Includes party "leaners" (see note 9).

Source: Canadian National Election Study (2004), post-election wave. N = 3052.

FIGURE 17.3 RESPONDENTS NOT IDENTIFYING WITH *ANY* POLITICAL PARTY, 1988 AND 2004

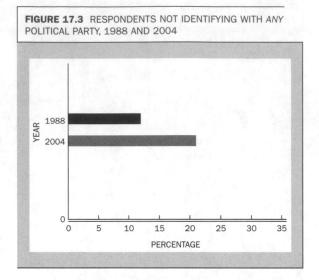

Source: Canadian National Election Studies (1988, 2004).

ing weak partisans. This distribution of partisan attachment does not suggest a return to the days of Liberal hegemony. The Liberal Party is considerably weaker today in terms of core support than it was in the 1960s and 1970s.

While the Liberals since 1993 seem to have settled at a lower level of support than they previously enjoyed, the Conservatives nevertheless remained well short of overtaking them, at least in the proportion of Canadians identifying themselves as supporters of the new party. But as the 2006 result demonstrates, this does not necessarily preclude a successful electoral appeal across party lines, and/or the migration of partisan attachment from one party to another.[10]

The ideological underpinnings of the Canadian party system are extraordinarily weak compared to party systems in many other Western democracies. While the terms "left" and "right" are widely used by political commentators and other elites in Canada, they do not resonate with much of the electorate. Figure 17.4 displays the ideological self-identification of Canadians surveyed in 2000. By far the largest component of the electorate is found in the political centre (39 percent), and 29 percent of respondents reject the concept of ideological placement entirely or

are unable to locate themselves on a left–right continuum. Just 31 percent of respondents describe themselves in ideological terms. Of these, 18 percent placed themselves on the right and 13 percent on the left. The observation that Canadian voters are not particularly ideological in their orientation to politics is not exactly new; we have known as much since the 1980s.[11] This relative lack of ideological fervour does not appear to favour the prospects of those who believe that the future of the Canadian party system lies in uniting the right or in presenting voters with more ideologically polarized choices. Neither a united right nor a more radical left would appear to be well placed to win the allegiance of a very large cross-section of Canadian voters on a continuing basis.

My conclusion is reinforced by the relatively weak linkage between ideological self-placement and party alignment (Figure 17.5). Even supporters of the Conservatives, the most ideologically coherent of the parties that contested the 2004 and 2006 federal elections, did not uniformly place themselves on the political right. Similarly, only about half of NDP supporters identify with the left. The ideological portrait of identifiers with the other parties was even more fragmented. Among the large and growing segment of the Canadian electorate that does not

FIGURE 17.4 IDEOLOGICAL SELF-PLACEMENT IN THE CANADIAN ELECTORATE

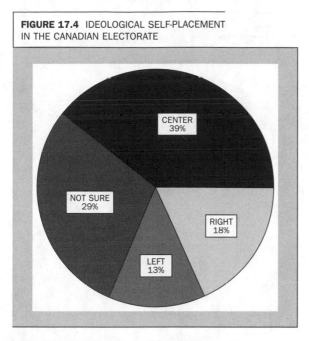

CENTER
39%

NOT SURE
29%

RIGHT
18%

LEFT
13%

Source: Canadian National Election Study (2000), campaign wave. N = 2691.

identify with *any* of the four main political parties, there are few adherents of either the left or the right.

Harper's success in the 2006 election came from his party's strategic decision to mount an appeal to the political centre, de-emphasize polarizing issues, and base the campaign on popular short-term fixes such as "accountability" and tax relief. This was essentially the key to the success of the Mulroney Conservatives in 1984 and 1988 and, to some extent, of the Diefenbaker Tories in the 1950s. It has also been the preferred strategy of the Liberals throughout much of their modern history. It was, after all, Mackenzie King whose formula for political success was to "campaign from the left, but govern from the right." The mention of particular leaders in this context is important. Given the weakness of ideology in the Canadian party system, along with the relative fluidity of issue and policy agendas, individual political leaders have assumed great importance in explanations of voting behaviour in Canada throughout much of its modern political history.[12] Parties have been most electorally successful when they have found a leader who

was able to capture the public imagination and reflect the mood of a particular time. Diefenbaker did this in breaking the Liberal hold on national politics in 1957–58 and Pierre Trudeau represents perhaps the clearest example of a leadership-driven politics in recent years. During the Trudeau years, the image of the leader came to define the party, rather than the other way around. It is thus not surprising that there are fewer Liberal partisans in the electorate now than during the Trudeau era. In the present political environment in Canada, there has not been any single political leader who has been able to capture the public imagination like Trudeau did. To some extent, this may be part of the reason why Canadian party politics appeared to stall around the weak 1993 alignment. Harper was more successful in the 2006 election in neutralizing some of the negative qualities of his image as a leader, although it would be stretching the evidence to argue that the two most recent elections turned as heavily on leader images as did some of those of the 1970s and 1980s. Nevertheless, it is clear that Harper's greater acceptability as a potential prime minister played a role in the minority outcome of 2006.[13]

In this political setting, voters do not make choices easily. It is not simply a matter of reaffirming support for a party or voting one's ideological identity. Surveys of the electorate consistently show that only half or fewer voters are able to decide how they are going to vote before the campaign actually begins (Figure 17.6). As the campaign progresses, more voters are able to reach a decision based on their assessment of the leaders, issues, and the context of a particular election. Increasingly, high-profile events such as the televised leaders' debates play a crucial role in this process. In a typical election, a significant number of voters remain "undecided," sometimes until the final days leading up to the election. This makes the actual campaign period vital to the election outcome, as the sharp turnaround in public opinion polls during the 2006 campaign clearly demonstrated.

FIGURE 17.5 IDEOLOGICAL SELF-PLACEMENT BY PARTY IDENTIFICATION, 2004

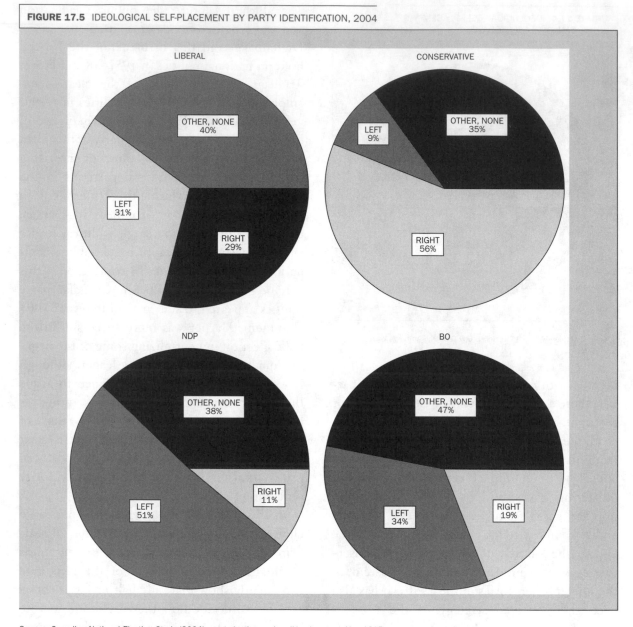

Source: Canadian National Election Study (2004), post-election and mail-back waves. N = 1615.

THE CONSEQUENCES OF BROKERAGE POLITICS

A certain style of politics has persisted through-out much of modern Canadian history and does not appear to have been significantly altered by events since 1993. The style makes for exciting election campaigns but not necessarily for a healthy democracy. Parties and their leaders become cynical and manipulative, and voters turn distrustful as they come to believe that the electoral choices presented to them are not meaningful. As one group of researchers wrote:

> Voters are profoundly and almost universally dissatisfied with brokerage politics. [Many] believe that the parties do not offer real choices and think that the parties fail to tell the voters about the really important problems facing the country. Moreover, there is virtual consensus

FIGURE 17.6 REPORTED TIME OF VOTE DECISION, 2004 FEDERAL ELECTION

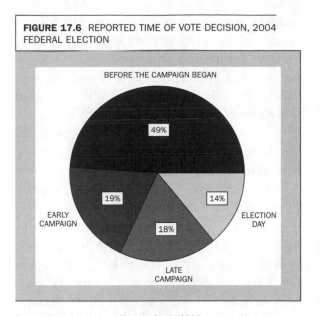

Source: Canadian National Election Study (2004), post-election wave. N = 2360.

FIGURE 17.7 ATTITUDES TOWARD POLITICS AND GOVERNMENT, 1988 AND 2004

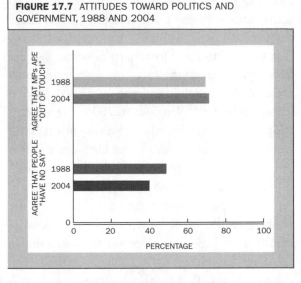

Source: Canadian National Election Studies (1988, 2004).

that political parties pay too much attention to winning elections and not enough to governing afterwards, and to gaining partisan advantage rather than to solving important problems. . . . 91% of respondents agreed that there was a big difference between what a party says it will do and what it actually does if it wins an election.[14]

As Figure 17.7 suggests, data from both recent and older surveys confirm the impression of voter cynicism. In 1988 and 2004, nearly half of all Canadians surveyed agreed that "the people have little or no say in what the government does." Nearly three-quarters of respondents in both surveys also agreed that "Members of Parliament lose touch with the people soon after they are elected." Survey findings of this type do not vary substantially from election to election and appear to have changed little over the past three decades.

The events that immediately followed the 2006 election seemed almost designed to reinforce such cynicism. When a previous Liberal Minister crossed the floor to join the new Conservative Cabinet within days of the election, there was widespread condemnation of his decision. At the same time, the appointment of a Conservative

Party campaign co-chairman to the Senate and his assignment to the Public Works portfolio, which had been a lightning rod of scandal in the previous government, brought further criticism. "Different party, same old tricks," wrote *Globe and Mail* columnist Jeffrey Simpson. "Is this how Harper ushers in a new era?" asked *The Globe and Mail* on its editorial page following the Cabinet appointments.[15] The new Prime Minister's Cabinet appointments might not have provoked such a reaction had they not appeared so much at variance with the Conservatives' resounding criticism over the course of the campaign of similar Liberal actions in the past. Voters who were hopeful that the change of government might strike a new tone of political accountability were quickly disillusioned.

Malaise in contemporary Canadian federal politics is also reflected in the declining turnout of voters in federal elections over the past two decades (Figure 17.8). While part of this decline can be explained by patterns of generational change and other demographic factors, there is little doubt that voter cynicism and the characteristics of the current party system have also contributed to the withdrawal of voters from the electoral process.[16] Dealigned voters with weak partisan attachments are more difficult to mobilize in elections. The strong regional patterns that have been evident in recent years have also contributed to the withdrawal of many Canadians from electoral participation because it has made elections less competitive in many areas of the country, and the choices presented less meaningful.[17] Turnout in 2006 rose slightly, in part because of the greater uncertainty regarding the outcome of that election. But it is unlikely that the pattern of decline has been broken because most of the factors underlying it remain in place. Voters in many parts of the country could easily believe that their vote would have little influence on the outcome of the election, either nationally or in their own constituencies. If they also believe that there is little real difference between the parties or that politicians cannot be trusted to keep their promises, the motivation to participate is further diminished.

The Canadian electorate has been distrustful of political parties and politicians for some time, creating the possibility that the political future in Canada could be much like the past. In the present political environment, all three of the interpretations advanced at the beginning of this chapter continue to have some degree of plausibility. Canada could be in the early stages of an ongoing process of realignment, in which some version of the present party system might yet solidify. Under this interpretation, the party system could eventually become more ideologically polarized, perhaps eventually leading to some type of new two-party configuration. But most of the present evidence indicates that this is not the most likely direction of any future reconfiguration of Canadian party politics, and the minority outcome of the 2006 election appears to reaffirm our skepticism regarding this interpretation. The second hypothesis—a return to Liberal hegemony—seems more plausible, even with the defeat of the Liberals in 2006. Given the thin Conservative minority, the Liberals could certainly recover and win a future election. But even if the Liberals recover, this interpretation is not the most compelling. The Liberal base is weaker than ever, and it was weak even before the sponsorship scandal took its toll. The Conservatives could just as readily convert their minority victory of 2006 into a majority in a subsequent election, particularly if the party's 2006 breakthrough in Quebec continues to undermine the hold of the Bloc on Quebec voters. But either of these possible outcomes would tell us little about the future of Canadian parties beyond one or two elections. In the past, Conservative governments, even some with large majorities, have had little staying power, and seeming Liberal hegemony did not insulate the party from sometimes crushing electoral defeats.

The interpretation that I have advanced here is that the Canadian electorate continues to be highly dealigned, in part because of the nature of brokerage politics. In this setting, elections are unpredictable and tend to be dominated by short-term issues, personalities, and events. With a dealigned electorate, the potential for sudden and unpredictable change is always high. Parties will continue to search for electorally successful formulae and to position themselves for short-term political advantage, even if that involves repudiation of past issues and ideological commitments. In a polity dominated by bro-

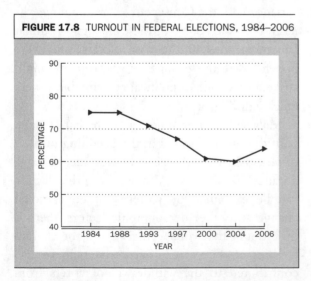

FIGURE 17.8 TURNOUT IN FEDERAL ELECTIONS, 1984–2006

Source: Elections Canada. On the World Wide Web at http://www.elections.ca.

kerage parties, an attractive new leader or a compelling issue easily ignites a process of sudden change. It happened in the elections of 1958, 1968, 1984, and 1993. Given what we know about the nature of the Canadian electorate, there is no reason to believe that it could not happen again, perhaps soon.

NOTES

1. R. Kenneth Carty, William Cross, and Lisa Young, *Rebuilding Canadian Party Politics* (Vancouver: University of British Columbia Press, 2000); R. Kenneth Carty, "Three Canadian Party Systems," in *Canadian Political Party Systems: A Reader,* ed. R. K. Carty (Peterborough: Broadview Press, 1992), 563–86.

2. Kaare Strøm, "A Behavioral Theory of Competitive Political Parties," *American Journal of Political Science,* 34 (1990): 565–98; Peter Mair, "Myths of Electoral Change and the Survival of Traditional Parties," *European Journal of Political Research,* 24 (1993): 121–33; Stephen Clarkson, *The Big Red Machine* (Vancouver: University of British Columbia Press, 2005), 3–27.

3. Neil Nevitte, André Blais, Elisabeth Gidengil, and Richard Nadeau, *Unsteady State: The 1997 Canadian Federal Election* (Toronto: Oxford University Press, 2000), 67–69, 127–135; André Blais, Elisabeth Gidengil, Richard Nadeau, and Neil Nevitte, *Anatomy of a Liberal Victory* (Peterborough: Broadview Press, 2002), 115–25.

4. Harold D. Clarke, Jane Jenson, Lawrence LeDuc, and Jon H. Pammett, *Absent Mandate: Canadian Electoral Politics in an Era of Restructuring* (Toronto: Gage, 1996), 15–21; Janine Brodie and Jane Jenson, *Crisis, Challenge and Change: Party and Class in Canada Revisited* (Ottawa, Carleton University Press, 1988).

5. Robert Alford, *Party and Society* (Chicago: Rand McNally, 1963), 250–86; John Porter, *The Vertical Mosaic* (Toronto: University of Toronto Press, 1965); Jon H. Pammett, "Class Voting and Class Consciousness in Canada," *Canadian Review of Sociology and Anthropology,* 24 (1987): 269–90.

6. Clarke et al., *Absent Mandate.*

7. Stephen Clarkson, "Disaster and Recovery," in *The Canadian General Election of 2004,* ed. Jon H. Pammett and Christopher Dornan (Toronto: Dundurn Press, 2004), 28–65.

8. The 2004 Canadian National Election Study (CNES) was conducted by André Blais, Elisabeth Gidengil, Neil Nevitte, Patrick Fournier, and Joanna Everitt. The 1993, 1997, and 2000 Canadian National Election Studies were conducted by André Blais, Neil Nevitte, Elisabeth Gidengil, and Richard Nadeau. The 1988 CNES, which is used as a basis for comparison in Figure 17.3 and subsequent figures, was conducted by Richard Johnston, André Blais, Henry Brady, and Jean Crête. The field work for all of these studies was carried out by the York University Institute for Social Research, and the studies were funded by the Social Sciences and Humanities Research Council of Canada. Neither the funding agencies nor the principal investigators are responsible for the analyses or interpretations presented here. Some of the findings of the 1997–2000 studies are reported in Nevitte et al., *Unsteady State,* and in Blais et al., *Anatomy of a Liberal Victory.* On the 1988 study, see Richard Johnston, André Blais, Henry Brady, and Jean Crête, *Letting the People Decide* (Montreal and Kingston: McGill-Queen's University Press, 1992).

9. There are different methods of measuring party identification in surveys. In the findings reported here, we use data from the post-election wave of the Canadian National Election Studies to maximize comparability with the older surveys. Respondents reporting any party "leanings" are counted as identifiers even though they may have rejected identification with a party in their first response.

This produces a somewhat more conservative estimate of non-identification than might be obtained by other methods of classification. The standard sequence of questions employed in the CNES surveys is: "Generally speaking, do you think of yourself as a Liberal, Conservative, NDP, etc.?" [IF PARTY] "How strongly do you feel—very strong, fairly strong, or not very strong?" [IF NO PARTY] "Do you feel a bit closer to any of the federal parties?" [IF YES] "Which party is that?" On some of the issues involved in employing different measures and methods of classification, see Richard Johnston, "Party Identification Measures in the Anglo American Democracies: a National Survey Experiment," *American Journal of Political Science*, 36 (1992): 542–59.

10. Lawrence LeDuc, Harold D. Clarke, Jane Jenson, and Jon H. Pammett, "Partisan Instability in Canada: Evidence from a New Panel Study," *American Political Science Review*, 78 (1984): 470–84; Clarke et al., *Absent Mandate*, 50–69.

11. Ronald D. Lambert, James Curtis, Steven Brown, and Barry Kay, "In Search of Left/Right Beliefs in the Canadian Electorate," *Canadian Journal of Political Science*, 19 (1986): 542–63.

12. Clarke et al., *Absent Mandate*.

13. Public opinion polls show that, at about the mid-point of the 2006 campaign, Stephen Harper overtook Paul Martin as "the leader who would make the best prime minister." His rating as a leader who made a "favourable impression" also rose sharply during the second half of the campaign. Strategic Counsel/*Globe and Mail*, Ekos Research/*Toronto Star* surveys (29 November 2005–21 January 2006).

14. Clarke et al., *Absent Mandate*, 180–81; André Blais and Elisabeth Gidengil, *Making Representative Democracy Work*, vol. 17 of the Research Studies of the Royal Commission on Electoral Reform and Party Financing (Toronto: Dundurn Press, 1991).

15. Jeffrey Simpson, "Different party, same old tricks," *The Globe and Mail*, 7 February 2006, A1; Editorial, *The Globe and Mail*, 8 February 2006, A8.

16. Blais et al., *Anatomy of a Liberal Victory*. See also Jon H. Pammett and Lawrence LeDuc, *Explaining the Turnout Decline in Canadian Federal Elections: A New Survey of Non-Voters* (Ottawa: Elections Canada, 2002).

17. Jon H. Pammett and Lawrence LeDuc, "Four Vicious Circles of Turnout: Competitiveness, Regionalism, Culture and Participation in Canada," paper presented to the Joint Sessions Workshops of the European Consortium for Political Research, Uppsala, Sweden, April 2004; Jon H. Pammett and Lawrence LeDuc, "Behind the Turnout Decline," in *The Canadian General Election of 2004*, ed. Jon H. Pammett and Christopher Dornan (Toronto: Dundurn Press, 2004), 338–60.

Chapter 18

French Quebec, the Quiet Revolution, and After:

GLORIES AND MISERIES OF FOUR UTOPIAS[1]

JEAN-PHILIPPE WARREN

This essay focuses on four visions of the ideal society ("utopias") formulated by the French population in Quebec in the past four decades. My starting point is the Quiet Revolution (1960–70). During the 1960s, Quebec undertook massive reforms aimed at getting rid of what many observers judged to be its backward character. Blaming mostly the Catholic Church's domination of the province, French Canadian intellectuals and militants dreamed of establishing a society in which democracy, tolerance, justice, and openness would prevail. This is how, in the space of just a decade, a largely traditionalist and closed society was transformed by the dreams of a new generation of *Québécois*.[2] This essay relates the story of these dreams and their fate.

The four utopias of the 1960s and the 1970s were as follows:

1. the realization of a thoroughly democratic political system;
2. the achievement of Quebec independence or the construction of a completely bilingual Canada;
3. the establishment of a socialist society ("social democracy"); and
4. the translation of the old language of values into a new humanism adapted to the technological age in the making.

Analysis of these utopias can help us better understand the ideologies and commitments of Quebec social movements during the past four decades, reveal the main political and social tendencies of this period, and, consequently, underline the challenges facing Quebec society today. You will see that, following two decades of struggle and great expectations (the 1960s and 1970s), a period of disillusionment set in. In this respect, Quebec was no different from other countries in the Western world, where the radical 1960s and 1970s eventually gave way to a more conservative era. Reassessing the utopias of the 1960s and 1970s will also serve to emphasize the importance of not forgetting them, even if they must now be understood in a new light.

1. DEMOCRACY

It is easy to forget today, but one of the chief debates that helped Jean Lesage and his Liberal Party get elected in 1960 turned on the question of political morality. The Union Nationale Party, led by Maurice Duplessis, dominated Quebec politics since the 1930s. Duplessis was premier from 1936 to 1939 and from 1944 to 1959. He turned patronage (e.g., hiring and giving government contracts to political friends) and corruption (e.g., accepting bribes) into a political system. Characteristically, Duplessis once started a speech by addressing his audience as "Électeurs, électrices, électricité" ("Male Electors, Female Electors, Electricity"), reminding voters in the small village he was speaking in

Source: © Jean-Philippe Warren (2006).

that they had better vote for his party if they wanted to get connected to the province's electrical grid.

Duplessis organized politics into an efficient machine for reinforcing his personal domination. Companies had to pay a "commission" for every government contract they obtained, and the regime's friends had to contribute to Union Nationale coffers if they expected personal favours. Duplessis was also careful to discredit the provincial Liberal Party. He accused it of being a refuge for French Canada's enemies. Did the Liberal Party not support compulsory military service in 1942, forcing the *Québécois* to fight "England's" war against Germany, as if Quebec were still an English colony, he persistently asked the electorate? Was the Liberal Party not a nest of dangerous socialists, as evidenced by its support for more state intervention in economic life? Duplessis's propaganda tarnished the reputation of everybody who stood in his way. Nor did he stop at words. He took action—often brutal action—to rid himself of opponents. He crushed the prolonged and bitter Asbestos strike (1948) by sending in the police to beat up the strikers. He imposed restrictive new regulations at Laval University that compelled Father Georges-Henri Lévesque to resign as dean of the *Faculté des sciences sociales*. And so forth.

One of the most famous articles published in Quebec in the 1950s was Gérard Dion and Louis O'Neill's "L'Immoralité politique dans la province de Québec" (1956). The authors denounced the "flood of stupidity" that Quebec was witnessing and the complete "perversion of conscience." Their words were harsh for they feared the destruction of democracy in Quebec. This is why, for both of them, an urgent reform of political morals by means of general civic education seemed necessary. "The work has to speed up before demagogues and would-be fascists render the masses so stupid that any effort to right the situation becomes impossible."[3] This was also what the intellectuals grouped around the *Rassemblement* (formed in 1956) and the *Unions des forces démocratiques* (formed in 1958) believed.

These two political organizations did not seek to become political parties. Rather, they sought to purify Quebec's politics by educating ordinary *Québécois*. "In 1958, French Canadians must begin to learn democracy from scratch," wrote the young Pierre Elliott Trudeau.[4] If the masses were not ready to exercise their political rights, the solution was not to abolish democracy altogether but to elevate political consciousness.

The generation that came of age after World War II was dedicated to establishing liberal democracy in Quebec like no generation before. At last, for instance, Aboriginal peoples gained the right to vote at the federal and provincial level in the 1960s. To be sure, there were violent elements in provincial politics, including people who thought traditional liberal democracy was a sham and were willing to plant bombs in mailboxes to prove their point. In 1970 the Front de Libération du Quebec (FLQ) proclaimed: "We wash our hands of the British parliamentary system; the Front de Libération du Québec will never let itself be distracted by the electoral crumbs that the Anglo-Saxon capitalists toss into the Quebec barnyard every four years."[5]

Believing Quebec was on the eve of a popular uprising, the FLQ kidnapped and murdered Pierre Laporte, Quebec Vice-Premier and Minister of Labour, plunging the country into the 1970 "October crisis," during which martial law was declared, federal troops marched into the province, and arbitrary mass arrests were made. Yet this outburst of violence cannot make us forget the peaceful and democratic way in which most of Quebec's political disputes were dealt with. Many democratic struggles elsewhere—notably the civil rights movement in the United States, which sought to heal much deeper and more painful wounds—witnessed bitter violence. Most of the members of the postwar generation believed that the people were the sole repository of power and that transparency was the cardinal quality of a democratic regime. This meant an insistence on participatory democracy (universal, mass participation in politics) and the eradication of corruption from public affairs.

Notwithstanding the absurdity of most of their claims, the radical groups of the 1970s (the FLQ, the Marxist-Leninists, the Maoists, extremists in labour unions, etc.) attacked liberal democracy for not being democratic enough and extended the critique of the parliamentary system as a system of corruption and favouritism.

In 1978 the ruling party, the *Parti Québécois*, adopted laws restraining companies and trade unions from contributing to the electoral funding of political parties and forcing the latter to state their incomes and expenses. Recently, the *Bloc Québécois* has been trying to adhere to these funding rules in Ottawa despite the fact that other federal parties do not follow similar principles and have no intention of doing so. Numerous other provincial laws confirm the commitment of *Québécois* to the health of their democracy.

In Canada, the Trudeau government did not have similar success in its attempt to change the electoral process and political organization in general. Of course, less needed to be done because most of Canada outside Quebec was already a vigorous, albeit imperfect, democracy in the 1970s. It is nevertheless obvious that Bay Street did not lose control over Parliament, that thousands of jobs for political friends were created in the 1970s, and that networks of political patronage remained strong. Characteristically, of the 25 cabinet ministers appointed to Trudeau's first government, 15 were given prestigious federal offices after they left politics.[6] Trudeau's commitment to establishing participatory democracy during his 1968 leadership campaign soon vanished, leaving Canadian politics in pretty much the same state as when he came to power.

This is not to say that Canada is not a democracy and should not, as such, be regarded with envy by the world community. It is to say that democracy, here and abroad, is a work in progress, and that *Québécois*, having made considerable headway in their province, must continue to fight for greater openness of public institutions at the federal and provincial levels. Major changes await us if we want to live up to the dreams of our predecessors. At the provincial level, one of these might involve reassessing the constituency-based, simple majority ballot. In the 1998 Quebec election, fully one-third of the deputies were elected with less than 50 percent of the popular vote in their ridings because so many people voted for losing candidates. Many analysts are now talking about partly adopting a system of proportional representation, as in Western Europe. In addition to the traditional vote for local candidates, this would involve people voting for a province-wide list of candidates established by each political party. It might take, say, 40 000 votes from anywhere in the province to elect each person on a party's list. In that case, few votes would be wasted and representation in the Quebec legislature would much more closely reflect the political will of the people. The fact that the percentage of people exercising their right to vote is slowly but inexorably dropping election after election is one indication among others that democracy in Quebec (and Canada as a whole) is amenable to improvement. The concentration of ownership of the Canadian press in the hands of a few giant conglomerates is another big problem area for Quebec and Canadian democracy.

2. A NATION IN THE MAKING

Louis Tardivel, the religious owner of the newspaper *La Vérité*, and Henri Bourassa, the founder of the newspaper *Le Devoir*, knew each other well and respected each other's commitments. But while Louis Tardivel wrote a novel (*Pour la Patrie*, 1895) in which he predicted an independent Quebec by 1945, Henri Bourassa wrote and spoke to convince English Canadians to help him build a bilingual and bicultural Canada respectful of the two founding nations. When Bourassa died in 1952, neither dream had become reality. The national question remained unresolved. The Quiet Revolutionaries split on this issue, most of the older half joining the federalist camp and most of the younger half joining the nationalist camp.

The historical context nurtured the dreams of both federalists and nationalists. On the one hand, nationalism had been discredited by the horrible atrocities of the fascist regimes during World War II. Furthermore, the Western European countries were trying to unite into a single political body, paving the way, according to optimists, to a world government. On the other hand, colonies around the globe (including, ironically, Canada, which adopted its flag in 1965, its national anthem in 1980, and repatriated its Constitution from London in 1982) were striving for independence from their metropolises while invoking the principle of self-determination recognized by the United Nations.

For French-Canadian federalists, Canada belonged to both francophones and anglophones even if the two founding peoples did not always act like equal partners. With this view in mind they helped to enact the Official Languages Bill (1969) in spite of strong resistance from conservative factions in English Canada, who feared so-called "French power." French-Canadian federalists believed that nearly every Canadian would eventually speak English and French fluently. Moreover, they felt that once Canada was a bilingual country, Quebec would not have the right to speak for all French Canadians.

In contrast, separatists did not believe Canada could ever be a true home for Francophones. English Canadians, they said, had never respected them. They argued, for example, that during World War II the federal government asked the provinces to temporarily hand over their control of income tax but never gave it back. Historically, the federal government even refused things as trivial as bilingual postage stamps, insisting instead on stamps extolling Canada's attachment to the British Empire. French Quebec, said the separatists, shared nothing with the rest of Canada. Moreover, lost in what appeared to be a North American ocean, many *Québécois* felt in danger of being assimilated to the English majority. Securing the *Québécois* nation could only be achieved through the political autonomy of the province, they concluded.

Quebec's last 40 years of history has been summarized by some analysts as a political struggle between sovereigntists and federalists. But these analysts fail to underline how much both camps came to share as they evolved:

1. *Culture as a state policy.* Despite their continuous quarrelling, Quebec federalists and Quebec separatists were both convinced nationalists, proud of being a citizen either of Quebec or Canada. Jacques Parizeau, leader of the *Parti Québécois* during the 1995 referendum, once said that he and Trudeau agreed on everything except where to put the national capital. And in fact, while the Quebec government was adopting programs to promote local culture, the federal government, under the guidance of those who exercised "French power," was mounting a campaign to protect Canadian culture from American influence. Artists, magazines, television and radio broadcasting, as well as thousands of institutions, associations, groups, and organizations received government funding conditional on promoting "Canadian content." The federal government gave itself the mandate of building a Canadian nation out of British, French, Aboriginal, and other elements, while the Quebec government imagined having a mandate to forge a Quebec nation out of (for the most part) the *Québécois*. Yet despite heading in different directions, the principles at the crux of Canada's and Quebec's actions were similar. Opposed when they were addressing Canadian cultural issues, they stood shoulder to shoulder at international consultation tables for the protection of local particularities. They tried to save Quebec and Canadian culture from the invasion of "McWorld" by creating state cultural institutions (Radio Canada, *Télé Québec*), distributing grants to artists and intellectuals (Canada Council for the Arts, Ministère de la culture), establishing quotas on "Canadian" and "Quebec" content, and controlling

investment in cultural institutions (some companies engaged in cultural production must be two-thirds Canadian-owned by law).

2. *Language as the only legitimate criterion for defining a nation.* A second area of commonality between sovereigntists and federalists involves the criterion they employ for defining a nation. They did not always agree on this matter. In the 1960s, the federal Commission on Bilingualism and Biculturalism had legitimized the "two equal founding nations" idea. In 1972, however, the federal government passed a bill on multiculturalism. Many Quebec nationalists accused Trudeau of betrayal, of watering down the idea of two equal founding nations. To the sovereigntists it seemed that other immigrant groups were now being awarded almost the same status as the *Québécois.* Partly in reaction, the Quebec government passed Bill 101 in 1977. Its aim was to protect not just the French language, but also the values and traditions of the *Québécois.* Yet in the 1980s and 1990s more and more Quebec nationalists came to acknowledge that a state can promote only language and that cultural diversity is not a dilution but an enrichment of national traditions. The Quebec nation many *Québécois* have come to believe in is a "nation of cultures"—very much like Canada with its multiculturalist policies—and not a homogeneous nation composed exclusively of people of French descent. For example, historian Gérard Bouchard, a leading separatist thinker, asserts that the *Québécois* should be defined "strictly by a linguistic criterion."[7] As a result of the widespread acceptance of this idea, promoting *Québécois* culture now involves little more than subsidizing the creation of cultural products in Quebec, regardless of their cultural content. This is similar to the situation in the rest of Canada, where cultural products created in Canada are equated with Canadian culture.

3. *Quebec as a people.* A third area of commonality between sovereigntists and separatists concerns the idea that French-Canadian Quebeckers form a *Québécois* people. The *Québécois* have come a long way since the nineteenth century, when they called themselves *Canadiens* to distinguish themselves from the British, and since the turn of the twentieth century, when they called themselves French Canadians to distinguish themselves from Canadians who spoke English. Today, the *Québécois* feel little or no attachment to their linguistic "brothers" and "sisters" in other provinces. For their part, the leaders of the provincial and federal Liberal parties speak of *Québécois* interests without even trying to convince the *Québécois* that they are members of the same family as Francophones outside Quebec. The same recognition was embodied in the ill-fated Meech Lake Accord, which was designed to entice Quebec to recognize Canada's constitution. The Accord recognized Quebec—not French Canada—as a "distinct society," that is, a society enjoying special status in Confederation.

Today the national question remains unresolved. The 1980 and 1995 Quebec referenda on sovereignty ended in bitter defeat for the sovereigntists. Trudeau's dream of a bilingual Canada is an almost complete failure, except in the Acadian part of New Brunswick and despite episodic vitality in other French-Canadian communities outside Quebec. Not only is French as a first language not progressing outside Quebec, its only chance of maintaining itself as a first language is to stay within Quebec's borders. The numbers are there to remind anyone of the fragility of the French fact in Canada. In 1971, the percentage of people speaking French at home outside Quebec was a mere 4.4 percent. In 1981, it was down to 3.8 percent. Ten years later, it fell to 3.2 percent. In 1996, it dropped to 2.9 percent. This picture is discouraging for anyone hoping to achieve

Henri Bourassa's and Pierre Trudeau's dream of a Canada which would be not just officially bilingual but where French as a first language would flower from coast to coast.

3. SOCIAL JUSTICE

The generation that came of age after World War II committed itself to erecting a welfare state in Canada and Quebec. (A "welfare state" guards citizens from the ravages of the market by providing some level of protection against ill health, unemployment, poverty, etc.) The federal and Quebec bureaucracies were in their infancy in 1940. Twenty years later, things had changed dramatically. Governments were playing a large and growing role in public affairs. In 1950, Quebec was, according to some observers, a "priest-ridden province." In 1980, it was a state-controlled province.

Trudeau made speeches in the 1950s on behalf of establishing socialism in Canada and flirted with the New Democratic Party. He was not alone. In Quebec, many people advocated state intervention in domains previously reserved for the Roman Catholic Church. Soon, education, previously controlled by the Church, came under state jurisdiction and state social programs replaced private charities.

An interventionist state was thought to be necessary for many reasons. The state was a rational institution in an age when efficiency and functionality became watchwords. In an age of universalism, it was viewed as a neutral and inclusive institution in which people of different national origins and religions could be treated equally. The state was regarded, moreover, as a means of "domesticating capital," that is, avoiding recurrent financial and industrial crises. Finally, an interventionist state was widely construed as a means of leading Canadians to the creation of a "just society" in which equality would prevail. Labour unions in particular were fighting for a more equitable distribution of wealth and power.

Many of Trudeau's articles in the 1950s constituted a defence of Keynesian economic theory. (John Maynard Keynes was the leading British economist who first advocated massive state intervention to end the Great Depression of 1929–39.) Thus, it is not surprising that under Trudeau's government state intervention reached new heights. The federal debt grew nine-fold under his administration. He fostered a national energy policy, restricted foreign investment in Canada, created regional development, programs, and so forth. Quebec did not trail behind for long. In the U.S. State Department, Quebec came to be known as "Cuba North." In a little less than a decade, Quebec created thousands of municipal councils and regional boards, hundreds of health institutions, innumerable social services, programs for the protection of agricultural lands, giant Crown Corporations such as Hydro-Quebec, and so on. The state intervention movement even radicalized itself in the 1970s. Concluding that socialism could never be implemented in Canada, some revolutionaries turned their hopes towards an independent Quebec. Pierre Vallières, for example, the author of the famous *White Niggers of America,*[8] intertwined nationalist sentiments with socialist beliefs.

The deep and prolonged recession of 1981–82, by far Canada's worst economic crisis since World War II, rattled the foundations of the welfare state ideologically and practically. Practically, it meant that the Trudeau spending years were over. In Quebec, the return of Liberal Robert Bourassa to power (1985) brought an end to the liberal spending policies of the *Parti Québécois* years (1976–85). However, privatization of government-owned enterprises and cuts in social programs did not reduce the size of the state as much as is sometimes thought. In fact, in absolute numbers, the state apparatus continued to grow along with Quebec's population. Government transfers (welfare payments, unemployment insurance, etc.) as a percentage of personal income even increased, from 10 percent in 1970 to 17 percent in 1990 to approximately 20 percent in 2000. In comparison with the United States, Quebec and Canada maintained their social-democratic proclivity. The continuation of a national health-care system is testimony to the country's disputed but still strong commitment to social democracy.

Ideologically the change was more drastic. The state changed its role from arbiter and organizer of the economy to a merchandiser of labour and a servant of the market. The new ideology (known as neo-conservatism in the United States but more accurately called neo-liberalism), does not oppose the state as such. It only wants the state to eliminate all values from its vocabulary save the value of cost-efficiency and let nothing other than the market determine social priorities. The neo-liberal state defines people more as paying clients than citizens with rights. This ideology accompanied the signing of the Free Trade Agreement between Canada and the United States in 1989 (largely supported by *Québécois*, in contrast with the rest of Canada), its broadening to include Mexico in 1993, and subsequent discussions to eventually create a free trade zone encompassing all of North and South America. This process can only contribute to a further subordination of politics to financial and industrial priorities and interests.

4. A NEW HUMANISM

The first publishing success in Quebec in the second half of the twentieth century was Jean-Paul Desbiens's *Les Insolences du frère Untel*,[9] a book in which the author, a young friar, declared war on Quebec's traditional culture. That 50 000 copies were sold in less than three months reveals how popular and long-awaited Desbiens's criticisms were. Desbiens criticized French-Canadian culture in three ways. First, he said, it was an outmoded island in the midst of a progressive American continent. The French Canadians might use "an American clock" but they lived in "the Middle Ages." The inventions of science, new literary currents, new conceptions in the arts—all this was censored by a clerical

authority that associated modernity with evil and erected ideological walls to "protect" French Canadians from the "perverse" influence of an English and Protestant continent. Second, according to Desbiens, French-Canadian culture imposed a cult of mediocrity on French Canada. "Joual" (the French dialect of the *Québécois*) was for him the self-evident syndrome of this cult. For Desbiens, Joual represented a defeat of the spirit and a laziness of the mind. It was evidence of the abysmal lack of education in the province. Not only did people speak Joual, he complained, they thought Joual. The language crisis was terrible and patent proof of the crisis of French-Canadian civilization, wrote Desbiens. Finally, he argued, French-Canadian culture advocated fear and obedience: "What we are practicing here is purity by sterilization, orthodoxy by silence, security by material repetition. We imagine there is only one way to walk straight, to go nowhere, only one way to never be mistaken, never search for anything, only one way to never get lost: sleep. We have invented a radical means of fighting the caterpillars: cut down the trees."[10] The Catholic Church's doctrine was one reason this situation came to prevail in Quebec, according to Desbiens. By insisting continuously on one's duties and not on one's freedom, by exercising its omnipresence and overwhelming authority over almost every field of activity, the clergy served as a sentinel against rebellious, dissident, and deviant attitudes and beliefs, ending up obliterating the very meaning of free will.

Contrary to what has often been stated, however, the Church was not inactive in the secularization of Quebec society. After all, Desbiens himself was a friar in the Mariste order. He was the expression of a new religious ethic that catalyzed the will for social reform and promoted the individual's triumph over authoritarian institutions. It is no coincidence that the Quiet Revolution took place during the Vatican II Council. Abbot Louis O'Neill, Father Lévesque, and committed Catholics like Fernand Dumont and Robert Lalonde drew from this new religious ethic the moral energy to confront the Catholic Church itself.

The search for a new culture took two directions, both closely connected to reform of the educational system. For a century, French-Canadian intellectuals had considered education the core of all reform. "Without school," said early-twentieth-century Quebec nationalist intellectual Lionel Groulx, "nothing is possible. With school, everything is possible." This is close to what many intellectuals of the 1960s believed.

Firstly, some intellectuals tried to adapt the classical colleges' humanism to the new conditions of a technological and modern society. Humanism, they argued, had to incorporate the developments of the human sciences, to be more open to other cultures and beliefs, and to be founded on the rights of the individual. A 1963 government report ratified this perspective: culture was not a catechism of questions and listed answers but a toolkit that enabled every citizen to prepare for the modern industrial world. The creation of the CEGEPS (two-year college) system in 1969 grew out of this report. Spending two years in CEGEPS between high school and university, each student would now have an opportunity to learn the basics of philosophy, humanities, and the social sciences, thus assimilating the lessons of a general but ever-changing humanism.

Secondly, some intellectuals, going further, insisted on a culture that would not only help individuals adapt to the new era, but would encourage them to question society as it was and strive for a better world. Sociologist Marcel Rioux, fearing a world in which all creativity would disappear under the steamrollers of machinery, technology, and computerization, associated education with the imaginative search for new possibilities: "To speak of culture in our modern society is to speak . . . of surpassing oneself through values, imagination, and creativity."[11] Rioux insisted among other subjects on the teaching of art in schools so as to introduce students to a world where they could be their own creation.

In the 1960s and 1970s, Quebec's culture flourished like never before, at least quantitatively. The Quiet Revolution brought about the creation of the *Ministère des Affaires culturelles du Québec*, the founding of many publishing houses (the number of titles published annually rose from 260 to 4 000 between 1962 and 1977), the establishment of the National Film Board, the popularity of *chansonniers* like Gilles Vigneault and Georges D'or, who were not just singers but cultural icons, and so on. Between 1960 and 1970, the number of university students doubled. The number of artists and art teachers grew from 683 to 3 805 between 1951 and 1971.[12] Television transformed itself from a medium of information to an agent of socialization.

More generally, the decline of the traditional nuclear family, the erosion of religious practice, the liberalization of sexual behaviour, and the emancipation of women deeply affected Quebec society. Looking back at the 1950s through the films of the era can be a big shock to anyone who is unaware of the rapid and radical cultural transformations that originated in the 1960s and created a vastly more open and progressive culture in place of the earlier conservatism. Unique to Quebec was the almost complete secularization of social life that was brought about by restricting the Catholic Church to a very narrow role in private affairs. In the 1960s, the "priest-ridden province" rid itself of the widespread influence of the priesthood.

The quest for a new culture—specifically, for a new humanism—ended with the rise of a consumer society. The great celebration of "we-ness" in the 1960s raised hopes of a more fraternal and convivial society. But the 1970s and 1980s opened the way to an increasingly individualistic society in which people were increasingly concerned with their own destiny. The 1960s also raised hopes for an authentic human culture that would enable every person to discover his or her real self. But disillusionment swiftly replaced this optimism. The pervasive influence of American culture—Hollywood cinema, Walt Disney philosophy, a fast-food mentality—jeopardized the formulation of a new humanism. As Rioux put it: "The Americanization of Quebec is, to my eyes, a most important and anguishing question. . . . Humanity, which was once condemned to a thermonuclear death . . . is now more and more threatened by a cultural death. . . ."[13]

Notwithstanding Rioux's condemnation, the consumer society made more and more inroads into Quebec culture. In 2000, 50 percent of Quebec households had two colour television sets, 46 percent owned a gas barbecue, and two-thirds were connected to cable TV. In 1990, 300 000 movie performances were shown on theater screens; in 2000, the number rose to about 650 000—and 85 percent of all movies were American productions. Instead of turning their liberty into an existential or spiritual search, the *Québécois* soon preferred inquiring about the latest car models. Instead of taking advantage of the cultural opportunities offered to them, they became couch potatoes enslaved to their television sets. At least, this is what the generation that came of age in the aftermath of World War II tended to believe. What was missing among the younger generation and in Quebec society as a whole, they said, was what Fernand Dumont called "transcendence." He wrote: "A society is not an aggregate of people pursuing their individual roads according to their interests; nor is it a closed field where factions struggle for their privileges independently of any rules other than the power of numbers or money."[14] A society, continued Dumont, must be capable of judging its inner value by resorting to some abstract transcendence. Failing to achieve such a judgment, a society condemns itself, according to Dumont, to disappearance as a distinct entity.

This cultural revolution had perhaps a deeper impact in Quebec than elsewhere in Canada, for the will to escape a closed and homogeneous religious universe resulted in calling into question all institutionalized authorities. But, in opposition to Rioux's and Dumont's harsh judgments, the general Americanization of French Canadian culture did not only mean the progressive establishment of an atomized and materialist society. It also meant the rise of pluralism, a greater tolerance toward different ways of living, and an attachment to simple and fundamental human values. "Beyond political rhetoric," concluded two sociologists on the basis of a national survey, "Quebec's uniqueness can readily be seen in the province's young people of the 1990s."[15] Among other unique features, Quebec's teenagers, they declared, are more open than teenagers elsewhere in Canada to premarital sex, homosexuality, and abortion, and they enjoy their family life more. Overall, their main characteristic seems to be a "lifestyle flexibility" that regards culture as a series of options and opportunities rather than a set of widely accepted values.

CONCLUSION

The reader has certainly noticed that the four great utopias of the Quiet Revolution did not materialize in contemporary Quebec, at least not completely. This observation allows me to reach three conclusions.

Conclusion 1: If one were obliged to summarize in a single sentence the development of Quebec after 1960, one would have to underline two radical social changes that are unique to Quebec history when compared to the rest of North America. First, with the Quiet Revolution, "French Canadians" began to call themselves "*Québécois.*" Second, clerical French Canada gave way to a state-controlled Quebec. But besides these two changes, the challenges Quebec faces today resemble pretty much those of every other Western society. For example, the fact that Quebec is a minority nation struggling for the recognition of its rights is not unique. In Canada, Aboriginal peoples are also trying to achieve national recognition. Corsicans in France, Basques in Spain, and the Scottish in the United Kingdom are only some of the other small nations searching for a way to preserve their language and to promote local autonomy through new political arrangements. It is one of the great lessons of the twentieth century that modern states have to find a way to accommodate basic human rights with the collective ambition of nations. Canada has not yet found all the answers to the dilemma nor the secret to equilibrium. But it represents one of the greatest social laboratories of what that equilibrium could be like and leads the way for other countries that today confront the same problems.[16]

Conclusion 2: The Quiet Revolution failed to achieve some of its goals. Bare statistics show the failure of the attempt to create a bilingual Canada. A sovereign Quebec now seems a remote dream. Canadian and Quebec social democracy are on the decline. Democracy is experiencing a crisis. There seems to be little desire to renew humanism. On the other hand, the Quiet Revolution accomplished a complete and largely beneficial transformation of morals and attitudes. For example, in spite of persistent sexism in many quarters, women have gained a status they lacked in the 1950s. Lately, *Québécois* have been found in national surveys to be very tolerant toward immigrants and visible minorities—in spite of a certain level of persistent racism (anti-Semitism, for example, has a long history in Canada, particularly in Quebec). Multiculturalism has brought about a recognition of Canada as a nation of nations. The Charter of Rights and Freedoms is accepted by the vast majority of the provincial population, the only question being whether it should have precedence over the National Assembly in Quebec City. It is worth noting that Quebec passed a *Chartre des droits et libertés de la personne* in 1975 (the provisions of which were extended in 1981) that has quasi-constitutional status and covers not only public law, like its Canadian counterpart, but also private law. The Quebec government was also the first provincial government to sign treaties with First Nations' representatives and has encouraged a new policy of negotiation instead of sterile confrontation.

Conclusion 3: I am not one to believe that a utopia is something that can be fully realized here and now. A utopia is first and foremost a source of inspiration. Obviously, democracy, nationalism, social democracy, and humanism have made inroads in Quebec over the years. But much more must be done if we want Canada to be a place where justice, tolerance, openness, and transparency prevail. If this lesson in humility is remembered, the utopias of the 1960s and 1970s, with all their excesses and their self-evident weaknesses, will not have been dreamt in vain. In this sense, they constitute a useful reminder that if the Canada of 2007 cannot be changed, the Canada of 2057 is yet to be built. That Canada, inescapably, we will have to build together.

NOTES

1. I thank Robert Brym and Valérie de Courville Nicole for their useful comments on a draft of this essay.
2. In this chapter, *"Québécois"* refers to French Quebeckers and "Quebeckers" refers to the entire population of Quebec.
3. Gérard Dion and Louis O'Neill, "L'Immoralité politique dans la province de Québec," *Le Devoir* (14 August 1956).
4. Pierre Elliott Trudeau, "Some obstacles to democracy in Quebec," *Canadian Journal of Economics and Political Science* XXIV: 3 August 1958: 303.
5. "FLQ Manifesto," on the World Wide Web at http://www.ola.bc.ca/online/cf/documents/1970FLQManifesto.html#top (23 November 2002).
6. Stéphane Kelly, "Pierre Elliott Trudeau et son maître. Une éducation politique," *Argument* (I, 1: Fall 1998) 29–40.
7. Gérard Bouchard, *La Nation québécoise au futur et au passé* (Montreal: VLB, 1999) 69.
8. Pierre Vallières, *White Niggers of America: The Precocious Autobiography of a Quebec "Terrorist,"* Joan Pinkham, trans. (Toronto: McClelland and Stewart, 1971). [First French edition, 1969.]

9. Jean-Paul Desbiens, *Les Insolences du frère Untel* (Montreal: Les Éditions de l'homme, 1960).

10. Ibid., 55–56.

11. Marcel Rioux, *Rapport de la Commission d'enquête sur l'enseignement des arts au Québec* (Quebec: l'Éditeur officiel du Québec, 1968) quoted in Pierre W. Bélanger et Guy Rocher, dir., *École et société au Québec: Éléments d'une sociologie de l'éducation* (Montreal: HMH, 1970) 462.

12. Marcel Fournier, *Les Génération d'artistes* (Quebec: IQRC, 1986) 97.

13. Marcel Rioux, "Remarques sur les industries de l'âme," *Question de culture*, 7, "*La culture: une industrie?*" (Quebec: IQRC, 1984) 50 and 49.

14. Fernand Dumont, *Raisons communes* (Montreal: Boréal, 1995) 218.

15. Reginald W. Bibby and Donald C. Posterski, *Teen Trends. A Nation in Motion* (Toronto: Stoddart, 2000), 115–36. [First non-abridged edition, 1991].

16. Michael Ignatieff, *The Rights Revolution* (Toronto: Anansi, 2000).

Chapter 19

Affluence, Power, and Strikes in Canada, 1973–2000

ROBERT J. BRYM

Common sense suggests affluence breeds contentment. On this assumption, people with secure jobs, good working conditions, and high wages are happier than people who face the prospect of unemployment, poor working conditions, and low wages. Moreover, according to the common-sense view, happier workers are less likely to strike. After all, compared to unhappy workers, their needs and demands seem closer to having been met. They appear to lack the deprivations that would motivate them to strike.

It follows from the common-sense view that there ought to be an observable association between measures of strike activity and measures of economic well-being. Figure 19.1, covering the 1973–2000 period, seems to suggest there is such an association.[1] The graph's horizontal axis shows *GDPpc* (Gross Domestic Product per capita), or the total value of goods and services produced in Canada in a year divided by the number of people living in the country at year end. GDPpc is an indicator of the economic well-being of the average Canadian. It is measured in constant (1992) dollars to eliminate the influence of inflation. In effect, this indicator of economic well-being shows the purchasing power of the average Canadian in a given year. Meanwhile, the graph's vertical axis shows *weighted strike frequency*, or the number of strikes that took place in Canada each year divided by the number of non-agricultural workers in the

country. The curve formed by annual scores on these two variables slopes downward. This suggests that when well-being is low, propensity to strike is high; and when well-being is high, propensity to strike is low. Affluence, it seems at first glance, does breed contentment.

Case closed? Hardly. GDPpc is an average, and averages can mask more than they reveal. For instance, GDPpc could conceivably rise when the purchasing power of high-income earners (a minority of the population) rises a lot and the purchasing power of middle- and low-income earners (a majority of the population) falls a little. In that case, rising GDPpc would mask the fact that most people are worse off.

Because workers who strike are unlikely to be rich, we need a better measure of workers' well-being than GDPpc. One candidate is the *unemployment rate*. Unemployment is more likely to affect ordinary workers than the well-to-do. Doctors rarely lose their jobs, and business executives, even if they are fired, can live relatively comfortably off savings in the typically short period before they find work again. On the other hand, unemployment is likely to result in a sharp decline in living standards for ordinary workers, and sometimes the period before they find a new job is protracted.

How then does strike activity vary with the unemployment rate? Figures 19.2 and 19.3 provide the surprising answer. During the first half

Source: Copyright © Robert J. Brym (2006). Originally published in James Curtis, Edward Grabb, and Neil Guppy, ed., *Social Inequality in Canada: Patterns, Problems, Policies 4th ed.,* (Scarborough: Prentice-Hall Canada, 2003). I thank Jonah Butovsky, John Fox, Morley Gunderson, Alan Harrison, Reza Nakhaie, Gregg Olson, and Michael Shalev for helpful comments on a draft of this chapter.

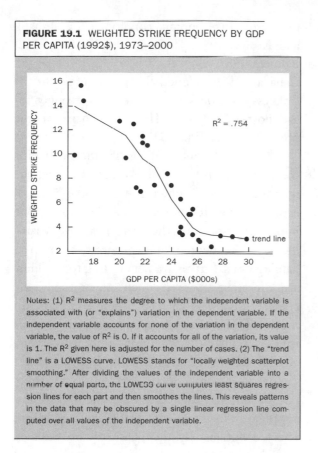

FIGURE 19.1 WEIGHTED STRIKE FREQUENCY BY GDP PER CAPITA (1992$), 1973–2000

Notes: (1) R^2 measures the degree to which the independent variable is associated with (or "explains") variation in the dependent variable. If the independent variable accounts for none of the variation in the dependent variable, the value of R^2 is 0. If it accounts for all of the variation, its value is 1. The R^2 given here is adjusted for the number of cases. (2) The "trend line" is a LOWESS curve. LOWESS stands for "locally weighted scatterplot smoothing." After dividing the values of the independent variable into a number of equal parts, the LOWESS curve computes least squares regression lines for each part and then smoothes the lines. This reveals patterns in the data that may be obscured by a single linear regression line computed over all values of the independent variable.

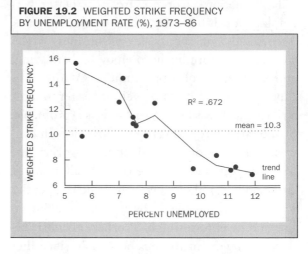

FIGURE 19.2 WEIGHTED STRIKE FREQUENCY BY UNEMPLOYMENT RATE (%), 1973–86

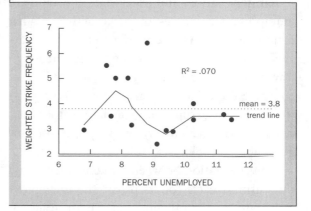

FIGURE 19.3 WEIGHTED STRIKE FREQUENCY BY UNEMPLOYMENT RATE (%), 1987–2000

of the 1973–2000 period, weighted strike frequency fell when the unemployment rate rose, and rose when the unemployment rate fell (see Figure 19.2). In other words, when workers were most economically deprived, they were *least* inclined to strike, and when they were most secure in their jobs, they were *most* inclined to strike. This is just the opposite of the common-sense view, outlined above. Equally unexpected are the results for the second half of the 1973–2000 period (see Figure 19.3). After 1986, the relationship between the unemployment rate and weighted strike frequency virtually disappeared. Thus, the trend line summarizing the association between weighted strike frequency and the unemployment rate shows little trend. What accounts for the inverse association between the unemployment rate and weighted strike frequency in the 1973–86 period? What accounts for the near disappearance of this inverse association after 1986? These are the intriguing questions I address in the remainder of this chapter.

STRIKE RESEARCH ON THE EFFECT OF THE BUSINESS CYCLE

The existing body of strike research goes a long way toward explaining the trend for the 1973–86 period, although not, as you will see, for the 1987–2000 period. Many strike researchers begin with the observation that capitalist economies undergo recurrent "boom and bust" cycles. During bad times, unemployment is high and business profitability low. During good times, unemployment is low and business profitability high. They then go on to note the existence of an association between the business cycle and strike frequency (Rees, 1952). They argue that, as unemployment falls, strike incidence rises.

That is because workers are in a better bargaining position during good economic times. Accordingly, at the peaks of business cycles workers are more likely to enjoy higher savings and alternative job opportunities. At the same time, workers know employers are eager to settle strikes quickly since business is so profitable. Strikes are therefore relatively low-risk. In contrast, during economic downturns, workers are less well off and have fewer job alternatives. They understand employers have little incentive to meet their demands because profitability is low and inventories high. Workers avoid strikes during troughs in the business cycle since they are riskier than in economic good times. From this point of view, workers' contentment, levels of felt deprivation, and other states of mind are unimportant as causes of strike activity. What matters is how *powerful* workers are. Their bargaining position or their ability to get their own way despite the resistance of employers is what counts. Said differently, strike research suggests we can arrive at superior explanations for variations in strike activity by thinking like sociologists, not psychologists.

The association between strike incidence and the business cycle (or its proxy, the unemployment rate) was first demonstrated empirically for the United States (Ashenfelter and Johnson, 1969) and shortly thereafter for Canada (Smith, 1972). Since then, researchers have shown that the association between strike incidence and the business cycle was a feature of most advanced capitalist countries in the twentieth century (Hibbs, 1976). However, later research also introduced three important qualifications to the argument.

First, before World War II, the North American system of collective bargaining between workers and employers was not well institutionalized. In Canada, for example, the legal right to organize unions, bargain collectively, and strike with relatively little constraint dates only from 1944. Before then, strikes were often fights for union recognition. They were therefore less

responsive to economic conditions (Cruikshank and Kealey, 1987; Jamieson, 1973 [1957]: 102; Palmer, 1987; Snyder, 1977). As a result, in Canada and the United States, the effect of the business cycle on strike incidence is stronger for the post–World War II period than for the pre–World War II period.

The second important qualification concerns the fact that, in much of Western Europe, the institutional environment mitigates the effect of economic conditions on strike frequency. One important aspect of the institutional environment is the degree of centralization of bargaining units. Strikes are negotiating tools. They are therefore more frequent during periodic contract renewals than between contracts. In much of Western Europe, however, centralized, nationwide bargaining among workers, employers, and governments means that entire sectors of the work force come up for contract renewal and negotiation at the same time. Thus, aggregate measures of strike frequency are affected not just by the phase of the business cycle but by the periodicity of contract renewal schedules. In contrast, the absence of a centralized bargaining structure in Canada and the United States makes aggregate measures of strike frequency more sensitive to the business cycle in North America (Harrison and Stewart, 1994; Snyder, 1977; Franzosi, 1989).

Union density, or the proportion of the non-agricultural labour force that is unionized, is another aspect of the institutional environment that influences strike activity. Unions educate workers and enable them to speak with one voice. Their organizational assets allow unions to mobilize workers. It follows that union density will influence strike action, although strike frequency is often less affected than are strike duration and the average size of strikes (Shorter and Tilly, 1971).

Finally, the third condition limiting the impact of the business cycle on strike frequency is political. In many Western European countries, left-wing or social democratic parties have formed governments or at least achieved representation in Cabinets. This has the effect of moving negotiations over the division of rewards in society from the labour market, where strikes are important bargaining tools, to the political sphere. Where labour is powerful enough to negotiate favourable income redistribution and welfare policies at the political level, industrial conflict tends to recede.[2] Agreeing to limit strike action has even been used as a bargaining chip in exchange for income redistribution and welfare concessions in Sweden, Germany, and other Western European countries. Thus, in the 1970s and 1980s, strike frequency in Sweden, for example, was relatively insensitive to the business cycle (Franzosi, 1989; Hibbs, 1978).

In sum, a substantial body of research demonstrates an association between the business cycle and strike frequency. Moreover, it shows that the association is strongest in North America in the post–World War II era because that is the setting least influenced by mitigating institutional and political variables (Paldam and Pedersen, 1982).

In the context of this research, Figure 19.2 is as ordinary as Figure 19.3 is puzzling. The strong inverse relationship between the unemployment rate and strike frequency for the 1973–86 period is wholly in line with expectations derived from the research literature. However, contrary to what we are led to expect by the research literature, there is little discernible trend for the 1987–2000 period. The unemployment rate is very *weakly* associated with strike frequency in the latter period. Said differently, cyclicality appears to have been largely wrung out of Canada's labour relations system in the last 14 years of the twentieth century, at least in terms of its influence on the incidence of industrial disputes. With respect to its impact on strike incidence, the business cycle was somehow repressed—and this in precisely the setting (post–World War II North America) where its impact was previously the greatest.

Why? What accounts for the repression of the business cycle as a determinant of the incidence of Canadian industrial disputes? That is the question on which the remainder of this chapter turns. An intimation of my answer lies embedded in my decision to divide the recent history of Canadian industrial disputes into two 14-year periods, as in Figures 19.2 and 19.3. Inspection of scatterplots suggested that a shift in the direction of the relationship between the unemployment rate and weighted strike frequency took place after 1986. Since data were available for 14 years following 1986, I chose to examine the relationship for a period of equal duration before 1987. That period ends in 1973.

Using 1973 as the cut-off is also justifiable on historical grounds, for 1973 was the year of the first oil shock. In that year, due to war in the Middle East, the price of oil on world markets tripled, intensifying already high inflation and galloping wage demands. As a result, a strike wave that had been growing since the mid-1950s gained force and crested in 1974–75. In the entire history of Canadian labour, the only strike action that matched that crest was the Winnipeg General strike of 1919 and the ensuing sympathy strikes that stretched all the way from Amherst, Nova Scotia to Victoria, British Columbia (see Figure 19.4). Understandably, therefore, the strikes of 1974–75 caused a strong reaction among government and corporate leaders. They soon took measures to make it substantially more costly for workers to strike. Thus, 1973 marks the beginning of an historical era, one aspect of which is the substantive focus of this chapter.

In the balance of this chapter, I outline how, from the mid-1970s to the 1990s, government and corporate leaders weakened unions and made it more difficult for workers to achieve their goals. These actions had the effect of making strikes less frequent and repressing the effect of the business cycle on the propensity to strike. As you will see, they explain the near-trendless trend line in Figure 19.3.

FIGURE 19.4 WEIGHTED STRIKE FREQUENCY, 1901–2000

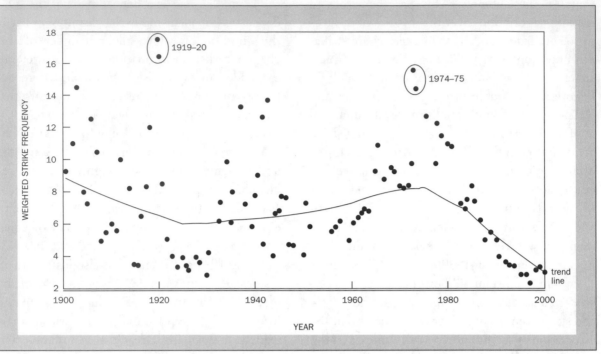

A NEW ECONOMIC AND POLITICAL CONTEXT

Government and business leaders reacted to the 1919–20 strike wave by sending in troops to restore order, throwing union leaders in jail, legislating strikers back to work, and changing laws to allow the deportation of British-born immigrants, who were thought to dominate the strike leadership (Bercuson, 1990 [1974]). Faced with a strike wave of similar proportions in 1974–75, government and business leaders again felt drastic action was necessary. However, the political, institutional, and cultural environment had changed between these two extraordinary episodes of labour unrest. As a result, strategies for controlling labour were different. In 1944, Canadian workers had won the right to organize, bargain collectively, and strike with relatively little constraint. In the context of three decades of post-war prosperity, their new rights allowed them to win substantial gains in real earnings and a massive expansion of state supports and services. In the mid-1970s, business leaders and governments sympathetic to business felt they had to control labour unrest while fighting wage gains and the growth of the welfare state. To accomplish these tasks, they organized a neo-conservative "counter-revolution" that continues to this day.

The neo-conservative counter-revolution was, however, motivated by more than just the strike wave that crested in the mid-1970s. Rising government debt and global competition also contributed to the decision to go on the political offensive (Johnston, 2001).

Government borrowing rose quickly in the 1970s and 1980s. By the end of that period, interest payments were consuming a quarter of the federal government's annual budget. With indebtedness threatening to cripple government programs, the neo-conservative claim that debt reduction is sound public policy made sense to more and more people.

At the same time, global competition was becoming fiercer. By the early 1970s, Japanese and West German industry had fully recovered from the destruction of World War II. Manufacturers in these countries were exporting massive quantities of finished goods to North America and other markets. In the 1980s, South Korea, China, and other countries followed suit. With growing global competition threatening the welfare of Canadian industry, big business had to develop new strategies to survive and prosper. One such strategy involved restructuring: introducing computers and robots, eliminating middle management positions, outsourcing parts manufacturing, and so forth. Another strategy aimed at increasing business opportunities and ensuring job growth by creating a free trade zone encompassing Canada and the United States (MacDonald, 2000).

Controlling labour while cutting debt, restructuring, and promoting free trade required deep ideological change. Business leaders therefore set about the task of redefining in the public mind the desirable features of the market, the state, and the relationship between the two. From roughly the end of World War II until the mid-1970s, labour demands focused on improving wages and state benefits. Now, an imposing ideological machine sought to convince the public that high wages and generous state benefits decrease the ability of Canadians to compete against workers in other countries. Massive job losses will result (the neo-conservative argument continued) unless wages are held in check and state benefits slashed. That was the main message of Canada's two neo-conservative, corporate-funded think tanks and pressure groups, the Fraser Institute, founded in 1974, and the Business Council on National Issues (BCNI), founded in 1976. The creation of these bodies in the mid-1970s signalled that, like its counterpart in the United States, the Canadian business elite was becoming more ideologically and politically organized and unified (Akard, 1992; Langille, 1987).

One important sign of neo-conservative success was the outcome of the 1988 "free trade" federal election (Richardson, 1996). Just four days before the election, a Gallup poll showed the pro–free trade Progressive Conservatives

with the support of only 31 percent of Canadians intending to vote. The anti–free trade Liberals enjoyed a commanding 43 percent of the popular vote while the anti–free trade New Democratic Party stood at 22 percent. At about the same time, an Angus Reid poll disclosed that most Canadians opposed free trade by a margin of 54 percent to 35 percent. A majority of Canadians apparently sensed that free trade might open the country to harmful competition with giant American companies, thus leading to job losses and deteriorating living standards.

Then, a mere 100 hours before the first votes were cast, a little-known organization, the Canadian Alliance for Trade and Job Opportunities (CATJO), swung into high gear. CATJO was funded exclusively by the BCNI. With a campaign budget larger than that of the two opposition parties combined, CATJO bankrolled a media blitz promoting the PCs and their free trade policies. A barrage of brochures, newspaper ads, and radio and television commercials supported the idea that Canadian prosperity depends on the removal of all taxes and impediments to trade between Canadian and the United States. CATJO argued that if goods and services could be bought and sold across the border without hindrance, and capital invested without restraint, good jobs would proliferate and Canada's economic future would be assured. The CATJO onslaught succeeded in overcoming some of the public's fears and drawing attention away from the opposition. On election day, the PCs won with 43 percent of the popular vote. The free trade agreement with the United States was signed just six weeks later.

The free trade agreement, later broadened to include Mexico, sharply increased competition for investment between jurisdictions, leading to a "downward harmonization" of labour policies (Gunderson, 1998). Just as water seeks its lowest level, capital that is allowed to flow freely between jurisdictions will seek the jurisdiction with the lowest costs and therefore the highest profit potential, all else the same. Increasingly, jurisdictions will compete for investment by offering outright tax concessions to investors and ensuring competitive labour costs in the form of lower state benefits, wages, and rates of labour disruption due to strikes. As Canadian workers learned, persistent demands for higher wages—indeed, failure to make wage and other concessions—increase the prospect of plant closings. Where capital mobility is unrestricted, it is only a short hop from southern Ontario to "right to work" states like Georgia or the Maquiladora free trade zone of northern Mexico. In this context, unions lose bargaining power and strikes become riskier actions with a lower probability of achieving their aims.[3]

The slew of government budget cutbacks that took place in the 1990s also had a negative influence on strike incidence. Since workers who go on strike sometimes quit or lose their jobs, declining income-replacing state benefits make strikes riskier for them. In other words, many of the cutbacks of the 1990s increased the potential cost of job loss to workers and therefore ensured that strike incidence would drop. Restricting eligibility for employment insurance and welfare were two of the most important policy measures affecting the readiness of workers to strike.

High government debt, intense global competition, and neo-conservative publicity and lobbying continued to push the Canadian electorate to the right in the 1990s. The Reform Party became the official opposition, its popularity aided by the defection of members of the working class, most of them non-unionized, from the Liberals and the NDP (Butovsky, 2001). The ruling Liberals, meanwhile, adopted much of the neo-conservative agenda. To varying degrees, all major parties supported the new industrial relations regime that had begun to crystallize in the mid-1970s.

A NEW INDUSTRIAL RELATIONS REGIME

Beginning in the mid-1970s, governments adopted a series of measures aimed at better controlling labour (Panitch and Swartz, 1993 [1988]).

Among them was the establishment of wage and price controls that limited only wages in practice yet claimed to require equal sacrifices from labour and business. That strategy was followed in 1975 by the Trudeau government establishing the Anti-Inflation Board for a three-year period. Blessed by business and condemned by the labour movement, the anti-inflation program suspended collective bargaining for all workers in Canada. By undermining the ability of strikes to achieve wage gains, it also dampened labour militancy. A similar approach was taken in 1982, when the federal government passed the Public Sector Compensation Restraint Act. The act imposed a two-year wage limit on federal employees, eliminating their right to bargain and strike. The provinces soon passed similar laws. In some cases, provincial cutbacks were even more draconian than those implemented at the federal level. Public employees in Quebec, for example, took a 20 percent pay cut. In 1991, the federal government announced a one-year wage freeze for federal employees, followed by a 3 percent limit on wage increases for the next two years. By 1993, even the Ontario NDP was backing wage restraint. In that year, the government of Bob Rae introduced a "Social Contract" that overruled the provisions of existing collective agreements and effectively reduced the wages of all 900 000 provincial employees for a three-year period.

A second method of labour control involved amending a variety of laws and regulations. For example, governments persistently broadened the definitions of "management" and "essential service," thereby denying many public sector workers the right to strike. Thus, in 1984 nearly 76 percent of public service workers negotiating contracts were designated as providing managerial or essential services. In the preceding set of negotiations, fewer than 47 percent of those workers were so designated. In addition, and to varying degrees, governments imposed restrictions on political strikes and secondary picketing (picketing beyond the plant or department affected by a strike). They increased employers' rights to fight organizing drives and employees' rights to attempt decertification. They banned strikes in designated work sites, weakened the ability of unions to discipline members who carried out anti-union activities, permitted unions to be sued, and, in most jurisdictions, allowed the use of replacement workers. One result of these actions was that, beginning in 1984, union density began to decline (see Figure 19.5).

Finally, throughout the 1980s, and particularly after Brian Mulroney's Progressive Conservative government was elected in 1984, federal and provincial governments increasingly adopted *ad hoc* back-to-work legislation to weaken workers' bargaining position and thereby limit strike action. Used on average only 0.2 times per year in the 1950–54 period, back-to-work laws were passed on average 5.0 times per year in the 1975–79 period and 5.4 times per year in the 1985–89 period.

At first, limiting the right to strike was widely viewed as a temporary measure necessitated by fear of a resurgence of the strike wave of 1974–75, the highest inflation rates Canada had ever seen, and the deep recessions of 1981–82 and 1991–92. However, limiting the right to strike became a matter of enduring if unstated public policy, largely because economic and political conditions required a less expensive and less militant work force. By the mid-1980s, a new labour relations regime had crystallized. One of

its main purposes was to render labour's ultimate bargaining tool—the strike—increasingly superfluous as a means of bargaining for improved terms of employment.

CONCLUSION: THE WITHERING AWAY OF THE STRIKE?

About 1960, some influential social scientists predicted that the strike was "withering away." The working class, they wrote, had become "embourgeoisified" due to growing affluence. Class conflict was supposedly becoming "institutionalized" in stable systems of collective bargaining. These developments were viewed as a sort of natural evolutionary process, part of the peaceful unfolding of the "inner logic of industrialization" (Ross and Hartman, 1960; Dahrendorf, 1959).

In the 1960s and 1970s, an international strike wave caught these social scientists by surprise. It cast doubt on the validity of their generalizations. Now, however, amid an international "resurgence of labour quiescence" (Shalev, 1992) that has lasted more than two decades, some observers may be tempted to argue that affluence has at last caused the strike to wither away. For them, the generalizations of 1960 may appear valid after all.

My analysis suggests we should avoid this conclusion. I have shown that a measure of average affluence (GDPpc) is inversely associated with weighted strike frequency but is a poor measure of the economic conditions that shape the lives of Canadian workers. The unemployment rate is a much better indicator of workers' economic conditions; and for the 1973–86 period, the unemployment rate varied inversely with weighted strike frequency. This suggests that the relative power or bargaining position of workers—not their level of affluence—determined their propensity to strike. Complicating the story, however, is a fact most researchers have overlooked. In the 1987–2000 period, the inverse relationship between the unemployment rate and weighted strike frequency nearly disappeared.[4] The business cycle had little effect on workers'

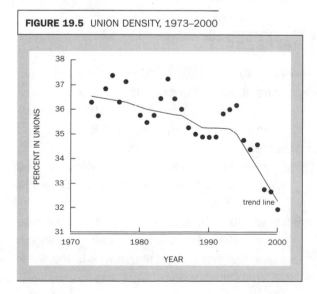

FIGURE 19.5 UNION DENSITY, 1973–2000

propensity to strike. The reason? Actions taken by employers and governments from the mid-1970s to the late 1990s—introducing free trade, cutting budgets for a wide range of government assistance programs, passing laws and regulations that undermined unions—disempowered workers and rendered the strike a less effective weapon.

In sum, the history of Canadian industrial relations since the mid-1970s suggests that the "inner logic" of industrial capitalism is driven by power, not alleged evolutionary imperatives such as the rising average level of affluence. Industrial relations systems *are* institutionalized forms of class conflict, that is, enduring legal resolutions of historically specific struggles between workers and employers. But "enduring" does not mean "permanent." Trends lasting a few decades should not be confused with the end of history. Industrial relations systems change when power is massively redistributed between classes. In Canada, for example, a massive redistribution of power in favour of workers took place from the mid-1940s onward, when workers won the legal right to unionize and strike and were in a position to extract increased disposable income and benefits from employers and governments. Another massive redistribution of power, this time in favour of employers, took place after the mid-1970s. The Canadian industrial relations regime was transformed on both occasions. The transition from the first regime to the second was marked by a change in the relationship between strike frequency and the business cycle. It follows that, however difficult it might be to imagine in the current industrial relations climate, another massive shift in the distribution of power in society could once again help the strike regain its former popularity.

NOTES

1. Data sources for this chapter are as follows:
   - *Population:* CANSIM (2002b).
   - *Gross Domestic Product per capita:* CANSIM (2002a).
   - *Strikes:* "Series E190-197 . . ." (2001); "Chronological Perspective . . ." (2001).
   - *Union membership:* "Series E175-177 . . ." (2001); Human Resources Development Canada (2001); "Union membership. . ." (2000).
   - *Non-agricultural workers* (1902–10 and 1912–20 interpolated): *Fifth Census . . .* (1915), Table 1, p. 13; *Labour Organizations . . .* (1973) pp. xxii–xxiii; *1994– 1995 Directory . . .* (1995) p. xiii; "Union membership . . ." (2000).
   - *Unemployment:* CANSIM (2001).
2. That is why the influence of union density on strike action peaks at intermediate levels of union density and then tapers off. In countries with the highest proportion of unionized workers, unions tend to exert considerable political influence.
3. As Morley Gunderson commented on a draft of this chapter, the argument developed here is also an argument about wage concessions. Moreover, for strike incidence to fall, the *joint* cost of strikes to both workers *and employers* must increase. In the present case, the cost of strikes to employers has increased, partly because strikes threaten the loss of global market share.
4. See, however, Cramton and Tracy (1994), who reach similar conclusions about the United States in the 1980s.

REFERENCES

Akard, Patrick J. (1992). "Corporate Mobilization and Political Power: The Transformation of U.S. Economic Policy in the 1970s." *American Sociological Review, 57*: 587–615.

Ashenfelter, Orley and George Johnson. (1969). "Bargaining Theory, Trade Unions, and Industrial Strike Activity." *American Economic Review*, 59: 35–49.

Bercuson, David Jay. (1990 [1974]). *Confrontation at Winnipeg: Labour, Industrial Relations, and the General Strike*, rev. ed. Montreal: McGill-Queen's University Press.

Butovsky, Jonah. (2001). *The Decline of the New Democrats: The Politics of Postmaterialism or Neoliberalism?* Ph.D. dissertation, Department of Sociology, University of Toronto.

CANSIM. (2001). "Unemployment Rate Age 15+ SA CDA." On the World Wide Web at http://chass.utoronto.ca/cansim/ (4 April).

———. (2002a). "G.D.P, Expenditure-Based, 1992$/Gross Domestic Pr at Market Prices." On the World Wide Web at http://chass.utoronto.ca/cansim/ (7 January).

———. (2002b). "Population of Canada, by Province/Canada." On the World Wide Web at http://chass.utoronto.ca/cansim/ (7 January).

"Chronological Perspective on Work Stoppages in Canada (Work Stoppages Involving One or More Workers), 1976–2000." (2001). On the World Wide Web at http://labour-travail. hrdc-drhc.gc.ca/doc/wid-dimt/eng/wsat/table.cfm (27 March).

Cramton, Peter C. and Joseph S. Tracy. 1994. "The Determinants of U.S. Labour Disputes." *Journal of Labor Economics, 12*: 180–209.

Cruikshank, Douglas and Gregory S. Kealey. (1987). "Strikes in Canada, 1891–1950." *Labour/Le Travail, 20*: 85–145.

Dahrendorf, Ralf. (1959). *Class and Class Conflict in Industrial Society.* London: Routledge & Kegan Paul.

Fifth Census of Canada, 1911, Vol. VI. (1915). Ottawa: Census and Statistics Office, Department of Trade and Commerce.

Franzosi, Roberto. (1989). "One Hundred Years of Strike Statistics: Methodological and Theoretical Issues in Quantitative Strike Research." *Industrial and Labor Relations Review, 42*: 348–62.

Gunderson, Morley. (1998). "Harmonization of Labour Policies under Trade Liberalization." *Industrial Relations* 53. On the World Wide Web at http://www.erudit.org/erudit/ri/v53no1/gunder/gunder.html (9 April 2001).

Harrison, Alan and Mark Stewart. 1994. "Is Strike Behavior Cyclical?" *Journal of Labor Economics* 12: 524–53.

Hibbs, Douglas. (1976). "Industrial Conflict in Advanced Industrial Societies." *American Political Science Review, 70*: 1033–58.

———. (1978). "On the Political Economy of Long-Run Trends in Strike Activity." *British Journal of Political Science, 8*: 153–75.

Human Resources Development Canada. (2001). Special tabulation on union membership, 1960–2000.

Jamieson, Stuart. (1973 [1957]). *Industrial Relations in Canada*, 2nd ed. Toronto: Macmillan.

Johnston, William A. (2001). "Class and Politics in the Era of the Global Economy." In Doug Baer, ed., *Political Sociology: Canadian Perspectives* (pp. 288–306). Don Mills ON: Oxford University Press.

Labour Organizations in Canada 1972. (1973). Ottawa: Economics and Research Branch, Canada Department of Labour.

Langille, David. (1987). "The Business Council on National Issues and the Canadian State." *Studies in Political Economy, 24*: 41–85.

MacDonald, L. Ian, ed. (2000). *Free Trade: Risks and Rewards.* Montreal and Kingston: McGill-Queen's University Press.

1994–1995 Directory of Labour Organizations in Canada. (1995). Ottawa: Minister of Supply and Services Canada.

Paldam, Martin, and Peder Pedersen. (1982). "The Macroeconomic Strike Model: A Study of Seventeen Countries, 1948–1975." *Industrial and Labor Relations Review,* 35: 504–21.

Palmer, Bryan D. (1987). "Labour Protest and Organization in Nineteenth Century Canada, 1820–1890." *Labour/Le Travail, 20*: 61–83.

Panitch, Leo, and Donald Swartz. (1993 [1988]). *The Assault on Trade Union Freedoms: From Wage Controls to Social Contract*, 2nd ed. Toronto: Garamond Press.

Rees, Albert. (1952). "Industrial Conflict and Business Fluctuations." *Journal of Political Economy, 60*: 371–82.

Richardson, R. Jack. 1996. "Canada and Free Trade: Why Did It Happen?" In Robert J. Brym, ed. *Society in Question* (pp. 200–09). Toronto: Harcourt Brace Canada.

Ross, Arthur M. and Paul T. Hartman. (1960). *Changing Patterns of Industrial Conflict*. New York: Wiley.

"Series E175-177: Union Membership in Canada, in Total, as a Percentage of Non-agricultural Paid Workers, and Union Members with International Affiliation, 1911 to 1975 (thousands)." (2001). On the World Wide Web at http://www.statcan.ca/english/freepub/11-516-XIE/sectione/sectione.htm#Unions (29 March).

"Series E190-197: Number of Strikes and Lockouts, Employers and Workers Involved and Time Loss, Canada, 1901 to 1975." (2001). On the World Wide Web at http://www.statcan.ca/english/freepub/11-516-XIE/sectione/sectione.htm#Unions (29 March).

Shalev, Michael. (1992). "The Resurgence of Labour Quiescence." In Marino Regini, ed., *The Future of Labour Movements* (pp. 102–32). London: Sage.

Shorter, Edward, and Charles Tilly. (1971). "The Shape of Strikes in France, 1830–1960." *Comparative Studies in Society and History*, *13*: 60–86.

Smith, Douglas A. (1972). "The Determinants of Strike Activity in Canada." *Industrial Relations*, *27*: 663–77.

Snyder, David. (1977). "Early North American Strikes: A Reinterpretation." *Industrial and Labor Relations Review*, 30: 325–41.

"Union Membership in Canada—2000." (2000). *Workplace Gazette: An Industrial Relations Quarterly*, 3 (3): 68–75.

Chapter 21

Work and Society:

CANADA IN CONTINENTAL CONTEXT

WALLACE CLEMENT

THE WORST OF BOTH WORLDS

In the late 1980s and 1990s, Canada became increasingly integrated into the U.S. economy through several free trade agreements. The agreements facilitated cross-border trade and investment. Closer integration of the two countries had some paradoxical effects. On the one hand, Canadians witnessed an erosion of their hard-won rights to various welfare-state benefits—state-funded medical services, subsidized higher education, and the like. In this sense, Canada became more like the U.S., where citizens have historically enjoyed fewer welfare-state entitlements than Canadians. On the other hand, Canada failed to participate fully in the "boom" economy of the U.S., at least until the altered circumstances at the turn of the century. For example, while the proportion of working-age Americans in the labour force remained exceptionally high throughout the 1990s, the corresponding proportion in Canada fell. After the turn of the century, this trend reversed. Thus, the Canadian labour market failed to emulate the American model while the system of Canadian citizenship entitlements began to do so. In terms of labour market and state benefits, then, Canada experienced the worst of both worlds. The question before us now is "What does the post-September 11th, 2001, era hold in store for us?"

COMPARING LABOUR MARKETS

Before 1981, Canada and the United States had nearly identical unemployment rates. During the 1980s, however, a 2 percent gap in unemployment rates opened between the two countries. The gap grew to 5 percent in the early 1990s, reached nearly 8 percent in 1999, and then began to decline.[1] In 2004, the Canadian unemployment rate was 7.2 percent while the U.S. rate was 5.5 percent, a difference of just 1.7 percent (see Table 21.1).[2]

The gap between Canadian and U.S. unemployment rates is due in part to Canada lagging behind the United States in its capacity to create new jobs, but other factors are at work too. For one thing, the United States imprisons more of its citizens per 100 000 population than any other country. Incarceration became particularly popular in the U.S. in the 1980s and 1990s. Today, more than two million Americans are behind bars and the rate of incarceration is more than six times higher than in Canada. The high incarceration rate keeps many hard-to-employ Americans out of the labour force while providing many jobs for police and prison guards.[3] Also helping to

TABLE 21.1 UNEMPLOYMENT IN CANADA AND THE UNITED STATES (IN PERCENT)

	1992–2002	2001	2002	2003	2004
Canada	9.0	7.2	7.7	7.6	7.2
United States	5.4	4.7	5.8	6.0	5.5

Source: Based on Table 0.3. Unemployment in OECD countries (source: *OECD Economic Outlook*, No. 77, May 2005) and Table A. Standardised unemployment rates in 27 OECD countries (source: *OECD Main Economic Indicators*, 2005), OECD Employment Outlook - 2005 Edition, © OECD 2005.

Source: Adapted from Wallace Clement, "Work and Society: Canada in a Continental and Comparative Context," presented in the Department of Sociology, Bishop's University, Lennoxville, 9 November 1999. Revised 2005. Reprinted by permission of the author.

keep the U.S. unemployment rate low is the growing population of "illegal immigrants." There are about twelve million illegal immigrants in the United States, most from Mexico.[4] That is proportionately far more than in Canada. Illegal immigrants are likely to experience higher unemployment rates than legal immigrants and non-immigrants, yet they are not calculated among the officially unemployed because they are in the country as "undocumented workers." Finally, the American armed forces comprise 0.5 percent of the American population but only 0.2 percent of the Canadian population. The higher level of militarization of the United States also keeps the American unemployment rate lower.[5]

Compared to the U.S., Canada was more deeply affected by the recession of the early 1990s and its population grew more quickly. These factors also contributed to the growing gap in unemployment rates between the two countries up to 1999. True, by the middle of 2000, Canada's unemployment rate fell to its lowest level in ten years (6.8 percent) compared to 4.0 percent in the U.S. But it is important to note that much of this decline was due to the growth of part-time, not full-time, jobs. Part-time jobs are less secure, pay less, and offer fewer benefits than full-time jobs. Not until 1998 did the number of full-time jobs regain their 1989 level, with most new jobs in this nine-year period coming from more precarious sources such as part-time work and self-employment.[6] Moreover, some of the decline was due to people dropping out of the labour force. Declining unemployment rates due to people dropping out of the labour force and taking part-time work are less impressive and less beneficial than declining unemployment rates due to the growth of full-time jobs.

One of the strongest patterns of change in Canada's labour force during the free trade era is the rise in self-employment. Self-employment accounted for three-quarters of all new jobs created between 1989 and 1997. The self-employed in 2004 comprised 18 percent of Canada's labour force. Ninety percent of these new jobs are in the service sector, led by business, health, and social services. Significantly, earnings of self-employed workers are more polarized than earnings of employees, resulting in a bigger earnings divide in the entire labour force. Thus, 45 percent of self-employed workers, compared to 26 percent of employees, earn less than $20 000 annually. At the other extreme, only 1 percent of employees, compared to 4 percent of self-employed workers, earn more than $100 000 annually.[7]

A Statistics Canada study contrasting labour market developments in Canada and the United States between 1989 and 1997 found that self-employment grew by 39 percent in Canada while the number of employees rose by only 1.6 percent. In the United States over the same period, both self-employment and employment in general grew by about 10 percent[8] (see Table 21.2). The difference in self-employment in the two labour markets is striking when one considers that self-employment accounted for four-fifths of total job growth in Canada and only one-tenth in the United States between 1989 and 1997. Equally stunning is the difference in the share of growth from part-time employment in the two countries. Canada's full-time employees took a major hit over the period. Thus, not only was Canada's job growth much slower than in the United States, it was characterized by the more rapid growth of so-called marginal or "contin-

TABLE 21.2 COMPONENTS OF EMPLOYMENT GROWTH, CANADA AND THE UNITED STATES, 1989–1997 (IN PERCENT)

GROWTH	CANADA	UNITED STATES
Total employment	6.5	10.4
Percent of total growth from:		
Self-employment	79.4	9.5
Part-time	47.8	6.2
Full-time	31.6	3.3
Employees	20.6	90.5
Part-time	47.3	20.4
Full-time	−26.7	70.1

Source: Adapted from the Statistics Canada publication "Labour Force Update," Catalogue 71-005, Autumn 1998, Vol. 2, No. 04, November 24, 1998, Table 4, page 17.

gent" jobs that offer less job security, lower wages, more seasonal work, and fewer benefits.

The growth of contingent jobs affects different segments of the labour force to varying degrees. Compare women and men, for example. A recent Canadian study reports that nearly two-thirds of women who have been employed in the paid labour force have had their work interrupted for six or more months. This compares to just over a quarter of men. Moreover, while 88 percent of women's labour force interruptions were due to family responsibilities in the 1950s, this figure fell to 47 percent in the 1990s. Meanwhile, economic reasons such as layoffs accounted for nearly a quarter of female labour force interruptions in the 1990s.[9] Another gender difference is evident in the proportion of women and men who work part time. In all countries, women are more likely than men to work for pay fewer than 30 hours a week. In the U.S. in 2004, about 8 percent of men and 19 percent of women worked for pay fewer than 30 hours a week. In Canada, the respective figures were substantially higher: about 11 percent of men and 29 percent of women.

Part-time work may be voluntary or involuntary. In Canada, an increasingly large share of the part-time labour force is involuntary, which is to say it consists of people who want to work full time but cannot find full-time jobs. Thus, between 1975 and 1994, part-time employment rose from 11 to 17 percent of the labour force, while those seeking full-time employment but having to settle for part-time work rose from 11 to 35 percent. In 40 percent of cases, the involuntary part-time worker was the primary earner in their family.[10] Finally, shift work is becoming more common, and the health and family implications of this development are unclear. For 2000–01, in the core labour force age group (18–54 years old) 30 percent of men and 26 percent of women had nonstandard work schedules (evening, rotating, or irregular shifts).[11]

We now seem to be on the edge of a new era with unclear outcomes. This period began with the attacks on the United States on September 11, 2001, and soon involved much economic dislocation and military mobilization. The U.S.

seems to have been especially hurt in employment terms, and has experienced modest employment growth since the attacks. In Canada, the picture is mixed: job growth has taken place in the state sector (mainly health and education) but has slowed in the private sector.[12] Whether the federal Liberals were forced to expand the state sector after they formed a minority government in 2004 we cannot say with any certainty. We do know that the labour market is in a state of flux, with the number of Canadian self-employed people still rising and the share of the labour force in part-time employment still higher than in the United States. Women continue to make up about 70 percent of part-time workers in both Canada and the United States. The part-time share of the labour force in Canada remains higher than in the United States (see Table 21.3). In 2004, part-timers represented 13.2 percent of the U.S. labour force and 18.5 percent in Canada.

It is important to stress the difference between the expansion of the "own-account" self-employed category in Canada and its contraction in the United States. (Own-account self-employed workers have no employees.) In Canada, the own-account self-employed category grew by 65 percent between 1987 and 1998, accounting for 80 percent of all self-employed people by 1998. Individuals in the own-account category earned only 53 to 68 per-

TABLE 21.3 PART-TIME EMPLOYMENT BY SEX IN CANADA AND UNITED STATES (as percent of total labour force)

Canada	1990	2001	2002	2003	2004
Men	9.2	10.5	11.0	11.1	10.9
Women	26.8	27.0	27.7	27.9	27.2
United States					
Men	8.6	8.0	8.0	8.0	8.0
Women	20.2	18.0	18.5	18.8	18.8

Note: Part time is less than 30 hours per week in main job. U.S. data for wage and salary workers only; Canada includes entire labour market, including self-employed.

Source: OECD, *Employment Outlook 2005* (Paris: OECD, 2005), Table E, p. 252.

cent of the average income of other workers in this period.[13] While Canada experienced a dramatic increase in the number of own-account self-employed workers and the number of hours they worked, both declined in the United States between 1987 and 1998. These findings show fundamental differences between the self-employed sectors in the two countries.[14] Self-employed Americans are much more likely than self-employed Canadians to hire employees and earn more. Should Canadians be concerned? Yes, primarily because these new jobs are of low quality compared with other forms of employment. We are not headed in the right direction.

CITIZENSHIP AND THE WELFARE STATE

On the basis of the foregoing discussion it seems safe to conclude that, since the advent of free trade in the late 1980s, Canada has not participated in many aspects of the boom economy enjoyed by its southern neighbour until it faced the attack of September 11th, 2001. Whether we examine labour force participation rates, unemployment rates, change in GDPpc, or growth in full-time non-contingent jobs, Canada has lagged behind the United States. That, however, is only half the story I want to tell. The other half has to do with the decline of welfare-state benefits or entitlements. Here Canada *has* begun to resemble the United States. That is largely because of free trade. If Canada kept welfare-state benefits much higher than U.S. levels, investment capital would tend to flow out of the country because total labour costs would be higher here. Free trade thus puts downward pressure on Canadian welfare-state benefits.

The main differences between Canadian and U.S. entitlements are in the realm of health care and postsecondary education. In the mid-1990s, just under 45 percent of American health-care costs were covered by government. In Canada, the comparable figure was just over 70 percent. Similarly, the Canadian government heavily subsidizes postsecondary education, while American postsecondary education is largely private.

However, these and other differences between the Canadian and American welfare states are weakening in the free trade era. Canadian government spending on health care and postsecondary education was cut throughout the 1990s. Tuition fees have gone up and private health care is making inroads, especially in Alberta.

Here I must distinguish entitlements based on employment from those based on citizenship. To the extent that access to health care is based on private insurance plans or plans paid by employers rather than awarded as a right of citizenship, health-care insurance is turned into a commodity. In Canada, basic health care, including doctor's fees and hospitalization, are covered by a nationally financed health insurance scheme. Other features of health care—dentistry, drugs, eyewear, types of hospital rooms, and so on—are covered either privately or through employment benefits. In Canada, employers face modest demands in wage negotiations for health-care coverage, whereas in the U.S., health-care insurance demands are high because state funding partially covers only the elderly and the poor.

For education, Canada's primary and secondary levels are fully state-funded with near-universal utilization of the system. Preschool child-care is a private responsibility, and a once-promised national daycare program still remains a dream, although some progress has been made in recent years. Postsecondary education is fee-based but tuition has traditionally been modest and all universities are public institutions. In the United States, a large proportion of primary and secondary students are in private schools because of the low quality of many state-funded schools. Postsecondary education is sharply divided between (1) state-sponsored institutions with high tuition fees and (2) private colleges with very high tuition fees.

In Canada, the contributory "employment insurance" scheme became more restrictive in the 1990s as eligibility criteria were tightened and a shrinking proportion of unemployed people were deemed entitled to benefits. People excluded from employment insurance are pushed into the means-tested welfare system. While

83 percent of unemployed Canadians qualified for employment insurance benefits in 1989, only 43 percent were eligible in 1997. This declining coverage resulted from 1996 reforms disqualifying "voluntary" job leavers and seasonal and part-time workers. Benefits were cut from 67 percent of previous salary to 55 percent. The result was a cash cow for the government; $19.5 billion in employment insurance contributions was collected in 1997 but only $12.5 billion was paid in benefits and administration.[15]

In terms of public expenditures on labour markets, Canada and the United States are not in the same league. Active labour market measures facilitate people's ability to find work. Passive measures compensate them for not working. While active labour market support diminished in Germany and Sweden in the 1990s, these countries remained active in their labour market support throughout the decade. Canada and Australia were high on passive support but low on active support and moderate overall. Japan and the United States were inactive and provided little even in the way of passive labour market support (see Table 21.4).

Compared to the United States, Canada spends more on employment services and labour market training. However, Canada follows the meagre U.S. pattern for youth measures, subsidized employment, and disability measures. During the 1990s, countries such as Australia, Germany, and Sweden dedicated more resources to actively combating unemployment. Canada is in the same league as the United States and Japan in this respect. Still, it is exceptional because, compared to these two countries, Canada suffers from high unemployment.

Canada's dramatic reduction in passive payments was achieved by cutting coverage, not by reducing unemployment, as in the United States. Indeed, Canada's unemployment increased as its expenditures decreased. In terms of its welfare-state expenditures, it is acting like the United States but it is doing so on a labour market foundation dramatically different from its neighbour's.

CONCLUSION

What, in the final analysis, can be said about the relationship between work and society during the free trade era in Canada? Work in Canada has become more marginal or contingent in many respects. There are more self-employed workers, more part-time workers, and more unemployed people (although by 2001 the unemployment gap between the two countries declined to the low level of the 1980s). Instead of becoming more like the American labour market, where people tend to work longer hours

TABLE 21.4 PUBLIC EXPENDITURES IN LABOUR MARKET PROGRAMS AS PERCENTAGE OF GDP, SELECTED COUNTRIES, 2003–2004

EMPLOYMENT	CANADA	USA	AUSTRALIA	JAPAN	GERMANY	SWEDEN
Services	0.17	0.04	0.19	0.26	0.28	0.24
Training	0.12	0.05	0.03	0.04	0.40	0.37
Incentives	0.02	0.01	0.01	0.02	0.11	0.15
Subsidized	0.03	0.01	0.10	0.00	0.20	0.04
Disabled	0.02	0.03	0.05	0.01	0.15	0.48
Compensation	0.77	0.37	0.74	0.46	2.27	1.22
Active	0.37	0.16	0.39	0.32	1.14	1.29
Passive	0.77	0.37	0.74	0.46	2.31	1.22
Total	1.14	0.53	1.13	0.79	3.46	2.51

Source: Based on Table H. Public expenditure and participant inflows in labour market programmes in OECD countries, OECD Employment Outlook - 2005 Edition, © OECD 2005.

during longer work lives, Canada has become a place where people work less because less work is available, especially good work in the public sector and large corporations. Postindustrialism has not been kind to the Canadian labour force.

In areas like unemployment insurance, the Canadian government is putting more stress on employment-based benefits that are typically unavailable for self-employed and part-time workers. The Canadian state has not yet declined to American levels because its citizens continue to insist on a higher level of social support. Canada stands between the American job machine with its abundance of cheap labour and the more supportive labour markets of Sweden and Germany.

Are Canadians, as citizens and workers, better off under free trade? We cannot answer this question fully because we will never know the outcome of alternative policy choices. Nonetheless, it seems that many Canadians have paid dearly for the path Canada's political leaders chose and its economic leaders demanded. The labour market and social service effects of September 11th, 2001, remain unclear, but indications are that the United States experienced more negative effects than Canada. By 2004, the United States appeared to be recovering from the effects of September 11, 2001, but new challenges loomed, including the effects of disastrous hurricanes on the Gulf Coast, the ongoing war in Iraq, and the rising price of oil. Canada has attached its employment wagon to an unstable and inequitable society to its south with disquieting consequences.

NOTES

1. See *Labour Force Update* (Ottawa: Statistics Canada, Autumn 1998), p. 3.

2. See Organisation for Economic Co-operation and Development, *Employment Outlook 2005* (Paris: OECD, 2005), Table 1.3, p. 20.

3. Bruce Western and Katherine Beckett, "How Unregulated is the US Labor Market?: The Penal System as a Labor Market Institution," *American Journal of Sociology,* 104 (4) (January 1999): 1030–60; H. L. Ginsburg, J. Zaccone, G. S. Goldberg, S. D. Collins, and S. M. Rosen, "Special Issue on the Challenge of Full Employment in the Global Economy, Editorial Introduction," *Economic and Industrial Democracy,* 18 (1997): 24; "U.S. surpasses Russia as world leader in rate of incarceration," *The Sentencing Project* (2001). On the World Wide Web at http://www.sentencingproject.org/brief/usvsrus.pdf (18 October 2002).

4. See Min Zhou, "Growing Up American: The Challenge Confronting Immigrant Children and the Children of Immigrants," *Annual Review of Sociology,* 23 (1997): 63–95; *New York Times,* 31 August 1997.

5. "Defence expenditure and size of armed forces of NATO and partner countries," *NATO Review: 2001.* On the World Wide Web at http://www.nato.int/docu/review/2001/defence0103-en.pdf (18 October 2002).

6. See Ekuwa Smith and Andrew Jackson, "Does a Rising Tide Lift All Boats? The Labour Market Experience and Incomes of Recent Immigrants, 1995–1998" (Ottawa: Canadian Council on Social Development, February 2002).

7. See *Canadian Social Trends* (Ottawa: Statistics Canada, Spring 1998), p. 28.

8. See *Labour Force Update* (Autumn 1998), p. 13.

9. See Janet Fast and Moreno Da Pont, "Changes in Women's Work Continuity," *Canadian Social Trends* (Ottawa: Statistics Canada, Autumn 1997), pp. 3–5.

10. Grant Schellenberg, "'Involuntary,' Part-Time Workers," *Perception,* 18 (1996): 3–4.

11. See Statistics Canada, *The Daily,* 25 July 2002.

12. See Statistics Canada, *The Daily,* 9 August 2002.

13. See John Baldwin and James Chowham, "The Impact of Self-Employment on Labour-Productivity Growth: A Canada and United States Comparison" (Ottawa: Statistics Canada, August 2003), pp. 10–11.

14. Ibid., p. 29.

15. See *Globe and Mail,* 13 February 1998, A3.

Chapter 23

Violence, Sex, and Drugs Among Canadian Teenagers

REGINALD W. BIBBY

VIOLENCE

During the past few years, adults have been increasingly concerned about teenage violence, stimulated in large part by a series of violent acts in Canada and the United States. On April 20, 1999, 12 students and a teacher were killed at Columbine High in Littleton, Colorado, followed on April 28 by the shooting of two students, one fatally, in Taber, Alberta. Ever since, threats of violence in schools across Canada have been seen as abounding.[1] A knife attack on the one-year anniversary of Columbine in April 2000 resulted in the wounding of four students and one staff member at Cairine Wilson High School in the Ottawa suburb of Orléans. In November 2000 a Toronto teen admitted he had shown classmates a list of fourteen students he planned to kill and had attempted to buy an assault rifle over the Internet to carry out his plan.[2] The same month a student was stabbed to death at Calgary's Lester B. Pearson High School.[3]

Parents are among those feeling new pressures. *National Post* columnist Jane Christmas described the ambivalence she felt when her 14-year-old wanted to stay away from his Hamilton school on the day of the Columbine anniversary. In the end, she decided to let him. But it required the confirmation of her mother, her doctor, and word of what happened in Ottawa— what she describes as three votes of confidence. "Did I overreact?" she asks, and then answers her own question: "I don't believe anything you do in the interest of protecting your child is an over-reaction."[4] The headline of her article referred to the times as "the age of Columbine."

Violence among young people has not been limited to schools. On November 14, 1997, Victoria teenager Reena Virk was beaten by a group of girls she'd sought to befriend, then drowned by one of the girls and a teenage male companion.[5] Eight young people, seven of them girls between the ages of 14 and 16, were charged, and one of the girls was subsequently convicted of second-degree murder and sentenced to five years in prison before she can apply for parole. Virk's mother told the presiding judge, "My dream to raise and love my child is shattered like a vase."[6] In November of 1999, 15-year-old Dmitri Baranovski was punched and kicked to death in a Toronto park by eight to ten males wearing balaclavas and blue bandanas who demanded cigarettes, drugs, and money from the victim and his friends.[7] Just two days later, a 14-year-old Toronto girl was found bruised and bleeding with cigarette burns on her back; she'd been tortured for two hours by four older teenage girls.[8] In November of 2000, a 14-year-old Edmonton boy was taken off life support two weeks after being brutally beaten beyond recognition by two older teens behind a junior high school.[9] And youth violence was further highlighted when an eight-year-old boy in Lytton, Quebec, used his father's high-powered rifle to shoot and critically wound a 64-year-old man, claiming he was shooting at a tree to scare the man.[10]

Source: Bibby, Reginald W. *Canada's Teens: Today, Yesterday, and Tomorrow*. Toronto: Stoddart, 2001. pp. 79–105. Copyright © by Reginald W. Bibby.

In light of these and other forms of violent acts—including child abuse, sexual assault, and suicide—it's important to hear what young people have to say.

Violence in schools is seen as a "very serious" problem by significant numbers of teenagers. But the difference by gender is fairly dramatic. Some 65% of females see the issue as extremely serious, compared to just 40% of males. Nonetheless, out of 18 issues posed, violence in schools is among those most widely cited by males as being particularly serious (see Table 23.1).

One 17-year-old male from a small northern Alberta city expresses his concern this way: "We have had threats and it makes me scared to come here and learn. I mean, just the other day there was a fight in our hallways." A 15-year-old who lives in a small community in northern Ontario says she doesn't feel safe at school, adding, "I could at any time be shot." But another female, 16, from Regina warns against stereotyping teens: "In reaction to the recent school shootings, I would like to say it isn't all kids in black who listen to Marilyn Manson, have black trench coats, and get beat up at school who do these kinds of things. I would never do anything that stupid and I am a goth, black trench–owning, Marilyn Manson–loving freak who gets picked on."

In addition to violence in schools, some 50% to 65% of females and 30% to 45% of males view *child abuse, teenage suicide, violence against women,* and *crime* as "very serious" problems. In each instance, the concern levels for females are significantly higher than those of males. About 35% of females and 30% of males see youth gangs as "very serious."

Beyond perception of the seriousness of these various issues, teens were asked if they have a *close friend* who personally has encountered violence or has had depression or suicide-related experiences (see Table 23.2).

- Some five in ten, led by females, say they have had a close friend who has been *severely depressed*, while four in ten indicate that they have a close friend who has *attempted suicide*. In both cases the levels for females exceed those for males.

- Almost 40% of males and 25% of females report that they have had a close friend who has been *physically attacked at school*; conversely, around 40% of females and 25% of males say a close friend has been *physically abused at home*.

- Three in ten females and just under two in ten males confide that they have a close friend who has been *sexually abused*.

- About 30% of males and 20% of females say a close friend has been a victim of *gang violence*.

TABLE 23.1 PERCEPTIONS OF SERIOUSNESS OF VIOLENCE, CRIME, AND SUICIDE

	% Viewing as "Very Serious"		
	NATIONALLY	FEMALES	MALES
Child abuse	56%	66	44
Violence in schools	50	59	40
Teenage suicide	49	60	36
Violence against women	42	51	33
Crime	40	49	29
Youth gangs	31	34	28

TABLE 23.2 EXTENT TO WHICH PROBLEMS HAVE BEEN EXPERIENCED BY A CLOSE FRIEND

	NATIONALLY	FEMALES	MALES
Has been severely depressed	48%	57	39
Has attempted suicide	41	50	31
Physically attacked at school	32	25	39
Physically abused at home	31	37	25
Has been sexually abused	26	32	18
A victim of gang violence	24	21	28

Some caution needs to be used in interpreting such findings; one's close friend may also be the close friend of others. To find that three in ten females has a close friend who has been sexually abused, for example, does not mean that three in ten females have been sexually abused; obviously the figure, based on such an item, is somewhat lower.

Still these findings suggest that the incidence of depression and suicide attempts, physical attacks and abuse is startlingly high. What is disconcerting is that the violence is frequently found not only at school but also at home.

A final note on bullying. Alan King's 1998 national health survey found that just under 30% of males and females in grade 10 reported that they had been bullied during the school term. Such physical, verbal, or psychological intimidation has few clear-cut correlates, other than being disproportionately directed at males who feel isolated. Bullying tends to be cyclical: those who are bullied bully, and in turn receive similar treatment.[11]

DIFFERENCES ACROSS THE COUNTRY

Overall there are few distinct differences in the perception and incidence of school and home violence among regions and communities, regardless of size (see Table 23.3). Simply put, perception and behaviour are distributed fairly evenly across Canada.

Concern about violence in schools is somewhat less in Quebec than elsewhere, despite the fact that students there are marginally more likely than others to say they do not feel safe at school; presumably such concern has been normalized. Contrary to what I suspect is widely believed, teens in cities of over 400 000 are slightly *less* inclined than young people living elsewhere to view school violence as "very serious," and no more likely than others to say they do *not* feel safe at school. Teens living on farms are the least likely to report that they have close friends who either have been attacked at school or physically abused at home.

TABLE 23.3 CONCERN ABOUT VIOLENCE BY REGION, COMMUNITY SIZE, AND BIRTHPLACE

	SCHOOL VIOLENCE A VERY SERIOUS PROBLEM	CLOSE FRIEND ATTACKED AT SCHOOL	NOT SAFE AT SCHOOL	NOT SAFE AT HOME	CLOSE FRIEND PHYSICALLY ABUSED AT HOME
Nationally	50%	32	22	7	31
B.C.	51	30	19	7	30
Prairies	49	32	17	5	30
Ontario	53	32	22	7	32
Quebec	43	33	27	7	33
Atlantic	54	30	21	8	27
North	53	34	19	2	31
>400 000	44	35	21	5	32
399 999–100 000	51	32	21	7	34
99 999–30 000	56	36	28	7	31
Cities/towns <30 000	53	29	21	8	33
Rural non-farm	52	32	18	7	27
Farm	50	24	19	6	25
Born in Canada	50	31	21	7	32
Born outside Canada	47	35	26	6	28

There is little difference in concern about violence at school and at home between young people born in Canada and those born outside the country. There is, however, a slightly greater tendency for teens who have come to Canada to say both that (1) they have a close friend who has been attacked at school and (2) they themselves don't feel safe at school. As might be expected, as teens from outside Canada share in Canadian life, their inclination to engage in offences comes to resemble those of teens born here—a pattern noted, for example, by Brandon sociologist Siu Kwong Wong in a recent study of Winnipeg teens of Chinese descent.[12]

Concern about youth violence has led to proactive measures in cities such as Toronto. In June 2000, a Youth Violence Task Force comprising Toronto police, Catholic and public school boards, and the transit commission recommended that:

- police officers be assigned to schools, recreational centres, and subway stations during lunchtime and after-school hours;
- police disclose conditions of release for young offenders to schools as permissible under the *Young Offenders Act*; and
- a young offender program be implemented to target high-risk, repeat offenders.

A member of the task force, 17-year-old Krista Lopes, noted the need to work together "to combat the ever-increasing problem of youth violent crimes," while Toronto Police Chief Julian Fantino noted that "the ol' thing is no longer adequate," adding, "We need to do things that are more strategic and we need to count on parents, politicians, educators, and certainly the police community and all others, but especially the youth, to turn things around."[13]

In order to understand current youth violence in relation to the past, it is important to first ask, what constitutes violence? By way of illustration, a 1999 survey of 2 000 grade 7 to 12 students in Alberta by the Canadian Research Institute for Law and the Family found violence to be highest among grades 8 and 9 students. Some 40% of grade 9 students, for example, admitted to slapping, punching, or kicking someone in the past year, compared to 32% of grade 12 students. About 16% of students acknowledged they had brought weapons to school, with the most common being illegal knives, replica weapons—mostly plastic guns, clubs, and bats. The least common were pellet guns and handguns. In addition, more than half the students surveyed said they had been victimized at least once during the past year at school; perhaps significantly, almost the same percentage said they had been victimized while they were *not* at school. The most frequent forms of victimization—similar in all Alberta communities—included being slapped, punched, or kicked, having something stolen, being threatened with bodily harm, and having property damaged. The least frequent included being attacked by a group or gang and being threatened by a weapon. Such survey findings prompted the Calgary police chief at the time, Christine Silverberg, to call for an expansion of school resource programs in junior high schools.[14]

It is clear from such research that "violence" is being applied to an extremely wide range of activities beyond beatings, stabbings, and shootings. Such a broad application of "violence" undoubtedly is associated with a "zero tolerance" response to any physically aggressive act toward another person. *Hear me clearly*: this is in no way to minimize the gravity of such acts today. But it is to say the bar that defines violence has been raised considerably over where it has been in the past. Adults also may be placing the bar at a higher level than where many teens—especially males, but also some females—are placing it. Among them is a 16-year-old female from a small town near Calgary who comments, "School violence has been around since schools came about. Let kids be kids," she says, "Don't punish them for wrestling. Punish them for guns and severe fighting."

A REALITY CHECK

It is worthwhile to compare our survey perceptions and reports with additional information on young people. A victimization analysis released in December 1995 by Statistics Canada using data from police departments indicated that teenagers are certainly vulnerable when it comes to violent crime. In fact, they are at greater risk of violent crime than either adults or children. Young people between the ages of 12 and 19 made up 20% of the victims of violent crime in the mid-'90s, even though they represented just 11% of the population. About 80% of violent incidents against teenagers were assaults, some 15% being of a sexual nature; most of the others involved robbery. Victims of violent crime were equally likely to be males and females; however, a large majority of victimized females were victims of sexual offenses, whereas males were more likely to be victims of assault and robbery. Police statistics also revealed that about five in ten violent incidents against teenagers involved acquaintances, and three in ten strangers, while two in ten were committed by family members, with parents implicated in half of those incidents.[15] Further, Statistics Canada survey data for 1999 show that young people 15 to 24 are reporting the highest rate of personal victimization, more than twice the national average. Seniors 65 and over, by the way, are reporting the lowest rates of victimization.[16]

In July 2000, Statistics Canada released a new report, also based on police records, revealing that the national crime rate in 1999 fell to its lowest level in two decades. Young people under the age of 20 were more likely than people in other age groups to commit both violent and property crimes. Youth crime, however, was down more than 7% from 1998 and was 21% lower than in 1989. The rate of youths charged with violent crime fell 5%, the largest year-to-year drop since the *Young Offenders Act* was introduced in 1984. While the 1990s saw an increase in violent crimes among females, the female rate as of 1999 was still only one-third of the male rate. The report reminded readers that many non-violent young offenders are diverted from the formal justice system, but also said that available statistics indicate the number of youths being diverted has also been decreasing in recent years.[17] Coincidentally, the same day the report was released, Britain released crime statistics for England and Wales, which showed a large jump in violent crime in those two countries over the past year.[18]

A third Statistics Canada report, made available in August 2000, is also worth acknowledging. An analysis of sentences given to young offenders (12 to 17) who were convicted in youth court during 1998–99 reveals that one-third were put in some form of custody. Males were more likely to be sentenced to custody than females. A comparison of the sentencing of adults and youths for the most common offences for nine of the most frequent offences—such as common assault, breaking and entering, and possession of stolen property—showed that young people were less likely to be placed in custody. But when they were jailed, they were more likely to receive longer sentences than the adults. For example, in the case of common assault, the report found that 65% of young offenders were sentenced to more than one month in jail, compared to 43% of adults.[19] Commenting on the report, Robert Gordon, the director of the Department of Criminology at Simon Fraser University, suggested the sentencing differences reflect public calls for stiffer penalties for offences involving young people.[20]

Taken together, these three reports indicate that (1) a disproportionate number of teens are victims of violent crime, (2) the rate of violent crime committed by young people has been decreasing in recent years, and (3) young offenders who are placed in custody tend to be punished to a greater degree than adult offenders. These findings document that teen violence is a serious problem. But contrary to widely held perception, teen violence has actually been declining. In addition, reaction to young offenders in recent years, in some instances at least, has been harsher than that shown adults.

Even in the face of the Calgary school homicide in November 2000, Dennis Eastcott, the founder of the Alberta Association of School Resource Officers and the officer in charge of Edmonton's youth and crime prevention services, maintained that statistics do not support the notion that kids are becoming more violent or are getting "out of whack." As for school violence, Staff Sgt. Eastcott commented, "Studies based on where kids are victimized show one of the safest places for them is at school."[21] Obviously not everyone agrees.

It therefore is not surprising that it's difficult to obtain a consensus on how to respond to so-called youth crime. At a conference of victims'-rights advocates held in Hamilton in October of 1999, Justice Minister Anne McLellan said that Ottawa would do what it thinks is right to deal with young offenders, regardless of pressure from the provinces. "Quebec is telling me: 'Your legislation is too tough.' Ontario is telling me: 'It's not tough enough.' Well, you know what that tells me? Canadians are generally right in the middle and I think our legislation reflects that balanced approach."[22]

SAFETY AT SCHOOL AND AT HOME

Although teens are aware of friends who have been attacked and abused, 19 in 20 say they feel safe at home, 16 in 20 feel safe at school.

| | % INDICATING FEEL SAFE | |
	AT HOME	AT SCHOOL
Nationally	93%	78
Males	94	79
Females	94	78

A national survey of 400 American teenagers, 14 to 17, conducted in April 2000 for *Time* magazine found 86% felt either "very safe" or "somewhat safe" from violence at school.[23]

SEXUALITY

Our sexually liberated society is characterized by considerable openness about sex, led by the media. If Pierre Trudeau took the government out of the bedrooms of the nation, the media takes us into the bedrooms of the nation on a daily if not hourly basis. TV programs such as *Sex and the City*, the *Sunday Night Sex Show*, and *The Sex Files* lead the way explicitly. But sex is to be found everywhere, spanning sitcoms, movies, stand-up comedy, and, for reasons well known to all of us, even nightly newscasts in the U.S. and Canada on a regular basis during 1999.

Craig Colby, the Toronto producer of *The Sex Files* that airs on the Discovery Channel, recently commented, "There's definitely a lot more permissiveness in society." Colby says that two events have been new groundbreakers—the Monica Lewinsky affair, which made oral sex and phone-sex discussion topics, and the memorable "Master of His Domain" episode on *Seinfeld*, that "completely destigmatized" masturbation.[24] Yes, these are days of sexual freedom and openness. And with the morning-after pill becoming more accessible to women, making it possible to prevent pregnancy within three days of intercourse,[25] some would argue that the incidence and enjoyment of sexual activity, marital and otherwise, will only increase.

In the midst of all this, adults worry a great deal about teenagers and sex for any number of reasons. And they should, if the words of this 17-year-old female from Hamilton are accurate: "Sex is like an everyday thing for teens now."

The survey shows that Canada's youth are divided almost evenly when it comes to sexual attitudes and behaviour, although males typically hold more liberal attitudes than females and are more sexually active (see Table 23.4).

- Approximately six in ten teens, led by males, maintain that *consenting adults* should be able to do whatever they want sexually. Moreover, the same proportion of males and a smaller proportion of females feel that con-

TABLE 23.4 SEXUAL ATTITUDES

	% "Strongly Approve" or "Approve"		
	NATIONALLY	FEMALES	MALES
Sexual Tolerance Limits			
Consenting adults doing whatever they want sexually	61%	67	56
Consenting teens 15 to 17 doing whatever they want sexually	56	66	46
Sexual Behaviour and Rights			
Sex before marriage when people LOVE each other	82	85	80
Sex before marriage when people LIKE each other	58	68	48
Sexual relations between two people of the same sex	54	41	66
Homosexuals are entitled to the same rights as other Canadians	75	62	87
A married person having sex with someone other than marriage partner	9	13	4
Cohabitation			
A couple who are not married living together	86	89	83
A couple having children without being married	63	61	64
Abortion			
It being possible to obtain a legal abortion when a female has been raped	84	85	83
It being possible to obtain a legal abortion for any reason	55	58	52

senting teens between the ages of 15 and 17 also should be able to do whatever they want sexually. One 17-year-old from the B.C. Interior sums things up this way: "I believe in people's rights to do whatever they want sexually, as long as it doesn't hurt any other living thing. In the case of teenagers, however, more thought has to go into it because they are less able to deal with accidental pregnancy than adults."

- Some 80% of young people approve of sex before marriage *when people love each other*, with little disagreement between males and females. In addition, close to 60% think that sex before marriage is all right *when people like each other*. Here there is a significant difference in opinion between males (68%) and females (48%). A Burnaby, B.C., 16-year-old says, "I'm worried about diseases in Canada; more people are having unprotected sex." The issues of birth control and pregnancy are expressed starkly by a 17-year-old from

Alberta: "Teens should have more information about protection if they are going to have sex. People should be told how to take birth control properly, along with the fact methods aren't 100% effective against pregnancy." She signed her comments, "A pregnant teen who was on birth control." Few young people would disagree: 92% maintain that "birth control information should be available to teens who want it." More possibilities, incidentally, are on the way. As you might be aware, a new monthly injectable contraceptive known as Lunelle, the first new birth control method since 1992, was introduced in the U.S. in late 2000. It is an alternative to Depo-Provera, an injectable drug that is given every three months. Both are administered by a physician.[26]

- About one in two teenagers (54%) approve of *homosexual* relations, with females (66%) considerably more likely than males (41%) to express approval. But 75%, led by females, maintain that homosexuals are entitled to the same rights as other Canadians. Among males expressing consternation is this 15-year-old male from Regina who says, "Gays should not have a special week or the right to adopt children." A grade 11 male from a small Alberta town comments, "One thing I would like to stress is that homosexuality is wrong. If they really want to be gay, they should do it in secret and not adopt kids." (See Figure 23.1.)

- Merely 9% of young people condone *extra-marital* sexual relations. It seems quite obvious that such behaviour has not been adding much to lives, however heralded it might have been by some at the time of the sexual revolution.

- *Cohabitation* receives the approval of almost nine in ten teenagers, while having *children without being married* is regarded as all right by about six in ten. Stigma in the latter case seemingly is higher for teenage single parents than couples. A 16-year-old in the Atlantic region says that, despite the fact that her boyfriend has stood with her in raising her child, "I get a lot of discrimination against my parenting skills."

- The availability of *legal abortion* when a female has been *raped* is approved of by some 80%, abortion *on demand* by just over 50%. One twelfth grader from Vancouver says he "applauds the availability of birth control in British Columbia" and adds that

"abortion should never be withheld under any circumstances." The introduction of the RU-486 pill as an alternative to surgical abortion may or may not alter such attitudes. The pill, which can terminate a pregnancy up to about seven weeks after conception, was approved and made available to some U.S. doctors in late 2000[27] and is being tested in Canada. It has been met with strong opposition from pro-life groups. RU-486 has been made available in France since 1989 and is also sold in Britain, Sweden, and China.[28]

In short, while one in two Canadian teenagers indicate that, in theory, consenting individuals technically and legally have "the right" to do what they want, teens nonetheless have some strong personal feelings as to what is sexually appropriate and what is not.

We asked teens pointedly how often they engage in sex. About 25%, including 27% of males and 22% of females, claim they have sex at least once a week (see Table 23.5). Around another 10% indicate they have sex two to three times a month, a further 15% say less often. Approximately 50% of teenagers say they never engage in sex, with this category including some 45% of males and 55% of females. Among them is a 16-year-old male from southern Alberta who comments, "None of my friends or anyone I know have had sex. My friends and I feel that you should not have sex unless you are married." As for the one in two who do engage in sex, a *Globe and Mail* editorial has put it this way: "There is a principal reason why people engage in consensual sex: They enjoy it. Liking sex has little to do with age. Thinking about sex in terms of preventing unwanted consequences rather than preventing the sex act itself simply recognizes the fact that teenage sex is, well, common."[29] In responding to the question of how often she engages in sex, a 16-year-old female from suburban Montreal may speak for much of the nation in admitting, "When the chance comes up." In her case, she says, it's "hardly ever."

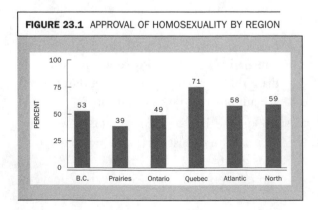

FIGURE 23.1 APPROVAL OF HOMOSEXUALITY BY REGION

SEXUAL ATTITUDES AND SERVICE ATTENDANCE

Differences in sexual attitudes are readily apparent between teens who attend religious services weekly versus those who attend less often.

	WEEKLY	% APPROVING LESS THAN WEEKLY
Consenting adults doing what they want sexually	38%	68
Consenting teens 15 to 17 doing what they want sexually	28	63
Sex before marriage when people LOVE each other	49	91
Sexual relations between two people of the same sex	25	62
Sex with someone other than one's marriage partner	4	10
Homosexuals entitled to same rights as other Canadians	59	79
A couple who are not married living together	57	94
A couple having children without being married	29	72
It being possible to obtain a legal abortion for any reason	24	64

A cautionary note: "engage" in sex undoubtedly means "sexual intercourse" for most teens, but not all. One 15-year-old female from Williams Lake, British Columbia, reminds us that "some people engage in sexual activity which does not include actual sex," and that "there is a lot more sexual activity between 'neck and pet' and 'sex.'"

In sum, around 50% of teens are currently sexually involved, and 50% are not. A national survey of teenagers carried out in the mid-1990s by Statistics Canada reports similar levels of activity and adds some further details. First, 44% of males and 43% of females had had at least one sex partner in the year that the survey covered. Second, 21% of teen males had sex with at least two partners, compared to 13% of females. Third, close to three in four males (71%) but only one in two females (49%) claimed that condoms were used.[30]

Yet our current survey findings on sexual activity underestimate the lifetime sexual experiences of teenagers, because the item is asking specifically about *current* sexual behaviour. Fifty percent of teens are not virgins. An additional survey item reveals that 15%–16% of males, 14% of females—are not sexually involved *currently*, but just 41% of teens (33% of males, 48%

TABLE 23.5 TEENAGE SEXUAL ACTIVITY

"About how often do you engage in sex?"

	NATIONALLY	FEMALES	MALES
Daily	6%	9	3
Several times a week	10	10	10
About once a week	8	8	9
2 to 3 times a month	7	8	6
About once a month	5	7	3
Hardly ever	13	14	12
Never	51	44	57
Totals	100	100	100

of females) say they have *never* been sexually involved. The "currently involved" and "previously involved" total consequently appears to be closer to 60%.

As for appropriate behaviour on dates, nine in ten teens think it is all right for two people to *hold hands* on the first date if they like each other and more than seven in ten approve of kissing on the first date (see Table 23.6 on page 250). *Necking and petting*, however, is seen by six in ten

TABLE 23.6 APPROPRIATE BEHAVIOUR ON DATES

"If two people on a date like each other, do you think it is all right for them to . . ."		
	YES, ON THE FIRST DATE	YES, AFTER A FEW DATES	NO
Hold Hands	89%	10	1
Males	92	8	<1
Females	87	12	1
Kiss	73	26	1
Males	78	21	1
Females	68	30	2
Neck and Pet	32	57	11
Males	43	50	7
Females	22	63	15
Have Sex	11	40	49
Males	18	50	32
Females	4	32	64

THE LIMITED IMPACT OF AIDS

"Has the existence of AIDS influenced your own personal sexual habits?"

	YES	NO
Males	58%	44
Females	62	38

teenagers as something that should not take place until after a few dates. Here, males and females differ significantly. Young women are much more inclined to indicate a few dates should have taken place, and about 15% don't think necking and petting should occur at all. In case you are wondering, no, we weren't all that excited about using the terms "necking and petting," but we wanted to use terms consistent with our previous surveys and, frankly, "making out" is too general. A 17-year-old from Nunavut was among those who wanted to make a distinction. Drawing an arrow to "necking," she said, "Yes, we did that after two months of going out. Me and my boyfriend neck, but I don't know what you mean by pet. If you mean 'feel up,' then no, never!" That's what we meant, and I think that's what most teens thought we meant.

Males and females differ sharply in their sense of when and if *sexual relations* are appropriate. Almost seven in ten males say sex is all right within a few dates, but fewer than four in ten females share their opinion.

Two common assertions of people observing the teenage sex scene is that the threat of AIDS has been (1) contributing to a reduction in sexual

activity and/or (2) resulting in more protected sex. While the first assertion is seriously in doubt, about 60% of teens who say they are sexually involved acknowledge that AIDS has influenced their sexual habits. The remaining 40% apparently have been relatively unfazed by the existence of the fatal disease. One 16-year-old, who lives in a small city in northeastern Quebec, seems to express the sentiments of many teens in this latter category when she says, "Since I have been sexually active, AIDS has existed. For me, nothing has changed."

DRUGS

Since at least the 1960s, considerable publicity has been given to the problem of drug use among young people. It remains an area of major concern for adults. For example, we saw earlier that some 25% of males and 15% of females note that they frequently have conflict with their parents over the issue of drugs. Parents' and adults' fears are not neutralized by what they sense is the ready availability of drugs. If anything, those fears may be heightened when they learn of the current survey's finding that no less than 44% of teenage males and 49% of females acknowledge they have a close friend with "a severe alcohol or drug problem."

There is little doubt that Canadian teens have ample access to illegal drugs. No less than 77% say that if they wanted to use drugs, it is "not very difficult" (26%) or "not difficult at all" (51%) to obtain them; 6% think it is "difficult" and the remaining 17% say they "don't know" (see Table 23.7). What's particularly striking is that access is not limited by whether or not

TABLE 23.7 ACCESS TO DRUGS

	% "NOT VERY DIFFICULT" OR "NOT DIFFICULT AT ALL"
Nationally	77%
Males	80
Females	74
B.C.	81
Prairies	76
Ontario	75
Quebec	78
Atlantic	80
North	81
<400 000	77
399 999–100 000	79
99 999–30 000	76
Cities/towns <30 000	80
Rural non-farm	75
Farm	76

someone is female or male, lives in one region of the country or another, or resides in a large city, small city, or a rural area. Illegal drugs appear to be just about everywhere. A 16-year-old in one Western Canadian city decries the availability of drugs where he lives:

I think the drug problem is very bad here. I mean, I try to stop doing drugs, but they are so readily available that it is very hard. There are so many drug traffickers in my school and I go to the best Catholic high school in the city. Kids need to be stopped from turning to drugs, but not by another one of the government's corny programs. Also, more stores should call for identification when people buy alcohol because I can buy it easily and I don't look a day over 16.

A grade 12 student from New Westminister says "drugs are available on today's streets" and that "it is easier to buy drugs than alcohol." A 17-year-old in Hamilton notes, "Drugs are everywhere. I can get marijuana any time I want, day or night." A 16-year-old in a small city north of Edmonton concurs: "Pot is so easy to get, and

cheap." Another Albertan, a 16-year-old male from a small town south of Calgary, takes the position that drugs are so readily available that laws should be relaxed: "I believe it shouldn't matter how old you are to buy liquor or cigarettes or pot because they are very easy to get if you are underage."

Availability, of course, doesn't equal use. A 15-year-old from Moose Jaw, Saskatchewan, observes, "There are a lot of drugs around here, but not all people use them." Yet the concern about drug abuse is shared by significant numbers of teenagers. As we saw earlier, almost one in two teens say that drug use is a "very serious" problem in Canada. One male, 16, who lives just outside Ottawa comments, "I really do feel that the use of drugs among teenagers is a big problem. I have many friends who engage in drugs weekly, daily, or monthly. I see this becoming more of a problem because I don't have a friend who hasn't at least tried drugs once or twice." A Grande Prairie, Alberta, teen expresses his alarm this way: "I strongly feel that heroin and crack cocaine are being strongly abused by teens and parents. This is breaking up families and lives. I am very worried about it and scared for the future of our society." A 16-year-old female from a small Ontario town acknowledges that the problem exists and offers an explanation as to why: "I think that in our town a lot of our drug and alcohol problems are because we have nothing to do—no movie theatre, no bowling alley, no mall, nothing."

Given the prevalent consternation and access, what actually is happening?

Some 28% of teenagers say they smoke *cigarettes* monthly or more often, 9% rarely, and 63% never. Female smoking levels are marginally above those of males (see Table 23.8 on page 252). These figures are consistent with Statistics Canada data for early 1999 that found 28% of teens, 15 to 19, to be smokers.[31]

Around 20% of teens say they drink *beer, wine, or other forms of alcohol* at least once a week, with the level for those under 18 only slightly lower than that of 15- to 19-year-olds as a whole. The

TABLE 23.8 DRUG USE AMONG TEENAGERS

"How often do you yourself . . ."			
	WEEKLY OR MORE	ONCE OR TWICE A MONTH	LESS THAN ONCE A MONTH	NEVER
Smoke Cigarettes	23%	5	9	63
Males	22	5	9	64
Females	24	6	9	61
Drink Beer, Wine, Other Alcohol	22	30	26	22
Males	29	29	22	20
Females	16	31	28	25
Under 18 total	18	29	26	27
Males	26	31	22	21
Females	14	31	29	26
Smoke Marijuana or Hashish	14	10	13	63
Males	19	11	13	57
Females	9	8	14	69
Use Other Illegal Drugs	3	4	7	86
Males	4	4	8	84
Females	2	4	7	87

weekly level for males is almost twice that of females; yet 75% of females drink at least on occasion, compared to 80% of males. One 15-year-old female from Edmonton helps to clarify the nature of alcohol use for some young people: "My parents often let me have wine or a cooler but I feel because of this I have grown a respect for alcohol. Because it's always available at home, I don't go out and get drunk with friends."

Approximately 15% of teenagers say they *smoke marijuana or hashish* weekly or more, with male use about twice that of females. However, about four in ten males and three in ten females admit to being occasional marijuana users.

Just 3% of young people acknowledge that they are using *other illegal drugs* on a regular weekly basis, including 4% of males and 2% of females. But again, occasional use is not insignificant—another 15% for males and 11% for females.

A 17-year-old from Montreal sums up the place of drugs in her life in a fairly matter-of-fact manner: "Every weekend I consume

alcohol when I go to a pub or go out to eat at a restaurant. When I go to a rave I take illegal drugs, but I only go about once a month." A grade 11 student who lives in a small community in New Brunswick explains her use of marijuana:

When you asked the question, "Do you smoke pot," I replied yes. This doesn't make me a drug addict. I'm getting an 80% average in school and doing well at work. I enjoy having a toke but I am very responsible. I never come to school or work high. I hope this shows that every teen who smokes pot is not a delinquent.

It's important not to lose sight of the fact that sizable numbers of young people maintain that they are *not* using drugs of any kind, including—in close to one in four cases—alcohol. Among them is another Montrealer, a 16-year-old female, who says, "Drugs do not interest me at all. I find cigarettes distasteful and I don't want to know anything about illegal drugs."

TOP FIVE MOST POPULAR DRUGS	
1. Marijuana	87%
2. Ecstasy	3
3. Hashish	2
4. Mushrooms	<1
5. Cocaine	<1

TWO AREAS OF CONTROVERSY

One drug that has become increasingly controversial is marijuana. Use is extensive and the public seemingly divided as to whether or not it should continue to be treated as illegal. Interest groups have been arguing that its effects, short-term and long-term, pale compared to legal drugs such as alcohol and nicotine. Those opposed argue that its affects are highly detrimental, contributing to short-term dysfunctions and long-term disabilities.

In late July of 2000, the Ontario Court of Appeal ruled that Canada's marijuana law prohibiting the possession of marijuana is unconstitutional and gave Ottawa a year to amend it. People who require marijuana for medicinal purposes can apply for an exemption; the Ontario court asked that the exemption be written into law. At the same time, the court upheld a lower-court decision prohibiting the possession of marijuana for recreational purposes.[32] On the heels of the decision, Ontario NDP leader Howard Hampton called for the decriminalization of marijuana, saying that too many people are being turned into criminals for "smoking a little pot," and that such a move would free up police to fight real crime.[33] Indications that marijuana use may be on the increase means the debate can be expected to intensify.

Young people are not lost for views on the topic. One in two favour the legalization of the use of marijuana, with males (58%) more likely to be in favour than females (42%). A 15-year-old male from Hamilton protests, "No matter what anyone says, marijuana is addictive," while a 16-year-old Calgary-area female offers these thoughts:

> I feel that the use of marijuana should not be illegal because it helps people relax; also, everyone does it nowadays so there is no way the law can keep it under control. If marijuana is illegal, then alcohol should be illegal, because it does the same things to your body and is just as dangerous or even more dangerous.

We saw earlier that 18% of teens say they attend raves monthly or more, with the figure for males (21%) higher than that for females (15%). The media have given extensive attention to raves; *Maclean's*, for example, carried a cover story entitled "Rave Fever" in its April 24, 2000, issue. Writer Susan Oh noted that many see Toronto as the rave capital of North America, and that ravers can "dance until dawn most weekends" in other cities such as Vancouver, Calgary, Edmonton, Montreal, and Halifax, as well as some other smaller locales.[34] Critics say that these all-night parties are replete with drugs, notably ecstasy, which was given emphasis in the *Maclean's* story. In Ontario, a 13-day inquest was held in May 2000 following the death of Allan Ho, 21, who died at a Toronto rave after taking ecstasy. The inquest resulted in 27 recommendations to ensure the all-night parties are safe.[35] Concern about ecstasy was heightened in late August 2000 with news that Canada Customs officials in Montreal had seized a record-breaking shipment of ecstasy that was on its way to Toronto.[36]

Raves, according to Toronto police chief Julian Fantino, are "threatening the very fabric of Canadian life." Others, however, say they represent a new cultural party expression and are no more problematic than party gatherings in the past—and typically less turbulent than gatherings in bars. Edward Adlaf, a research scientist at Toronto's Centre for Addiction and Mental Health, has said, "In many ways, the concerns raised over the rave scene are not that much different than for rock concerts in the 1970s." He points out that, in Ontario, about 60% of students who attended raves in the past year used cannabis but no other illegal substance. Just over 4% of all students surveyed had taken ecstasy in the past year.[37] A June 2000 article in *Time* magazine argued, "First we had the Beat Generation; now we have the Beats-per-Minute Generation. And it's not just about ecstasy." Rave culture, said writer Christopher John Farley, has started to exert a potent influence on pop music, advertising, films, and even computer games. According to some observers, rave culture has become youth culture. Drugs may or may not be part of "the rave scene."[38]

One of our survey participants, a 17-year-old male from Kelowna, B.C., has the following to say:

> I know lots of kids who go to them and I went to them extensively myself. The thing is drugs! So many hard drugs are taken by kids ages 14 to 25 it's amazing. I've done ecstasy about 10 times and it was really fun, although I won't do it again, and I was able to stop unassisted. I know of kids who go to every rave that's put on (about 1 to 2 times a week) and do ecstasy, crystal, mushrooms, smoke dope, use acid, drink, huff nitric acid, snort coke. People don't really know about this underground rave culture and parents would freak if they found out their 15-year-old daughter went to raves, got f . . . d out of her mind, and hooked up with some older guy. I can see how kids get addicted to raves but the drugs are the scary thing and it makes me laugh that parents have no clue!

Despite such alarming reports, journalists such as Kevin Grace maintain that a consensus is forming in some cities, including Toronto: attempts to ban raves only drive them underground. He cites one suburban-Vancouver municipal councillor who says, "They're not something I would ever go to, but my parents' generation had the same opinion of the dances we went to when I was young."[39] *Calgary Sun* columnist Bill Kaufmann writes, "The hysteria that swept city hall in the wake of an isolated stabbing incident following a rave was amusing to behold. It's as if raves have just arrived in Calgary in the past few weeks. In fact, they've been filling halls, party rooms and underground venues for years with little fallout." Predicts Kaufmann, "This current manifestation of youth culture—like so many others before it—will play itself out."[40]

So what do the data actually say?

To begin with, 6% of teens tell us that they go to raves once a week or more, 5% say they go two to three times a month, and another 7% about once a month. A further 18% say they "hardly ever" attend raves, and 64% say they never do. Almost 50% of monthly-plus ravers come from cities of 100 000 or more, but these consist of only about 15% of the teens in those same cities. Surprisingly, 40% of those who say they attend raves at least once a month come from communities of fewer than 10 000, suggesting that the term "rave" has come to have a fairly broad interpretation. Keeping things in perspective, approximately 20% of the young people living in those smaller communities go to raves that often.

An examination of general drug use among young people who attend raves and those who don't shows that rave-attendees are more inclined than non-attendees to use marijuana and other illegal drugs (see Figure 23.2). It is not clear where exactly such use is taking place. However, what is clear is that about 40% of teens who attend raves at least once a week say that they *never* use marijuana, and almost 70% claim they *never* use any other illegal drugs, including ecstasy. In short, lots of teens who attend raves claim they are partying without drugs.

Tracy Ford, a social worker with the Ministry of the Attorney General in Toronto and described as "a former enthusiast of the rave scene," is a member of the Party People's Project (PPP), a community-based group formed to protect the rights of ravers. Writing in a publication of the Alberta Alcohol and Drug Abuse Commission in late 2000, she maintains that false stereotypes of violence and rampant drug use have been used to discredit raves. What is required, she suggests, is not the outlawing of raves, but rather a combina-

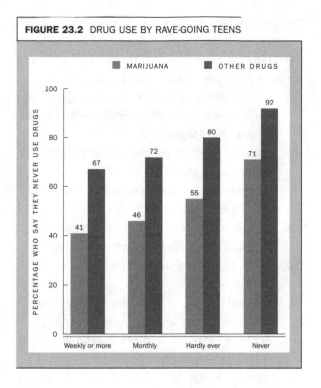

FIGURE 23.2 DRUG USE BY RAVE-GOING TEENS

tion of support, trained supervision, and education that can reduce rave-related harms. "The harm reduction model," she says, "accepts the choices of young people, and supports them, rather than criminalizing them." Ford writes:

> The rave community is a place where young people can find a creative and open network of individuals that love to dance and love music. Young people have basic civil rights to associate, express themselves and enjoy the same freedoms accorded all Canadians in their leisure time. Whatever our concerns about the safety of young people, we must find options that will foster their development, and support their ability to make informed choices.[41]

There is little reason to disagree.

NOTES

1. See, for example, the *National Post* story of April 21, 2000, "Threats of violence abound in schools since Taber, Columbine," by Ian MacLeod.

2. "Teen pleads guilty to making hit list of students," Canadian Press, Toronto, November 28, 2000.

3. Robert Remington and Chris Wattie, "$30 debt seen as motive in killing," *National Post,* November 21, 2000.

4. Jane Christmas, "A parent's dilemma in the age of Columbine," *National Post,* April 21, 2000.

5. For a summary article on the sentencing of one of Virk's assailants, see Rod Mickleburgh, "Virk's killer gets minimum sentence," *Globe and Mail,* April 21, 2000.

6. "Virk's killer off to prison," Canadian Press, Vancouver, April 20, 2000.

7. Details are provided by Jim Rankin and Michelle Shephard in their article, "Teen beaten to death didn't defend himself," in *Toronto Star,* November 17, 1999.

8. See Michelle Shephard, "Four teens charged with torturing girl, 14," *Toronto Star,* November 18, 1999.

9. Ian Williams, "Teens charged with murder after boy's death," *Edmonton Journal,* November 17, 2000.

10. "Kid says he used dad's gun to 'scare' man he shot," Canadian Press, Lytton, Quebec, November 27, 2000.

11. Alan J. C. King, William F. Boyce, and Matthew A. King, *Trends in the Health of Canadian Youth,* Ottawa: Health Canada, 1999:23.

12. Siu Kwong Wong, "Acculturation, peer relations, and delinquent behaviour of Chinese-Canadian youth," *Adolescence* 34, 1999: 107–19.

13. "Advisory group recommended to reduce youth crime," Canadian Press, Toronto, June 22, 2000.

14. "Junior high violence shocks officials," Canadian Press, Calgary, May 8, 2000. For a summary of a parallel earlier study in Calgary, see Joanne J. Paetsch and Lorne D. Bertrand, "Victimization and delinquency among Canadian youth," *Adolescence* 34, 1999:351–67.

15. *The Daily,* Statistics Canada, December 19, 1995.

16. *The Daily,* Statistics Canada, November 2, 2000.

17. "Crime rate drops to 20-year low," Canadian Press, Ottawa, July 18, 2000.

18. "British statistics show jump in violent crime," Reuters, London, July 18, 2000.

19. "Sentencing of young offenders," *The Daily,* August 1, 2000.

20. "Teens given more jail time than adults for same crime," Canadian Press, Vancouver, August 1, 2000.

21. Janine Ecklund, "Schools safe, say police," *Lethbridge Herald,* December 1, 2000.

22. "Ottawa, provinces disagree on youth crime," Canadian Press, Hamilton, ON, October 4, 1999.

23. "The Perception Gap," *Time,* April 24, 2000: 40–41.

24. "The Sex Files on Discovery pushing the envelope," Canadian Press, Toronto, October 4, 2000.

25. See, for example, Vanessa Lu and Richard Brennan, "No-prescription test for morning-after pill," *Toronto Star,* September 8, 2000.

26. "Injectable birth control approved in U.S.," Associated Press, New York, October 6, 2000.

27. Tanya Talaga, "American women get approval to use abortion pill RU-486," *Toronto Star,* September 29, 2000.

28. Graeme Smith, "Doctors to test French abortion pill here," *Toronto Star,* July 7, 2000.

29. Editorial, "The consequences of sex," *Globe and Mail,* December 1, 1999.

30. "Multiple-risk behaviour in teenagers and young adults," *The Daily,* Statistics Canada, October 29, 1998.

31. "Tobacco use," *The Daily,* Statistics Canada, January 20, 2000.

32. "Pot possession law ruled unconstitutional," Canadian Press, Toronto, July 31, 2000.

33. "Ontario NDP wants marijuana decriminalized," Canadian Press, Toronto, August 2, 2000.

34. Susan Oh, "Rave fever," *Maclean's,* April 24, 2000:39–43.

35. "Inquest urges steps for safer raves," Canadian Press, Toronto, June 1, 2000.

36. "Ecstasy seized in major drug bust," *Globe and Mail,* August 22, 2000.

37. Cited in Susan Oh, "Rave fever," *Maclean's,* April 24, 2000:41.

38. Christopher John Farley, "Rave new world," *Time,* June 5, 2000:42–44.

39. Kevin Michael Grace, "Spontaneous congestion," *The Report,* July 24, 2000:47.

40. Bill Kaufmann, "Rave hysteria amusing," *Calgary Sun,* Jun 5, 2000.

41. Tracy Ford, "Regulating the rave: Keeping ravers safe in Toronto," *Developments,* AADAC, Oct/Nov 2000.

Chapter 25

Race and Crime:

A CRITIQUE

JULIAN V. ROBERTS AND THOMAS GABOR

Canadian criminologists have been challenged recently by the work of a professor of psychology, Philippe Rushton, who claims to have uncovered evidence of significant interracial differences in many areas of human behaviour, including criminality (Rushton, 1987, 1988, 1989). In January 1987, Professor Rushton delivered a paper at the American Association for the Advancement of Science conference in San Francisco (Rushton, 1987). He proposed a genetically based hierarchy in which Blacks (who supposedly evolved earlier than whites or orientals) were, *inter alia*, less intelligent and law-abiding than whites and orientals. Rushton asserts that there are substantial interracial differences in crime rates, and that these are accounted for by genetic factors. We shall examine later the credibility of genetic explanations of variations in crime rates. First, it is important to address the context of these assertions, and their likely impact upon society.

Rushton's speculations about race and crime have achieved national coverage exceeding that accorded any research project undertaken by criminologists (*The Globe and Mail*, 1989). Part of the reason for this is the aggressive posture adopted by Rushton: he has been interviewed in several newspapers and has appeared on several television programs with national audiences. In contrast, the reaction from criminologists, but not other professional groups (*The Globe and Mail*, 1989), has been muted. His monopolization of media coverage may, we believe, have had a detrimental impact upon public opinion. It is important, therefore, that criminologists in Canada respond to his statements. While Rushton's claims about racial influences upon intelligence have been challenged, his assertions about crime have not.

THE EFFECT OF RUSHTON'S VIEWS ON PUBLIC THEORIES OF CRIME CAUSATION

The race/crime controversy has important consequences for public opinion in the area of criminal justice. Many of the important questions in the field of criminology—such as the relative deterrent effect of capital punishment—cannot be addressed by experiments. Accordingly, criminologists have used sophisticated correlational procedures to untangle the relative effects on crime of correlated variables such as genetic and environmental factors. The existence of a simple statistic, then, such as the overrepresentation in some crime statistics of certain racial minorities, will by itself convince few scholars. Criminologists have become sensitized to the possibility of alternative explanations for apparently straightforward relationships. Members of the public, however, are not so sophisticated in drawing inferences from statistical information. In fact, a great deal of recent research in social psychology has documented numerous ways in which the layperson is led into making unjustified inferences from material such as that which appears in newspapers (Fiske and Taylor, 1984; Nisbett and Ross, 1980).

Source: Excerpted from "Lombrosian Wine in a New Bottle: Research on Crime and Race," *Canadian Journal of Criminology* 32, 2 (April 1990): 291–313. Reprinted by permission of the Canadian Journal of Criminology.

Rushton's theories may affect public opinion in this area for several reasons. First, as already noted, the average layperson may not readily seek alternative (i.e., nongenetic) explanations for the overrepresentation of Blacks in certain types of crime. Second, laypersons are less likely to realize that studies on race and crime are essentially correlational, rather than causal, in nature. Third, the race/crime hypothesis comes from a highly credible source, namely a well-published and tenured university professor. Fourth, it is vital to remember that, to the average member of the public, crime is a relatively unidimensional phenomenon: it usually involves violence, loss of property, and is a consequence of a "criminal disposition." Members of the public tend to regard offenders as a relatively homogeneous group (Roberts and White, 1986) varying somewhat in their actions but not their motivations. Criminologists have long been aware of the deficiencies of this perception of crime; the multidimensional nature of crime and the complexity of motivation render sweeping statements about the etiology of crime invalid. Finally, but not last in importance, some people may be particularly receptive to racial explanations of crime. Thus, views such as those expressed by Professor Rushton may have the unintended effect of inflaming racism in Canada.

Furthermore, Rushton's views received what many laypersons might interpret as substantial support within days of the news media's coverage of his San Francisco address. On February 16, a representative of the Toronto Police Force released statistics showing that Blacks were overrepresented in the crime statistics in the Jane–Finch area of Toronto (*The Toronto Star*, 1989). These data are likely to be misinterpreted by members of the public to constitute evidence supporting a genetic explanation of crime.

For the vast majority of the public, the mass media constitute their primary source of information about crime and criminal justice. Public conceptions of deviance are a consequence of what people read, hear, and see in the media. An abundance of research has demonstrated a direct correspondence between public misperceptions of crime and distorted media coverage of criminal justice issues (Doob and Roberts, 1982). Since criminologists have failed to refute Rushton in the news media, we have also relinquished access to the one means of influencing public opinion on this issue. Criminologists may be highly skeptical of Rushton's opinions in the area of crime, but the only way that this skepticism can affect the public is through coverage in the news media. Once again, we note that while Rushton has been criticized by various behavioural geneticists (such as David Suzuki), his assertions regarding race and crime have remained uncontested.

We believe, therefore, that it is important to address the hypothesis that inherited racial traits affect crime rates. We shall examine some methodological issues relating criminality to race. A comprehensive survey of the literature on this topic would occupy a whole issue of a journal; we can only highlight the research findings and point out what we perceive to be the principal flaws in Rushton's argument. We shall draw upon data from Canada, the United States, and the United Kingdom. Finally, it should be made clear from the outset that we are addressing Rushton's theory as it pertains to the phenomenon of crime. We are not behavioural geneticists, to whom we cede the question of whether the general theory of racial differences withstands scientific scrutiny.

THE SCIENTIFIC ARGUMENT: EMPIRICAL RESEARCH ON RACE AND CRIME

PROBLEMS WITH THE DEFINITION OF RACE

Rushton relates an independent variable (race) to a dependent variable (crime). The interracial comparisons cited by Rushton are predicated on the assumption that people are racially pure. Each racial "category" is held to be homogeneous, but this is now accepted by contemporary anthropologists and biologists to be an antiquated and dangerous myth. Centuries of interbreeding reduce Rushton's rather crude tripartite classification (Black, white, oriental) to the level of caricature. For example, Radzinowicz and King (1977) note that in the United States, close to 50 percent of those classified as Black are over half white by lineage (see also Herskovits, 1930; and, for a study of offenders, Hooton, 1939). Many American whites, as well, have some Black ancestry; Haskell and Yablonsky (1983: 95) note that:

> Estimates of the number of Blacks who have "passed" into the white society run as high as 7 million. In addition to those millions who have introduced an African mixture into the "white" population of the United States in the relatively recent past, there must have been millions of Africans who were assimilated into the population of Spain, Portugal, Italy, Greece, and other Mediterranean countries. Descendants of those people are now part of the "white" population of the United States.

Wolfgang and Cohen (1970) cite data showing that no more than 22 percent of all persons designated as Black, in the United States, were of unmixed ancestry. Fully 15 percent of persons classified as Black were more white than Black (Wolfgang and Cohen, 1970: 7). The pervasiveness of such racial overlap calls genetically based racial theories of crime into question. (For the rest of this article, for convenience only, we shall continue to refer to interracial differences. This does not mean we endorse the racial trichotomy of Blacks, orientals, and whites advanced by Professor Rushton.) Finally, it is important to bear in mind that crime statistics deal with race as a sociological and not a biological category. In short, the independent variable, as it were, is highly problematic. Now we turn to the dependent measure, official and unofficial measures of crime.

THE ISSUE OF OVERREPRESENTATION IN OFFICIAL CRIME STATISTICS

Rushton's evidence for a genetic influence consists of the overrepresentation of Blacks in official statistics of crime in the United States, the United Kingdom, and elsewhere. Specifically he asserts that:

> African descended people, for example, while constituting less than one-eighth of the population of the United States or of London, England, currently account for over 50% of the crimes in both places. Since about the same proportion of victims say their assailant was Black, the arrest statistics cannot really be blamed on police prejudice. (Rushton, 1987: 3)

There are at least two factually incorrect elements here, but first we offer a general comment regarding the issue of overrepresentation.

A simple correlation between two variables does not constitute evidence of a *causal* relationship. A multitude of other confounding factors must be ruled out before one can contemplate a causal relationship. Even if the relationship between race and crime holds up after careful secondary analyses, this is hardly convincing evidence of genetic influences. The fact that parental alcoholism is correlated with alcoholism in the offspring does not prove a genetic component to alcoholism. Alcohol abuse can be a learned behaviour as well. The same argument applies to the race/crime relationship.

Another point is relevant to the issue of a disproportionate involvement in crime. Virtually every society contains racial and ethnic groups, usually minorities, who are more criminally active in certain crimes than the rest of the population. According to Rushton's theory of criminal behaviour, Native Canadians should display lower, not higher, crime rates than the non-Native population. Unfortunately for the theory, this is not true. The overrepresentation of Native offenders in the criminal justice statistics has been apparent for some time (Griffiths and Verdun-Jones, 1989; LaPrairie, 1989). Explanations in terms of the social strata in our society occupied by indigenous peoples can easily explain these findings; Rushton's racial theory cannot. According to Rushton's typology this group, being oriental or mongoloid, should display lower, not higher, rates of criminality.

According to Rushton's genetic explanation of crime, the crime rates for Blacks should be higher than the white crime rates, *and* the rates for Native Canadians should be *lower* than the non-Native population. The two categories (Blacks and Native people) are genetically dissimilar; their rates of criminality should reflect this difference (relative to the white population). The fact is that both Black Americans and Native Canadians share an elevated risk of certain kinds of criminality (relative to the comparable white populations in their respective countries). Such an outcome is, of course, perfectly consistent with a sociological explanation: both minority groups share a protracted history of constrained social opportunity, as well as overt discrimination.

Also in Canada, French Canadians are the most active in the crime of robbery (Gabor et al., 1987). In England, Irish immigrants have been overrepresented in crimes of assault for years (Radzinowicz and King, 1977). In Israel, the Arab population and non-European Jews are more criminally active in conventional crimes than the European Jews (Fishman, Rattner, and Weimann, 1987). Such overrepresentation, then, is the rule rather than the exception across different societies.

To return to Rushton's suggestion, two errors can be identified. First, he cites data published in the *Daily Telegraph* (a British newspaper) showing that Blacks account for over 50 percent of the crimes in the United States and the United Kingdom (Rushton, 1988). By any measure, this is a considerable exaggeration. If he refers to all reported crimes and not merely index crimes, Blacks account for about 29 percent of all persons charged in the United States (United States Department of Justice, 1989). Index crimes are those included in official crime indices; they exclude many white-collar crimes, for example.

As well, aggregate statistics based on index crimes alone misrepresent the true picture. Crime is not, as suggested by Rushton's publications, a homogeneous category of behaviours. While Blacks in the United States account for over 60 percent of arrests for robbery and almost 50 percent of arrests for murder, they account for about 30 percent of arrests for burglary and theft, less than 24 percent of those arrested for arson and about 20 percent of those arrested for vandalism (United States Department of Justice, 1987). Using Rushton's own data, Blacks are underrepresented in crimes like tax fraud and securities violations. In fact, arrest statistics for white-collar crimes such as fraud and embezzlement are significantly higher for whites. Treating crime as a unitary phenomenon obscures this diversity. These variations reflect differential opportunities for offending, and not, we submit, offence-specific genetic programming.

Differential Treatment of Blacks by the Criminal Justice System

Finally, arrest statistics reflect, to a degree, the more rigorous surveillance by police to which minorities are subject. Data on this point are hard to obtain; the magnitude of the problem is hard to quantify. Nevertheless, the recent release of the "Guildford Four" in England, after fifteen years of imprisonment following a wrongful conviction based upon fabricated police evidence, reveals the dangers posed to minorities by an overzealous police force.

Research in the United States sustains the view that the police are more likely to arrest and charge Blacks (Black and Reiss, 1967; Lundman, Sykes, and Clark, 1978). Wolfgang and Cohen (1970: 71) summarize some of this research:

> In comparing arrest statistics for Blacks and whites, it is important to remember, then, that one reason for the high arrest rates among Blacks is that they are more likely to be stopped, picked up on suspicion and subsequently arrested.

Furthermore, the bias does not remain at the police station: British data (Landau, 1981; Landau and Nathan, 1983) show that prosecution is more likely for persons of Afro-Caribbean origin. Bias persists at most critical stages of the criminal justice process. As Paul Gordon (1988: 309) noted, summarizing data on the issue:

> Black people's experience of the British criminal justice system shows clearly that the rhetoric of the law does not accord with the reality of its practice. The law is not colour-blind, but a means by which Black people have been subject to a process of criminalization.

Most recently, Albonetti and her colleagues (1989) have demonstrated that while the influence of race upon pretrial decisions is complicated, white suspects have the edge over Black suspects.

To summarize the data on contact with the criminal justice process, American Blacks are clearly overrepresented in violent crime statistics, slightly overrepresented in property crimes, and underrepresented in white-collar crimes. In order to explain this diverse pattern, one has to strain the genetic explanation beyond the breaking point. Are Blacks genetically predisposed toward street crimes while whites are programmed to commit white-collar crimes? A far more plausible explanation exists: social groups commit crimes as a consequence of their social situations and in response to prevailing criminal opportunities. This environmental perspective explains more findings and requires fewer assumptions. The law of parsimony, then, clearly favours environmental over genetic theories of crime. In short, Rushton's explanation of crime by reference to genetic influences requires acceptance of the position that specific antisocial behaviours are directly related to genetic structure. Modern behavioural geneticists would undoubtedly reject this view.

OVERREPRESENTATION AND ALTERNATIVE SOURCES OF CRIME STATISTICS: VICTIMIZATION SURVEYS AND SELF-REPORTED CRIMINALITY

There is convincing evidence that arrest data exaggerate the true incidence of Black criminality. Two alternative sources of information on crime make this clear. Overall, FBI data indicate that 46.5 percent of all violent crimes reported to the police are committed by Blacks. However, the victimization survey conducted by the U.S. Department of Justice found that Blacks account for only about 24 percent of violent crimes (United States Department of Justice, 1986). Which source presents a more accurate picture of crimes actually committed? With regard to crimes of violence, data derived from victims would appear to be more accurate than arrest data. But it is not just victimization surveys that cast doubt upon the official statistics. A third source of information on crime patterns also shows discrepancies. Rojek (1983) compared police reports with self-reports of delinquency. In the police database, race was a significant factor in several offence categories, but this was not true for the self-reports. Other studies using the self-report approach (Williams and Gold, 1972) have found a similar pattern: no difference between Black and white respondents (Pope, 1979) or only slight differences (Hirschi, 1969).

Unreported versus Reported Crime

Another explanation for the elevated incidence of Black offenders in official crime statistics concerns the issue of unreported crimes. As we have noted, official crime data indicate that Blacks are more likely than whites to commit certain crimes (personal injury offences) and less likely than whites to commit other types of crimes. The problem with crime statistics is that the reporting rate is highly variable, depending upon the offence. The types of offences committed by Blacks are more likely to be reported than the offences committed by whites. Any examination of aggregate crime statistics is going to overestimate the true incidence of crime committed by Blacks relative to the amount of crime committed by whites.

To conclude, the extent of overrepresentation of Blacks, even in those offences where it occurs, has been exaggerated. In perhaps the most comprehensive study to date which relates crime to race, Michael Hindelang (1982) tested various theories that attempted to explain interracial differences. He concluded that the theories of delinquency that best explain the patterns of data were sociological rather than biological. These included Merton's reformulation of anomie theory (Merton, 1968), Cloward and Ohlin's opportunity theory (Cloward and Ohlin, 1960), and Wolfgang's subculture of violence theory (Wolfgang and Ferracuti, 1982).

A final word on the crime statistics utilized by Rushton consists of a caveat: recorded crime is exactly that: it is only a small fraction of all reported and unreported crime. A recent article by Tony Jefferson (1988: 535) makes the point succinctly:

> We do not *know* what the real rate of Black crime is, nor whether it is on the increase. Take robbery for instance. The British Crime Survey reveals that only 8% of robberies were recorded. If those figures applied to London this would mean that there is a suspect for only 1 in 100 robberies. The comparable figure for burglaries would be 5 in 100. This means that *whatever* the arrest figures, and whatever the victim identifications, the "unknown" element is so great, especially for those crimes where Black "over-representation" is seen as greatest, as to make all estimates of Black offending strictly conjectural.

When there is sound reason to suppose that the police are more vigilant with regard to Black suspects and offenders, it is clear that if we were able to replace reported with unreported crime rates, the interracial differences would diminish still further.

Self-report studies provide insight in another area as well. While Professor Rushton associates "lawlessness" with being Black, there is overwhelming evidence indicating that most people, at one point or another, commit acts for which they could be prosecuted. As an example, in a now classic study, Wallerstein and Wyle (1947) surveyed 1700 New York City residents without a criminal record. Fully 99 percent admitted to involvement in at least one of 49 offences. This evidence suggests that rule breaking is normal activity on the part of most citizens in Western societies. The selection of norm violators to be prosecuted therefore is critical to an understanding of who becomes officially classified as a criminal. Many observers of the criminal justice system believe that race may be a key factor affecting that selection process. Another classic study, Hartshorne and May's (1928) investigation of children, also showed that dishonesty was both pervasive and situation-specific. There was little cross-situational consistency: children that were dishonest in one situation were honest in others. This emphasis on the social situation as the determinant of behaviour is consistent with an environmental view of crime, and inconsistent with Rushton's genetic theory. (A large body of evidence, drawn from longitudinal, self-report, experimental, and observational research, suggests that law breaking is widespread in North American society.)

WITHIN RACE COMPARISONS

Comparisons over Time

In the next two sections, we examine variation in crime rates within race, but across time and cultures. If genetic factors have an important impact upon crime, rates should be relatively stable within race, across both time and cultures. This, however, is not the case. Further undermining Rushton's thesis are the temporal and cross-cultural variations in crime patterns for the Black population. Street crime by Blacks in the United Kingdom has only recently increased significantly. Just over a decade ago, Radzinowicz and King (1977) were able to write that, with the exception of prostitution and other victimless crimes, the Black community was as law abiding as other Britons. Any increase in crime rates within a generation obviously cannot be attributed to genetic factors. This point was made recently by Anthony Mawson (1989) in the context of explanations of homicide in terms of Darwinian selection (Daly and Wilson, 1988). Mawson (1989: 239) notes the inability of biological explanations of homicide to account for fluctuations in homicide rates over a short period of time:

> Thus, it seems doubtful whether a selectionist explanation can be applied to changing homicide rates, even those occurring over a thousand years.

The same argument applies in the context of Rushton's work: increases in offending by Blacks over a period of ten to fifteen years cannot possibly be explained by reference to genetic influence.

In the United States as well, the proportional involvement of Blacks in crime has risen over the past few decades. One major factor in this rise has been the proliferation of illicit drug usage. Heroin use became pervasive in the 1950s, and "crack" cocaine is creating an explosion of violent crime in this decade. As well, the erosion of taboos relating to interracial crimes has been associated with increased victimization of whites by Blacks (Silberman, 1978). A third major development has been the greater accessibility of firearms. These are three potent environmental factors affecting Black criminality. One would be hard-pressed to find a genetic explanation for the changing criminal activity pattern of a race over such a short period of time.

Comparisons across Jurisdictions

The variations in Black, white, and oriental crime from one society to another also demonstrate the potency of environmental factors in the etiology of crime. Levels of violent crime in the American South are greater for both Blacks *and* whites than they are in other parts of the country. As well, there is substantial variation in the homicide rates for Blacks in different American states. For example, in Delaware the homicide rate for Blacks is 16.7 per 100 000. This is considerably lower than the homicide rate for Black residents of other states; in Missouri, for example, the rate is 65 per 100 000 (Carroll and Mercy, 1989).

Cross-national, within-race comparisons make the same point. Black Americans have a higher homicide rate than their more racially pure counterparts in Africa: this fact directly contradicts Rushton's thesis. The author (Bohannan, 1960: 123) of a study of African homicide concludes:

> if it needed stressing, here is overwhelming evidence that it is a cultural and not biological factor which makes for a high homicide rate among American negroes.

More recent data (International Criminal Police Organization, 1988) demonstrate the same variations: the homicide rate per 100 000 inhabitants varies from .01 (Mali) to 29 (Bahamas) and 22.05 (Jamaica). It is noteworthy also that the Caribbean homicide rates are far in excess of even the African countries with the highest rates (e.g., Rwanda, 11 per 100 000; Tanzania, 8 per 100 000). This despite the fact that residents of the Caribbean are more racially mixed than Blacks from Africa. According to Rushton's theory, homicide rates should be higher not lower in the more racially pure African states.

Furthermore, orientals do not constitute a monolith of law-abiding citizens. The homicide rates in the Far East also vary considerably, from 39 per 100 000 residents in the Philippines to 1.3 per 100 000 in Hong Kong. In Thailand, the homicide rate exceeds the rate of homicide in Japan by a factor of twelve (International Criminal Police Organization, 1988). In all these comparisons, the genetic explanation falls short.

The magnitude of these intraracial differences suggests that the potency of environmental factors to explain crime rates far exceeds that of genetic factors. In statistical terms, these data imply that the percentage of variation in crime rates explained by genetic factors is negligible, if it exists at all.

VICTIMIZATION PATTERNS

There is another form of overrepresentation of which Professor Rushton appears unaware: Blacks are at much higher risk of becoming the victims of violent crime. In the United States, Black males are 20 times more likely than whites to be shot, cut, or stabbed, and Black females are 18 times more likely to be raped than white women (Wolfgang and Cohen, 1981). Black Americans are also more likely than whites to be victims of burglary, motor vehicle theft, assault, robbery, and many other offences (United States Department of Justice, 1983). Although Blacks constitute only 12 percent of the general United States population, over 40 percent of homicide victims are Black. See Barnett and Schwartz (1989) for recent data showing Black victimization rates to be approximately four times higher than white rates. The same trends are apparent in other countries, such as England. The over-representation of Blacks as victims is substantial, yet no one has posited that such overrepresentation is due to a genetically based susceptibility to criminal victimization. While this finding is not inconsistent with an explanation based upon genetic factors, it does underscore the importance of environmental factors such as propinquity and accessibility. Violent crimes are a result of an interaction between offender and victim. To posit an overriding genetic basis of crime is to ignore the role of the victim and situational factors (Boyd, 1988; Wolfgang, 1958). When we examine the dynamics of the violent crime most commonly associated with Blacks—armed robbery—we readily see the importance of situational determinants. Actually, recourse to physical violence occurs only in a small minority of robberies. Usually the violence that does occur arises in response to victims who resist the robbers' demands (Gabor et al., 1987). The violence, therefore, is often instrumental and situation-specific.

If Blacks are more likely to be both offenders and victims in relation to certain types of crime, then a plausible explanation for their overrepresentation on both counts is that they tend to live in areas in which violence is a normal consequence of stress, threat, and frustration. This essentially is Wolfgang and Ferracuti's (1982) subculture of violence thesis. Aside from living in environments where violence is normative behaviour, Blacks tend disproportionately to live in poverty. Furthermore, they are overrepresented among urban dwellers. Economic status and urban residence are linked to a number of crime indices. A fair examination of Black and white criminality would therefore necessitate comparison between persons situated similarly in society.

But even the presence of a correlation between race and certain indices of crime, after other plausible environmental factors have been pointed out, does not demonstrate a genetically based race/crime link. As Charles Silberman (1978) has pointed out, the experience of Black Americans has been very different from the experience of any other disadvantaged group. The generations of violence, deprivation, disenfranchisement, and exclusion from educational and vocational opportunities to which they have been subjected has not been shared by any other ethnic or racial group. Moreover, much of this racial discrimination persists, to this day, and in this country, as recent research has documented (Henry and Ginzberg, 1985). Discrimination of this kind can engender social patterns and attitudes toward authority that lead to law breaking.

Careful epidemiological research can result in samples of Black and white citizens that are "matched" on many important background variables such as social class, income, education, age, and family size and composition. Comparison between such groups is preferable to comparison based upon unmatched samples, but the effects of long-term discrimination, brutality, and oppression over generations cannot be captured by the most rigorous multiple regression analysis. As John Conklin (1989: 140) notes:

> to argue that Blacks and whites of similar backgrounds will have the same crime rate is to argue that centuries of discrimination have had no long-term effects on Blacks that are conducive to criminal behavior.

Our opposition to Rushton's views should not be interpreted to mean that we deny the existence of any genetic influences upon human behaviour. Rather, we take issue with the attribution of racial differences in criminality to genetic factors. In our view, there is little scientific basis for his rather sweeping assertions about the relative "law-abidingness" of different racial groups. The few statistics he provides are susceptible to a multitude of highly probable alternative explanations derived from an environmental perspective. Given the incendiary nature of the theory and its policy implications, we feel that the burden of proof is upon Professor Rushton to provide more convincing data than the few ambiguous statistics he has to date brought forth. We leave it to others (Lynn, 1989; Zuckerman and Brody, 1989) to evaluate the scientific credibility of Professor Rushton's genetic explanation of other phenomena such as: intelligence, sexual restraint, personality, political preferences, and the efficacy of the German army in the Second World War (*The Globe and Mail*, 1989). In the area of criminality, his evidence, in our view, falls short of discharging a scientific burden of proof.

NOTE

The authors would like to acknowledge that this manuscript has benefited from the comments of Michael Petrunik (University of Ottawa), the editorial committee of the *Canadian Journal of Criminology,* and two anonymous reviewers.

REFERENCES

Albonetti, Celesta, Robert Hauser, John Hagan, and Ilene Nagel. 1989. "Criminal justice decision making as a stratification process: The role of race and stratification resources in pre-trial release." *Journal of Quantitative Criminology* 5: 57–82.

Barnett, Arnold and Elliot Schwartz. 1989. "Urban homicide: Still the same." *Journal of Quantitative Criminology* 5: 83–100.

Black, D. and Albert Reiss. 1967. *Studies of Crime and Law Enforcement in Major Metropolitan Areas.* Washington, DC: Government Printing Office.

Bohannan, Paul. 1960. *African Homicide and Suicide.* Princeton, NJ: Princeton University Press.

Boyd, Neil. 1988. *The Last Dance: Murder in Canada.* Toronto: Prentice-Hall.

Carroll, Patrick and James Mercy. 1989. "Regional variation in homicide rates: Why is the west violent?" *Violence and Victims* 4: 17–25.

Cloward, Richard A. and Lloyd Ohlin. 1960. *Delinquency and Opportunity: A Theory of Delinquent Gangs.* New York: Free Press.

Conklin, John. 1989. *Criminology.* (Third edition.) New York: Macmillan.

Curie, Elliot. 1985. *Confronting Crime.* New York: Pantheon.

Daly, Martin and Margo Wilson. 1988. *Homicide.* New York: Aldine.

Doob, Anthony N. and Julian V. Roberts. 1982. *Crime: Some Views of the Canadian Public.* Ottawa: Department of Justice.

Fishman, G., Arye Rattner, and Gabriel Weimann. 1987. "The effect of ethnicity on crime attribution." *Criminology* 25: 507–24.

Fiske, Susan T. and Shelley E. Taylor. 1984. *Social Cognition.* Reading, MA: Addison-Wesley.

Gabor, Thomas, Micheline Baril, M. Cusson, D. Elie, Marc LeBlanc, and André Normandeau. 1987. *Armed Robbery: Cops, Robbers, and Victims.* Springfield, Ill.: Charles C. Thomas.

The Globe and Mail. 1989. February 11: 14.

Gordon, Paul. 1988. "Black people and the criminal law: Rhetoric and reality." *International Journal of the Sociology of Law* 16: 295–313.

Griffiths, Curt and Simon Verdun-Jones. 1989. *Canadian Criminal Justice.* Toronto: Butterworths.

Hartshorne, M. and M. A. May. 1928. *Studies in Deceit.* New York: Macmillan.

Haskell, M. R. and L. Yablonsky. 1983. *Criminology: Crime and Criminality.* Boston: Houghton Mifflin.

Henry, F. and E. Ginzberg. 1985. *Who Gets the Work: A Test of Racial Discrimination in Employment.* Toronto: Urban Alliance on Race Relations and the Social Planning Council.

Herskovits, Melville J. 1930. *The Anthropometry of the American Negro.* New York: Columbia University Press.

Hindelang, Michael. 1982. "Race and Crime." In Leonard D. Savitz and N. Johnston, eds., *Contemporary Criminology.* Toronto: John Wiley.

Hirschi, Travis. 1969. *Causes of Delinquency.* Berkeley: University of California Press.

Hooton, Ernest A. 1939. *Crime and the Man.* Cambridge: Harvard University Press.

International Criminal Police Organization. 1988. *International Crime Statistics* 1985–86.

Jefferson, Tony. 1988. "Race, crime and policing: Empirical, theoretical and methodological issues." *International Journal of the Sociology of Law* 16: 521–39.

Landau, Simha. 1981. "Juveniles and the police." *British Journal of Criminology* 21: 27–46.

——— and G. Nathan. 1983. "Selecting delinquents for cautioning in the London metropolitan area." *British Journal of Criminology* 28: 128–49.

LaPrairie, Carol. 1989. *The Role of Sentencing in the Over-Representation of Aboriginal People in Correctional Institutions.* Ottawa: Department of Justice.

Lundman, R., R. Sykes and J. Clark. 1978. "Police control of juveniles: A replication." *Journal of Research in Crime and Delinquency* 15: 74–91.

Lynn, Michael. 1989. "Race difference in sexual behaviour: A critique of Rushton and Bogaert's evolutionary hypothesis." *Journal of Research in Personality* 23: 1–6.

Mawson, Anthony. 1989. "Review of *Homicide*" (Daly and Wilson, 1988). *Contemporary Sociology* March: 238–40.

Merton, Robert K. 1968. *Social Theory and Social Structure.* Glencoe: Free Press.

Nisbett, Richard and Lee Ross. 1980. *Human Inference: Strategies and Shortcomings of Social Judgement.* Englewood Cliffs, NJ: Prentice-Hall.

Pope, Carl E. 1979. "Race and crime revisited." *Crime and Delinquency* 25: 345–57.

Radzinowicz, Leon and Joan King. 1977. *The Growth of Crime: The International Experience.* London: Penguin.

Roberts, Julian V. and Nicholas R. White. 1986. "Public estimates of recidivism rates: Consequences of a criminal stereotype." *Canadian Journal of Criminology* 28: 229–41.

Rojek, Dean G. 1983. "Social status and delinquency: Do self-reports and official reports match?" In Gordon P. Waldo, ed., *Measurement Issues in Criminal Justice.* Beverly Hills: Sage.

Rushton, J. Philippe. 1987. "Population differences in rule-following behaviour: Race, evolution and crime." Paper presented to the 39th Annual Meeting of the American Society of Criminology, Montreal, November 11–14.

———. 1988. "Race differences in behaviour: A review and evolutionary analysis." *Personality and Individual Differences* 9: 1009–24.

———. 1989. "Race differences in sexuality and their correlates: Another look at physiological models." *Journal of Research in Personality* 23: 35–54.

Silberman, Charles. 1978. *Criminal Violence, Criminal Justice.* New York: Vintage.

The Toronto Star. 1989. February 17: 20.

United States Department of Justice. 1983. *Sourcebook of Criminal Justice Statistics.* Washington, DC: Bureau of Justice Statistics.

———. 1986. *Criminal Victimization in the United States.* Washington, DC: Bureau of Justice Statistics.

———. 1987. *Sourcebook of Criminal Justice Statistics.* Washington, DC: Bureau of Justice Statistics.

———. 1989. *Sourcebook of Criminal Justice Statistics.* Washington, DC: Bureau of Justice Statistics.

Wallerstein, James S. and Clement J. Wyle. 1947. "Our law-abiding lawbreakers." *Probation* 25: 107–12.

Williams, Jay and Martin Gold. 1972. "From delinquent behaviour to official delinquency." *Social Problems* 20: 209–29.

Wolfgang, Marvin. 1958. *Patterns in Criminal Homicide.* Philadelphia: University of Pennsylvania Press.

——— and Bernard Cohen. 1970. *Crime and Race: Conceptions and Misconceptions.* New York: Institute of Human Relations Press.

———. 1981. "Crime and race: The victims of crime." In Burt Galaway and Joe Hudson, eds., *Perspectives on Crime Victims.* St. Louis: C.V. Mosby.

——— and Franco Ferracuti. 1982. *The Subculture of Violence.* Beverly Hills: Sage.

Zuckerman, Marvin and Nathan Brody. 1989. "Oysters, rabbits and people: A critique of 'race differences in behaviour' by J. P. Rushton." *Personality and Individual Differences* 9: 1025–33.